Unchained Melody

JACQUELINE CLARK

Ark House Press
arkhousepress.com

© 2023 Jacqueline Clark

All rights reserved. Apart from any fair dealing for the purpose of study, research, criticism, or review, as permitted under the Copyright Act, no part may be reproduced by any process without written permission.

Unless otherwise stated, all Scriptures are taken from the New International Translation (Holy Bible. Copyright© 1996, 2004, 2007, 2013 by Tyndale House Foundation. Used by permission of Tyndale House Publishers Inc., Carol Stream, Illinois 60188. All rights reserved.)

Some names and identifying details have been changed to protect the privacy of individuals.

Cataloguing in Publication Data:
Title: Unchained Melody
ISBN: 978-0-6459938-1-3 (pbk)
Subjects: REL012170 [RELIGION / Christian Living / Personal Memoirs]; REL012040 [RELIGION / Christian Living / Inspirational]; BIO026000 [BIOGRAPHY & AUTOBIOGRAPHY / Personal Memoirs];

Design by initiateagency.com

With a thankful heart, I dedicate this book to my precious Saviour, Jesus who has shown His unconditional love and grace, by giving up His own life to save mine. I pray that this story will be a source of encouragement to take hold, and to hide in your heart the Greatest Story of All, the Holy Bible that has the power to transform lives, and to shine the light of Christ on the darkness.

I thank my dearest family for their love and support over the years, and pray earnestly that the Lord will continue to work through them with His love and grace.

All Glory and Honour to Him.

Introduction

This book is based on a true story with particular real life experiences and situations adapted and modified, with a mixture of fiction to suit the setting. There are pseudo names of characters to protect and preserve anonymity. The story starts with Melody's childhood, from her place of birth, India, to arriving in Australia in 1969. It tells of her experiences of adapting to a different way of life, and assimilating into a Western culture, such a contrast from her place of birth. From a colourful school life as a child growing up, her adult life also took many turns, through a rollercoaster of tragedies, emotions and fun times. The journey will make you laugh out loud, and then cry as Melody faces tragedy and heartache.

After leaving a corporate role, she took up her calling with further studies in psychology including theology to become a practitioner in the field. During this time, she encountered various spiritual battles, and came face to face with evil. It was terrifying as it challenged her in many ways. Yet these experiences taught her the power of the cross, and trust in Jesus Christ as the Sovereign Lord.

Consequently, the book contains accounts of cases that reflect the unseen spiritual world taking form. Confidentiality is essential in counselling and psychological practice, and all case descriptions, names and events have been altered including private particulars to preserve the anonymity of her patients without distorting the essential reality of the experience with her patients.

Psychotherapy is very rarely a brief process and can take a long time to work through. In this book she has addressed some highlights and difficult situations to indicate the horrific and insidious reality of the darkness of evil, contrasted with the magnificence of the light that the message of Salvation through Jesus Christ brings to our dark world.

In this book she has presented a holistic view of the whole person including the physical, mental and spiritual, with a Christian worldview. Her worldview had developed over the course of her life as presented in the book, as she was being transformed into a Believer of Christ. It was the Holy Spirit that began its work in her, sanctifying her daily to the person she is today - her true identity in Christ Jesus.

If the book raises any past life- threatening issues or crisis' please contact Lifeline for 24 hour support. If there is any threat of domestic violence please contact the RESPECT line for support and advice.

The book is NOT recommended for children or young persons under the age of fifteen years old as it discusses some adult issues and traumatic experiences.

INTRODUCTION

> **LIFELINE - 13 11 14**
> Crisis Support. Suicide Prevention.

Lifeline
www.lifeline.org.au
Lifeline is a national charity providing all Australians experiencing a personal crisis with access to 24 hour crisis support and suicide prevention ...

I'm feeling suicidal...
Thoughts of suicide can be frightening, confusing. If you or anybody you know are feeling this way, please call the number below for assistance.
Call **13 11 14** *(24/7 Crisis Support and confidential support from trained professionals)*

Our Services
Lifeline provides compassionate support for people in crisis.

RESPECT - Domestic Violence Hotline
(24 Hour Call Service)
1800 737 732

Chapter 1

A Colourful Journey Begins

I write this story looking back at the number of memories, and stories intertwined like a multi coloured tapestry, with reflections of pictures, beginning in the mind of a four year old, now taking on a more intricate and sophisticated interpretation. Each picture ingrained in my vast memory bank with an elaborate story behind it. I was such an ordinary person, like anyone on the street, but lived to tell an extraordinary story based on real life events, amazing people in my life, and the discovery of the supernatural world that led me to a transformed life. Now as an older person, I look back at my younger self, longing for the opportunity to guide her through the darkness into the glorious light. The journey took me to the edge of a cliff face, where I began to fall, with raging fear, but there was one thing that kept me safe, that restored my brokenness.

The journey begins at the age of four looking forward to immigrating to Australia, a land of mystery and intrigue, a remote place that was new, a little scary and exciting all at the same time. My name is Melody and I love to sing, a name that I had to grow into. I see my life in pictures and images, each having a little memory attached to it. Not many words, but emotion and colours that told an enchanting story. This is my story, exciting, scary and sometimes quite dark. In the midst of the darkness there were bright shining lights that lit up those dark places, and chased away the shadows.

I was standing at the gate, looking into the sky and seeing a large plane flying over. What would it be like to fly over the fluffy clouds and see the land and sea merge into each other. I had told all my friends in my town that I was going to a new country, a place that I could not pronounce, Horses tail ya (Australia)....funny but a big word for a little girl. They did not know what I was talking about.

It was the late 1960's and the start of a new decade in the 1970's and life was very simple. It was all about wearing the most daggiest outfit with mix matched colours, flares, beads and whatever took your fancy. I remember walking down the streets of India, going to the market with my family and taking in the smell of spices, fruit, and sewage all at the same time, and it was a place that I knew as a little girl. People often shouted, chanted and horns constantly tooting, with a mixture of bikes and those that could afford cars.

Richmond Town, a suburb of Bangalore, India was a busy little town with open spaces, farm land, large properties on compounds. My mother's family lived on an acreage with a large family home, various other dwellings, two of them being servants quarters, a granny flat for my great-grandfather, sheds and a chicken coop. At the back of the garden was an old cottage that was in need of repair. The cottage was bare, except for a chair, and old cupboard. The corner of the room had lots of spider webs, and the walls were full of lizards, or fly-catchers that enjoyed this cottage and food source. The cottage was creepy and I always had an uneasy feeling about entering the room.

A few weeks ago, I happened to overhear my Aunties and Uncles talking about a stray goat that wandered into the compound, and after riding it and teasing it, they hid it in the cottage and locked it up. It had a heavy creaky door that I could not open. The windows were very high up, with slats of glass, like shutters. The windows could not be opened up entirely. The next morning my Uncle Roy went to check on the goat and found an old lady huddled in the corner with no sign of the goat. He asked her how she got in with the door being locked, but she did not answer, just glared at him. He also asked about the goat but she would not answer. My Uncle felt an icy presence that he could not explain, and my Aunty saw the old woman through the slat windows. The woman would not leave, sitting in the one position until Roy left the room, with the door open.

My Uncle Roy talked about the strange mystery, and the cold presence that left him speechless. The woman seemed to be able to look into his soul, in a taunting evil way that made him flinch. He wanted to run out of there and yell, but tried very hard to compose himself. He talked about this for days during family meals, as he could not explain how this happened.

The compound was quite large, and away from the outbuildings and cottage, there was a paddock for the farm animals, with a cow, goats and various dogs that found their way into the compound. Also there were a few cats that took up residence near the cottage. The cats were feral and not very friendly. They were always fighting one another, hissing at me, and they terrified me. They were creepy and wild, and many times I thought they could attack me, especially as I walked past the cottage. After hearing the story from Uncle Roy I tried to avoid the cottage, especially at night time. This was the same cottage where we would hear tins rolling on the roof, hoping that there were just cats or monkeys.

The next morning, it was the weekend and time to go to the market. With a small bag in tow, I was sitting in a basket in the front of my Dad's bicycle holding onto two bananas under my arm to prevent the cheeky monkeys from stealing it and this was a feat in itself. Watching the traffic, cars, cows, cycle rickshaws and people…wow the people came from everywhere and it was a scary experience for me in this big crazy world.

My Dad, Anthony stopped along the way to speak to his friends. He would always introduce me saying, "This is my daughter, Melody," and was very proud of his little girl.

I would always say, "Very nice to meet you," as my parents taught me to be cordial and friendly. His friends would often comment on my fair skin and black hair. I didn't know why they made a big deal about my skin colour, as I still had a light brown complexion. My Dad had dark brown skin, brown eyes, a moustache and shining white teeth. He had a square face with a prominent jawline, while my face was quite pointy. I had his high nose, and his dark brown piercing eyes. My Mum had a pointy face but with high cheekbones and dark hair. Everyone used to tell her how pretty she was, and she loved to dress up. She was very slim with a tiny waist.

My Mum Jesintha met my Dad, Anthony at a dance in the local town. My Dad was quickly smitten, and they danced the night away to Elvis Presley's song Love Me Tender, and then other sixties music. It was their first love for both of them, pure and innocent. After they got married the following February, I was born nine months later. A honeymoon baby!

Getting to the market seemed to take forever, as we meandered around the cows and fought off the monkeys who were after my bananas. The cows were always treated very well, and I remember constantly trying to keep out of their way, with my mother saying every little while, "Melody watch out or you will be trampled." I did not understand why these cows were so decorated and adored, another question that I pondered about in my four year old brain.

Would Australia be so exciting as my home in India? Last week I watched a snake charmer come into the farm property to take away the King Cobra that took up residence in the yard. My usual chores were to collect eggs from the hens in the chook house. As I picked up an egg, I noticed that they were empty or hollow. I told my mother, and we discovered that a snake was penetrating the egg and sucking out all of the contents. This was very exciting!!

The snake charmer tapped on the gate, and I let him in. He said something in his language - a Hindu dialect that I did not understand. He looked around as I tried to explain what happened with the egg. I could not find my mother, grandmother or any other family member. The man just came in and looked around. He found a hole in the yard near the chickens and started poking around. I noticed that he had a few fingers missing, little stumps in its place.

He put his hand in and the snake came out hissing and seething with anger. I was standing a metre away and enjoyed seeing this man tempting the snake out of the hole. Then, the man started shouting and holding his hand, and he was motioning me to move away. The snake bit his hand, the next thing I saw was the man with an axe, and he cut off his bitten finger. The blood spurted everywhere and I started to scream. The snake began to come out of the hole, and I could hear my mother in the background calling me. I ran into the house, scared and startled at what I just saw. This picture will remain with me for some time. The smell of blood, sweat and spice from this man evaded my senses, and made this experience very real.

Over dinner, I told my family about the snake and the experience with the snake charmer. They did not find this exciting but scolded me about allowing the man into the property, and then standing so close to watch. I was only four, and didn't know about the dangers of a King Cobra snake.

The next day, the snake charmer with the turban sat outside my gate with his finger bandaged up. He had caught his prize and while he played the flute type instrument, the King Cobra appeared from within the basket and began to dance. The snake had a very prominent marking on its head, a regal presence, whilst being quite evil and conniving, which is an interpretation looking back at the picture etched in a little girl's brain. He was lashing out at this man from time to time, then the snake looked at me and tilted its head. Was he coming after me? I was certainly in striking distance, and realising this I moved back, scared.

A month later the man disappeared and so did the snake. Did this man die? Did the snake finally kill him? I asked the servant and kitchen hand and no-one seemed to know. People move on from town to town to make some money so hoping that the show continues on, for some other little child to recollect and talk about years down the track.

There are so many stories and pictures that I can recall during that time in my childhood. As I talked to my mother, Jesintha of the memories she helped me to put them into context, and filled in all the blanks with explanations.

My great grandfather, Papa had a flat at the back of the farm property, where he spent endless days collecting buttons, categorising them into sizes, colours and shapes. He would show me his collection and I would help him sort them as he showed me. I was not sure where he got all these buttons from, and how he found the interest to collect and store this. I thought at the time that this was a valuable collection, which one day he would hand on to some deserving person.

Papa would talk to me for hours about his boyhood and all the mischief he got up to. He spent days hunting in the bush, experiencing the jungle with tigers, elephants and snakes. He talked about camping in the middle of the jungle, watching and hoping that he could survive the night and not be a late night snack for the predators.

I listened to all these stories for hours upon hours, and kept him company. He was lonely, having lost his dear wife some years ago to illness. He was not able to move around much because of his slight stature and he used to tell me that his bones were aching and he had no strength. He often reflected on the day, sometime soon where he would be given a new body in Heaven, and he longed for that day.

As I counted the buttons, I put aside the large flat round ones and began to build a tower. Did Papa have enough buttons to build a tower? It began to be a game of trying hard not to let it fall. I looked around the room, a smallish and tidy room with a bed, a comfortable soft sofa and an old looking big radio. Papa sat on the sofa for ages listening to the radio and hearing stories. It kept him in touch with the world. He often told me about these stories, and one day I hope to recall some of these, buried deep within my memory vault.

I was going to miss Papa, leaving him to go to Australia. Will he ever be able to come and visit me and show me his button collection? I could not understand how these buttons became so much part of his life. Is this what old people do, I asked my Mum? How sad it seemed to me for someone to have had such an adventure-filled life, to then spend his last few years collecting buttons and stamps. I told Papa that he could come to Australia and find more interesting buttons, and explore the land while he was at it. I remember him laughing and laughing, and shaking his head with amusement!

"Melody… you are so full of life and wonder! Don't ever lose that!" He said with his Indian accent. I thought it was very funny too!

On Saturday afternoon, Uncle Billy the youngest was around twelve years of age, and didn't like me calling him uncle, so it was just Billy. He was full of mischief and loved building cubby houses in the compound, out of bricks, stones, sheet metal and whatever he could find in the street. I would go and sit in the cubby house and let him cook something on the fireplace he made. He would catch any random birds, take off the feathers and cook it on the fire. I didn't know what I was eating but it tasted okay. My Mum would be furious about eating random birds and would always tell me not to eat anything. Anyway I enjoyed the adventure, watching Billy building and hunting around the backyard.

The chickens were there to lay eggs, and were also a food source, so Mum always reminded me of that. They were not pets. However, she could not let go of little 'Brownie', this tan and white chicken who chirped when she saw my Mum. I even saw my mother pick up and cuddle this little chicken.

I suggested that she get rid of the cats that were really feral and annoying. They would often hassle the chickens in the backyard and my Mum's favourite one named Brownie. She just loved Brownie who was so tame and obedient. When my Mum went into the yard, Brownie would come straight to her and peck around the dirt, making noises of excitement. It was so cute to watch and I did not know that chickens could be affectionate and tame.

It was Sunday morning, and our family went off to the local church, an old building with lots of colourful statues of Jesus, Mary and other angels. It was a holy place, with windows that the light bounced off into a myriad of colours like a rainbow. My mind would often wander distracted by the sun shining through, and seeing the patterns and reflections all over the building.

What was the priest talking about? He kept saying the same thing over and over again, and everyone would say Amen. What was God like? I thought about how tall God would be, and how powerful and smart He was to make the whole world. I remember seeing books with pictures of Jesus surrounded with lots of children. Jesus must have really liked kids like me, and thought they were important enough to talk to them. I really liked Jesus and I wanted to meet Him one day.

I liked the singing in the church and tried to copy the words. It sounded like I was in heaven, with lots of beautiful voices singing and telling us how wonderful God is. I wanted to sing and I hummed along to the tune, trying to remember the words so I could continue singing at home.

Sunday was always a special day at home, where all my aunties and uncles joined us for a meal. There was always lots of laughter and funny stories told over lunch, and I really liked listening. I always had so many questions, and I would keep the conversation going, with each one of my relatives building on the story until it was too much to take in.

I was going to miss my aunties, Pammy and Francesca when I go to Australia. They really gave me lots of attention, spoiled me in so many ways, being the first niece, I guess. I told them that I was going to strap them up to the plane, and they could come with me. Or I was going to carry them in my arms, if that was all possible. It is the imagination of a four year old who thinks they are invincible. They laughed out loud, telling each other how cute I was, and that they were going to miss me. I remember feeling scared about this adventure, going to a new country with lots of people I didn't know. How was I going to make friends? Where were we going to live? I would miss this farm and the animals, but not the snake. Dad told me that there were some wild animals in Australia like sharks, spiders, kangaroos and lots of snakes. It sounded like a scary place and I imagined these kangaroos jumping all over the place. They were odd looking animals with a huge tail and strange legs, but I was hoping that they were friendly.

I was also going to miss the servants who were kind and looked after me while Mum was at work. They were friendly and enjoyed hearing my stories. I felt sorry for them, because they had ordinary clothes and really depended on my family for food and shelter. Thankfully my Grandpa and Nanna were staying in India, so they could continue to support them. Having such a large property was very useful as we could offer these poor people a job, food and shelter, and support their entire family. My grandparents were very generous and looked after these people so well.

Chapter 2

Australia Bound - A Great Land Of Opportunity

L ooking out of the window of the aeroplane I could see the fluffy clouds, bouncing like fairy floss. Sitting near the window I could see below, the sea and the many colours of the land below. It was scary at first taking off and hearing the rumble of the engine below, and the huge wings at the side.

Mum told me that we were flying first class, whatever that meant. My great uncle was the general manager of the airline and managed to get us these tickets. It meant I was able to travel in style, eat whatever I wanted and sleep in a comfy type of bed. I could not imagine sitting up in a seat for a long time.

The plane had a lower deck with a staircase near the front of the plane. I went for a wander and realised that the floor below was so crowded with lots more people. I liked being upstairs with areas that you could watch movies, and sit on the couch and colour in. The air hostess was very friendly and went out of their way to keep me busy with activities.

At times I was feeling quite sick, and even had to vomit. I had never travelled on a plane so Mum told me it was travel sickness. The air hostesses gave me ice-blocks and lemonade so that I could feel a lot better. After a little while the sickness stopped and I was able to have some fruit and snacks.

We were travelling to a place called Perth then taking another plane over to Sydney, Australia. I was so excited to take this trip, and missed my Dad who was waiting for us in Sydney. My Dad left India three months earlier to find a place to live, get a job and wait for us.

I was looking out of the window of the plane, seeing the coastline of waves so bright blue with the white sand. How beautiful was this country, with the waves lapping against the sandy coast? I don't remember ever seeing sand like this in India. Our family holidays were at a beach but it was nothing like this.

The plane landed at the Perth Airport and climbing down the high stairs I almost tripped. I only had small legs and it was a long way down. The air hostess had to help me because my Mum was carrying my baby sister, Jenny.

It seemed forever, with the excitement building up to get to our destination, Sydney and see my Daddy, who I missed for such a long time. Feeling ill with the travel, dizziness set in and I wanted to lie down, but knew I had to board another plane soon.

Before long we were up in the air again, and flying over the sea enroute, then across the red and orange land. It was so dry and I could not see any houses, just lots and lots of emptiness with no signs of life. It was so different from India with lots of towns, congestion, smog and people everywhere. I was wondering what Sydney was like and whether it was as beautiful as Dad said it was.

Another four hours and we finally landed. I was so happy and ready to hop down the stairs to the tarmac. My Dad was waiting at the airport in Sydney with a big grin. He had such white teeth and it shone through the crowd. He kept grinning and waving at us as we made our way through the landing area, with lots of people asking us questions, and then collecting our suitcases.

Dad gave Mum and I a big hug and told us he was so happy to see us. My sister, Jen started crying as she must have recognised my Dad, and not knowing what had happened to him. How do you explain this all to a two year old? Jenny just kept crying and we couldn't console her.

The apartment was three stories, and had lots of stairs to climb. It was small compared to the farm and compound we were living in. Inside was a sofa, some chairs and a table with plants here and there. My Dad did a good job setting up, even though he came with very little.

It was scary living in a different place. I really missed my home, extended family and the servants. I was so used to the hustle and bustle of people, the markets and lots of animals, and here I was in an unfamiliar place with my family. It was scary for a little girl moving to a new country and feeling that I was just ripped out of a life I knew, a life that was comfortable. However, to cope with the huge change, I had to see it as an adventure which appealed to my curiosity and willingness to explore. Dad told us that life was going to get difficult for us in India and we would be better off in Australia. I did not understand this at the time.

The next day, I awoke and thought I had dreamt the whole thing, imagining that I was home in my soft bed in India. I looked around and it was real, I looked at the bare walls and thought it needed some colour. Anyhow I can fix this, I thought to myself.

Going to the shops to buy some vegetables was interesting. The shop was quite small and everything was displayed. I saw some bananas and asked my Dad to buy some. I said in a cheeky voice, "Will the monkeys steal my bananas Daddy?"

My father in a rather comical tone said, "No there are no monkeys here, only you, cheeky monkey." I just laughed and wondered what animals I was going to encounter on the street.

Dad was looking for a house, because my cousins were coming from India and we needed a larger place to stay. The next month or so seemed forever, and I was going crazy cooped up in this small flat. I wanted to go for walks in the park, and stay outside and play. However my Mum said I couldn't go alone, so I would draw and paint to keep busy.

When my birthday finally came around, my Dad came home with a small guitar, called a ukulele and I enjoyed playing it. I made up songs and I would pass my time singing and playing. Mum made some dumplings with coconut which was my favourite. After dinner, we even had a chocolate cake that was very spongy and creamy. The cakes were so different here, but I really enjoyed it.

Sitting on the balcony, I could hear the children playing in the park, and birds would come and sit on the railing and sing along with me. I would imagine myself back in India with all the noise, people shouting as they walked by the house. I didn't know what to do with all this silence. When I closed my eyes it was so quiet and still, and not a horn blowing, chimes, or people talking.

I asked my Mum why it was so quiet here in Australia, and she said because there were a small number of people here. So I was a little scared, thinking that we were on some deserted island and alone. It was scary for a five year old to understand what this means. Also I could not see any people that looked like us.

The house we moved into was in the Inner West of Sydney. It was dark, gloomy and very scary. It looked quite small from the outside with dark brick, and it had a porch out the front with a swinging front door. It was fun to swing on this door, back and forwards.

Inside the house was a dark hallway which had rooms flowing from it. It had a fireplace in the corner, and the walls had designs on it. At least this place was colourful and we could brighten it up with lots of lights. We could play hide and seek as there were plenty of places to hide. The kitchen was large and very orange. It reminded me of India with lots of bright colours.

The backyard was large with steps leading down from the back door. There were lots of trees and shrubs all around. Mum was happy to see a mulberry tree in the yard, with lots of leaves and fruit. She said that I could climb it and pick up the fruit. I couldn't wait to taste these berries. Towards the back of the yard was this mound of dirt, 6 feet long by 3 feet wide, and it looked like a grave. There was a white rock on the top with some writing on it. I didn't know what this was but my parents told me not to go near it, which was not the right thing to say to me. It made me more curious and I was drawn to find out what this was.

I pondered it for days, thinking that I could dig a little and see if there was anyone under it. What if it was a grave, or a monster came out and killed me. It really scared me and I could not wait to tell my cousins when they arrived.

At the back of the fence there were some etchings and designs in white paint. I was wondering what that was. It looked like a person with a face and red eyes. When I stood at the back door, I thought it may be an Aboriginal standing there with a spear. I had learned about Aboriginals, and that they were the first people to live in Australia. They looked like some Indians back home, but were fierce hunters. I was afraid of them because of the paint on their faces and body.

My first day at school was terrifying. The teachers were dressed in black long dresses which covered their heads, and a white outline around their faces. I didn't know what sort of costume this was, and I had not seen this anywhere before. They were called nuns and lived together in a big house and prayed all night. That sounded very boring to me, I mean who would like to teach all day, and then pray all night? They could not have fun and explore, but lived a life of solitude and dedication. I thought to myself, "Wow, what sort of God wanted us to live this dreary life, being punished and suffering?"

My uniform was a dark blue tunic with a white shirt, and I had to wear a large brimmed hat. Mum said I looked very cute, but I was very scared to go to school. Having to march every morning, then go to church once a week to hear a man dressed in white talk about God, was not much fun for me. I didn't understand this language, even though they were speaking English it sounded very angry and a little scary. He was so different to the priests back home. For a moment I thought the man in white was God, and he spoke really loud and everyone was scared. I looked at the other boys and girls with fear on their faces, and wondered why they were so scared. Was this man going to punish us?

I walked around the playground trying to make friends. They would say to me, "I don't understand your language…you sound really weird." I had an Anglo Indian accent and would often roll my head and eyes to express myself, something that I learned growing up in India. My classmates would ask me where I was from and I told them that I was an Indian. They would immediately put their hand on their mouth and make this funny sound. They would ask me if I ate people and had a spear. I really didn't understand why they did these funny things everytime I said the word ' Indian.'

Later that night I mentioned this to my family whilst having dinner. My Dad said, "Maybe they are watching cowboys and indians on television or the movies and think you are one of those." We didn't have a television yet so I was not aware of this. My Dad told us that we were going to get a television next week, and I could not wait.

Every morning at school, we lined up at the classroom and we were given a small glass bottle of milk. We had to drink this up very fast then go to the main area for assembly. Standing there, I often daydreamed about a happier place, where there were not all these rules, and instructions that I did not understand. It was really overwhelming to adapt to all this change, and not understand why. I had so many questions but who would I ask? I could not even put this into words to describe this panic overflowing, my stomach churning so that I felt that I was going to choke and die. How was I going to survive this?

I just followed the other kids when I did not understand, or they would tell me. I met this girl Maria who had a way to explain things to me. She told me that she was from Italy, and her parents did not speak English. She was the only one in her family that spoke English. Maria would only speak Italian at home. Maybe she understood how I felt. The only other way is for me to pick up the twang, and words that I had not heard before.

Mum gave me a tin lunch box which formerly held biscuits in it, and it had a beautiful mountain, a river and a valley on the lid. I would have sandwiches and a piece of fruit with a lolly to make me feel a little better. I guess Mum knew how scared and anxious I was about school.

One day I opened my lunch box and saw a chapati with jam and some fruit. I was terrified that the kids would laugh and tease me about this. I tried to cover it up and slowly ate it as I was very hungry. One boy yelled out, "She is a wog, she has wog food." I asked him what a wog was and he told me that because I came from another country and ate different food that I was a wog. I was getting angry and wanted to cry as everyone looked at me and sniggered.

"I am an Indian," I yelled back in a loud voice. The boy burst out laughing and started to make these funny sounds, tapping his mouth whilst he danced in a circle. Now that we had a television I understood the shows about cowboys and indians. So I told the boy with a defiant voice that if he didn't stop with the teasing that I would 'scalp him'. He stopped immediately with fear, looked at me then ran off to tell the nun in his loudest voice, so that everyone could hear what I had said. This was so embarrassing!

The nun came over to me, looking down with an angry expression. "Now Melody, did you tell Scott that you were going to 'scalp him'?" she said with a funny tone. I looked at her, trembling but still quite angry about all the teasing and ridicule. I looked up at her, "Yes I stammered…he was teasing me and calling me an Indian, making funny noises and I asked him to stop…"

The Nun interrupted me, sniggered and said, "Do you understand what that is?"

"I watched cowboys and Indians and they say these things when they get mad, so I thought I would try that," I said with my Indian accent. She asked me to sit on a bench, and I thought I was in trouble. I just wanted to go home and cry. Tears spilled down my face as I tried to be brave and fight back the flow. I could not let these kids see me cry.

Moments later she returned and told me to go back to class, with no explanation. Maybe she thought it was funny, and I was very relieved that I was not in trouble. However the teasing continued and Scott would still do his funny dance and tap his mouth like some lunatic. I would just put my hands on my hips and frown at him.

Later that night I told my Mum and Dad about the teasing and what I had said. They laughed and laughed and told me that was very cute. I didn't see why this was so funny, when it was annoying me. Mum told me to ignore Scott and all the other kids that were teasing me, as they were looking for a reaction. It did not make sense to me.

The bell rang and it was time for the marching and assembly. I lined up behind all the other students in my class and we marched once around the school. When we finished, it was time to go to our class room and drink our milk. Sometimes the milk was lukewarm and tasted sour, but I was afraid to tell the teacher. I would tell Maria and she would blurt it out. She was a good friend that looked out for me at times. However, there were times when she joined in with the teasing. I could not trust her.

It was time for church today, and as we entered the building I took a seat then knelt down. I prayed to Jesus, that he would be with me, and help me with school. It was great that I could softly speak to him without saying a word. I did not want the other kids to know what I was praying about. I bet He knew how I was feeling and could help me through this. I thought about the prayer that our parents had taught us and we said every night before bed

'Gentle Jesus, meek and mild, look upon a little child. Pity me and suffer me to come to thee Bless... and so we begin to put our petitions forward'. I said this prayer in my head and then listed all the people I had left behind in India. I really missed my extended family and friends.

I was always looking forward to getting home and exploring the backyard. I loved the mulberry tree and would often get the berries all over me, and even make myself ill from eating too many. They were soft and juicy and would dissolve like a burst of sunshine in my mouth. It made me think about India and all the fruit trees in the compound.

Whilst I was trying to climb the tree, a bird flew into the side of the shed and fell to the floor. It was a black bird with a yellow beak. It was injured so I knelt down and scooped it up in my hands and took it inside to show my Mum. My Mum knew lots about animals and could help fix this bird. We were able to find a bird cage in the garage and I put some soft cloths at the base and put the bird into it. It would be appropriate to give this bird a name, so I called it Peter.

From time to time during the night, I would wake up and check on it. It was hardly moving and every time I called out, it would chirp as it was trying to tell me something. It was feeling cold and I tried to cover it up to keep the bird warm.

The next day, the bird was moving slightly but had not eaten. I thought I would go and collect some worms and bugs to feed it. So before school I ventured out into the backyard digging around the mound for worms. Surely if there was a dead body underneath, there would be worms. I heard about this from the Bible, that our body turns into worms.

I found some big juicy worms and could not wait to feed this to Peter. Surely this would make him better. I left some water in a container and hopefully he would be better once I returned from school.

It was another tough day of school with teasing about the way I looked, and how I spoke. I don't think anyone knew about India. I just told them all that they were ignorant and should go and ask their parents about the country of India before calling me a 'Red Indian' or 'Comanche'. I had wavy blue black hair, dark brown eyes with a high nose, with tanned skin, a warm brown. Mum said that I always had such a sparkle in my eyes, with a cheeky grin which was my signature look. Did I actually look like an American Indian? My sister Jenny looked more like that, and I started calling her a Comanche.

The only thing I liked about the church was the singing of choruses and hymns. I loved to sing and it sounded so wonderful as the music and voices bounced off the walls and roof. It really felt like heaven, and I was visiting.

The man in the white robes jumped up with lots of energy and started preaching, talking about the miracles of Jesus. Jesus was in the business of performing miracles so that people would believe. Yet so many people saw this but still did not believe. I did not understand how this could happen because if I saw a miracle then I would believe.

The Priest then asked us if we had anything to pray about, but no one responded. I felt so sad about Peter, my minor bird and thought that Jesus could heal his broken leg. I put my hand up and told him that I wanted prayer for Peter who had a broken leg.

The man in the robe asked everyone to join in and pray for Peter that God would heal his broken leg and make him better. The Priest in a powerful tone said, "Almighty God, maker of Heaven and Earth, we lift Peter up in prayer, and ask for your healing touch on his leg. We pray that he will be restored to good health, so that he may serve you and give you glory Amen."

I thought it was very kind of the Priest to pray like that for a pet bird. However, the Priest had forgotten to ask me who Peter was and spoke of him as if he was a person. He asked me, "Is Peter your younger brother?" in a deep tone.

In a soft voice I said, "Peter is my injured pet bird that fell off a tree."

The man sighed and looked at me with disbelief. I was scared, did I say something wrong? The children all sniggered and laughed, and Sister Bernadette asked them to be quiet and called out, "Melody come with me!" I trembled as I left the church, sobbing because I had thought I was in a lot of trouble.

Sister Bernadette gave me a stern look and asked if I was joking or playing some prank. However she could see that I innocently wanted my bird to be healed and the Priest told us about the miracles of Jesus. Surely Jesus who loved little children also loved animals?

I said in a small voice and holding back the sobs, "Am I in trouble? What did I do wrong?"

She looked at me then sighed again, "No... you are not in trouble, but prayers in church are for people and not animals," she said in a matter of fact way. I sat on the bench outside the Headmaster's office for a little while until I stopped crying.

I could not understand why school was so traumatic, but every day I was learning something new, including some difficult lessons. My stomach would be in knots most of the day, as I tried to work out what was going on. I also seemed to be invisible at times, when the teachers would look over the class and not make any eye contact with me. Why were they always shouting, telling kids off and just plain cranky? Dad said because they wanted to get married and they were frustrated!

Finally my cousins arrived from India, and we had some company and lots of noise, yeah! They were smaller than me so since I was the eldest I could teach them all what I had been learning at school. Charlie was three and half and his sister Cary was an infant. Charlie was mischievous like me so often the three of us Jenny, Charlie and myself would play out in the back garden climbing the trees and throwing the ball around.

They could not wait until I got home from school, and we played and played for a long time until it was time for dinner. I taught them how to pull the wallpaper off the walls to make designs, climb the mulberry tree and how to put white glucose powder on their faces. When they looked in the mirror, they were terrified thinking it was a ghost. I thought it was really funny, but told them it was only powder. They would often pull my hair and scratch me but that did not bother me because I was having fun and so were they.

I told them about the grave in the backyard, and it had a body beneath the dirt. They often played near it but we were all too scared to step on it in case the skeleton jumped out of the grave and pulled us in. I would sit and tell them scary stories about the ghost in the grave, and it was waiting for someone to step over it. When the ball landed near the grave, we would take turns of fetching it, but always looking out for one another.

They also discovered the mulberry tree, and before long we had lots of stains on our clothes. We ate so many mulberries that when dinner came around, our stomachs were full and we had belly aches and could not eat. Our Mum would ask me, "Melody, did you eat any mulberries?"

In a soft tone I would say, "We only tasted one or two."

Mum would interject, "Only one or two? Show me your tongues!" This would always give it away as our tongues, hands, feet and arms were all purple. My cousin and sister could hide it as their skin was darker than mine. Being the eldest, I was always the one in trouble.

Aunty would say, "Melody you are teaching the young ones mischief?"

I would say back with a cheeky voice, "But they are enjoying themselves." Mum would tell me not to lie but I did not want to get in trouble. Deep down I really did not feel good about lying to my Mum, especially as she always caught me out.

Chapter 3

Mischief and Intrigue

We often had parties, and got together with our extended family, and it was so much fun. We had music in the background, and my cousins, and friends would play with the ball in the backyard. We also played card games and there was a lot of noise. It reminded me of home and now I was beginning to like Australia.

When I arrived home from school the next day, there were two geese in the backyard. I said with excitement, "Wow we have some new pets," and ran inside to tell my sister and Charlie. However, before long I found out that the geese were wild, and they chased me. They could bite hard and I ran around the backyard screaming. Every time I went to the backyard they would chase me. Maybe my Mum was tired of me eating all those mulberries, and bought some geese to scare me away.

My Mum told me that they were going to eat these geese, and I could not believe that. I thought they were pets, so I started to make friends with them. I think they eventually got used to me and left me alone from time to time.

One day, I took a plastic bowl out with me, and told my cousin that I was going to put this bowl on the goose's head. They did not believe me, but as I stepped down the stairs and threw the bowl and it landed on the goose's head. The goose pushed it off but came running for me and my naughty cousin, and sister locked the back door so I was stuck with this angry bird chomping on my backside. I could see the faces of my cousin and sister in the window laughing and watching me scream and kick off the bird. It was not funny but they kept laughing and laughing and eventually let me in. I was shaking, having been bitten on my bottom and legs and did not think this was funny.

Before long the goose was on the table ready to eat! My Mum loved to curry everything, fresh chickens, ducks and goats to name a few. Thankfully the geese were not too friendly because then I would have declared it a pet, and that's where it crossed the line. I could not eat my pets, even if I was super hungry!!

I was sure the house was haunted, as at night there was lots of noise with scratching, and tin cans rolling on the roof. Later my Mum discovered that there were a couple of large rats that took up residence in our kitchen cupboards. Now it was my Dad's job to get rid of them. We set some rat traps with cheese and it did not disappoint. The next day, the rats lay motionless in the trap with blood smothered all over it. It was disgusting! I had never seen rats so big before. Before long, the noises stopped so I assumed that it was the rats that created all the drama.

Dad found the open spaces in the cupboard and patched them up. There were also some food sources in the garden, as we would put our vegetables and cuttings for compost. They loved the smells and the decaying vegetables.

Over dinner that night, Mum told us that she was going to work part time to save for a house. She had arranged for a lady down the road, Mrs Levinsky, to look after us until she returned home. This was another thing that made me anxious, not knowing who this lady was, and what to expect. I decided to make it another adventure, hoping that this lady was as lovely as our neighbours Mr and Mrs Jones, who became my adopted grandparents.

On Friday afternoon, the weather was very cloudy so I thought I would bring cheer to people that walked by our house by singing the new songs I had learned at school, Yes Puff the magic dragon. I took out my ukulele and strummed and sang on the front porch. Before long I had a small gathering of people, mostly older folk but a few young children and they listened and listened, then clapped. It was exhilarating to see their happy faces, smiling at me and it really cheered them up. On the way back, a lady dressed in black came over to me and handed me a bag of lollies to share with my sister and cousins. "Thank you Miss," I said with a big smile. She was then saying something in another language and smiling at me.

I talked this over with my parents and cousin, Charlie and told them that it was special to make people smile and brighten up their day. The following Monday, I rushed home from school, and did my homework. I came up with an idea to put a bowl on the wall of the front porch and put up a sign 'Lollies Please!' Off I went to work at my first busking job, singing all the songs I had learned at school including a few hymns from Church. Mum and Dad came home to a small crowd of people standing in front of our house listening and clapping when I had finished. I would clearly announce the next song and tell them a funny joke. It was so much fun and at only five and half years of age, I felt so grown up.

By nightfall, I had bags and bags of lollies to share with my family. Mum would say, "Melody you are going to get rotten teeth if you keep this up." I had to come up with another plan. That night I pondered over ideas in my head as to how I could help my parents buy a house. My Dad had to work two jobs, with shift work and we hardly saw him. I thought I could help save up for a new house, yes that was a great idea!!

At school we had some free time, so I made a poster with some cardboard that read, 'Money please for a new house'. I had to check with the teacher about the spelling and she helped me. The teacher asked me about the poster and I explained that I was singing on my porch, and the poster was to collect money. She looked at me with a puzzled expression and said that I needed to ask my parents for permission. That did not make any sense to me, as it was a surprise, and I didn't want them to know about collecting money for the new house.

So for the next week, on Wednesday, Thursday and Friday I would place my bowl on the porch and sing Yellow Submarine, Puff the Magic Dragon, Jesus loves me and What a wonderful friend is Jesus, a song which I made up some of the words. People stopped by and placed coins and some notes in the bowl. They asked me about the new house, and hoped I would not be leaving the suburb as they would miss my singing and smile. There were so many nice people that I made a lot of friends in the local area.

This busking continued for a few weeks, until one day My Dad came home early to a crowd of people in our front yard. He asked me what was going on, and I told him about my singing and making people happy. "Oh No!" I screamed.

He saw the sign and quite astonished looked down at me and smiled. "This is what you have been up to, Melody," he said in a smug tone.

He went inside and told my mother who was busy bathing my sister and preparing dinner. She just thought I was singing from time to time and people stopped by with lollies. She did not know about the sign requesting money. I only wanted to help my parents, and thought of contributing.

I had learned about kindness from my Bible stories of how Jesus reached out and touched so many lives. I wanted to be like Jesus and bring joy to people, and at the same time help my parents who were always working.

Chapter 4

Close Encounters with Danger and Strife

It was a very cold day, and my feet were frozen, and even though I had socks on and a blanket around me, I shivered. It was not this cold in India and I don't remember ever sitting near the heater like I was in Australia.

We went to a large shopping centre with Mum, Dad and my sister Jenny to buy some clothes and presents. It was so much fun to go up and down the escalators, looking at all the colourful shops. We even saw some Indian people and Mum went over to talk to them. My Mum was very friendly and she was always hunting for spices and asking people if they knew where to buy Indian goods. These Indian people told us to go to Bondi where there was a shop that sold Indian sweets, and lots of spices and dhal. My Mum was very happy to hear this, but we had no idea where Bondi was, let alone how to pronounce this name.

There was a dark looking man with fancy clothes singing at the shopping centre at Roselands, and Dad recognised him from the television. His name was Kamahl and I thought wow he must be famous if he didn't have a last name. He had a powerful voice and sang on the stage at the shopping centre. Everyone seemed to know him and after he finished the applause was deafening.

After he had finished, my Mum and Dad went over and introduced themselves and they chatted and laughed. We hardly saw anyone from India and Kamahl had been here longer than we had. He still sounded very Indian and wobbled his head like my parents. Even I had wobbled my head from time to time. He was friendly and also told my parents about this shop in Bondi that sold curry stuff, and Indian sweets. We said goodbye and left this man to mingle with the crowd.

We shopped and shopped and I accidentally stepped away from my parents and found my way down the escalator. "Oh no, I had lost my parents and could not find them," I gasped as I pulled on a stranger's jumper. I had told them that I was lost and could not find my parents. I began to cry and just stood near the escalators and waited. I prayed, "Jesus please bring my parents back."

After a short while, My Dad was standing with me and took my hand. "It is okay Melody, we found you. Mum is waiting upstairs with your sister", he said with a gentle voice. He seemed very calm but my Mum was in a panic, and I could see it on her face. I told her that Jesus was with me and I was okay. She scolded me and told me to hold her hand. That was the end of my shopping adventure for the day.

It seemed to take forever to find this place called Bondi. My Dad had to look up a book for directions and then stop along the way to ask people.

The shop reminded me of India, and as soon as I walked in the spices hit me like a bulldozer, it went up my nose and made my eyes water. The man in the store was burning incense and it was irritating all my senses. I did not understand why people burnt these senseless sticks, maybe to take away the sewage smells, cow dung that littered the street and gutters. I was always looking out for this to avoid stepping into these slushy pieces of dirt that stunk. Phew! However, Australia was not like that, and I did not see one cow on the street.

Mum was so excited looking at all the spices, tasting the sweets and buying heaps of goods. The man had a funny name called Ezi Moses and I laughed, because he was supposed to be Indian, but he was actually a Jew. I just could not wait to get out of this shop and spend the afternoon at the beach. The water was so blue, with frothy waves that tossed the sand about.

I ran straight into the water and it jumped through the waves. It was so much fun, and I screamed and laughed as the water pushed me back, and I even fell a few times. My Mum was sitting on the beach with Jenny, as she was terrified of the sound of the waves. My Dad was walking along the shore watching me frolicking around and enjoying the waves.

I started to step out and then a large wave caught me by surprise and I went under the water. I remember swirling around like a washing machine as the rip started to take me out. I was really scared as I drank in the sea water and fought for air. Then I felt a hand pull me up, and looked up and it was my Dad. I gasped for air and began coughing and spluttering. I couldn't walk for a moment, and my Dad carried me out of the sea. Next moment I was lying on the towel and coughing up the salty water, my nose stinging and I began to cry. Mum began shouting and panicked, thinking that I was going to die or something. This made me more afraid, as I was trying to breathe, whilst coughing up the water that I had swallowed. A lifeguard came over and checked on me. He told my Dad that the rip was quite strong and that he saved me in time. He also mentioned that we were supposed to swim between some flags which made no sense. Thankfully, I was going to be okay.

The beach in India where we holidayed from time to time did not have such powerful waves. It was very calm and I was not afraid. Afterall the beach was special to me, because it was the first time I walked after 13 months of being carried around and crawling, with my parents worrying that I was unable to walk. It was the beach that I first began to take my first steps then run into the water. Mum and Dad cheered so loudly as if it was some kind of miracle! Well the running part so quickly was a miracle! I must have stored up all this energy and developed firm muscles and agility in order to have been able to run so quickly.

After a little while I went back into the waves but made sure I didn't venture too deep. The lifeguards told us to swim in a particular area away from the dangerous rips. That was my first near drowning experience of being caught in a rip. I had lots of news to tell when I went to school on Monday!

Mum and Dad told me that we would regularly go to Bondi to pick up these Indian goods, and so there will be plenty of opportunities to go to the beach and swim. Obviously in winter, the water was way too cold but I always loved watching the ocean lapping at the rocks, crashing during high tide and those silly birds they call seagulls swooping at me.

That Saturday, Mum and Dad came home with a little white puppy for us. It was such a cute dog, with big brown eyes, short blonde hair and I knew what to call it. I named the dog Susie, and it would wag its tail, and spin around. I figured it must have really liked the name, because everytime I called it, it would get excited and show off.

I looked forward to getting home from school so that I could play outside with the puppy. I would often wrap it up in an old cloth and walk around holding it like a baby. I was so besotted with the dog, and it was so mischievous. Puppies loved to explore and find interesting things to keep them busy but most of all mischief. Susie would often take off with our shoes and chew on them. We now had to make sure we put our shoes in the cupboard or up high. Susie would also go out on the street and our neighbours would have to bring the dog back.

A few months later, we discovered that Susie was a male dog, with a female name. I tried to change her name to Sam but he would not respond. So the name Susie stuck! This was a bother as I would often explain what had happened and that Susie was my favourite name and the dog looked like a female, so cute and feminine. However, the mischievous streak and hyperactivity were red flags, but I could not see that.

Winter was very cold, and our dog had to sleep on the porch or sometimes we would sneak him into the back room. That night, I went into my parents room and looked for something warm to dress Susie. I found my mothers white jumper that she had not worn for a while. It had a polar neck and was warm and fluffy. I put this on Susie, and took a pair of scissors and cut holes for his eyes and snout. I also cut the sleeves so that I could put Susie's feet through and he could walk around. "Perfect, now you can be warm," I said feeling very proud of myself for coming up with the idea.

In the morning around four o'clock we had a milkman come and deliver milk in bottles to each home and this was a service for most people. Every week we received a bill and put the money out to be collected. In those days, not everyone had cars so this was a convenient way to ensure people received milk.

This morning, I heard an alarming squeal that echoed in the house from outside. My heart jumped as I could clearly hear, "Oh my God! What is that?" Then the shattering of glass on our porch. My Dad jumped out of bed and went to check. It was the milkman who had dropped the bottles of milk, and was bleeding. His hands were covered with blood and the stains were splattered all over the floor, with the fragments of glass and milk. It looked like strawberry milk in some spots. He stood there shocked and said "I thought I saw a ghost crawling around!! What is that?" My Dad looked around and saw Susie sitting in the corner with a jumper on, two big brown eyes peeking through the holes of the jumper, with an elongated shaped head. Yes it did look like some sort of creature! My Dad ran inside and got some towels and a bandage, to patch up the wound.

Dad helped the milkman into the house as he was stumbling all over the place, maybe by the loss of blood and shock. We gave him a glass of water and banaged his hand to stop the bleeding. My Dad offered to take him to the hospital but he said that his mate was in the truck and could take him there if needed. Thankfully we managed to stop the bleeding, and the milkman felt a lot better. I stumbled into the room, and said that I was very sorry because I put the jumper on my dog to keep him warm. I was teary because I thought I would be in a lot of trouble. The milkman said that was a very good idea but it totally frightened him, as Susie sat in the corner and growled at him like a demon. The man said, "It looked like a ghost and I am a real chicken." I thought to myself, *Wow, this man has seen ghosts before!*

Later that morning, my Mum scolded me for not asking permission to cut up her jumper for the dog. She liked the jumper and was going to wear it during the winter. I understood why she was mad, but I felt really sorry for Susie having to sleep outside in the cold. I promised that I would not do that again.

Chapter 5

A New Home

It was time to leave this house and move to a place out south west of Sydney, miles and miles away. Mum and Dad found a white cottage in suburbia and it was elevated, which was always a good thing I heard. It was quite small but cosy. The worst thing about it was the toilet being located outside in a little shed. I imagined having to go in the middle of the night in the dark with a torch. It was also very smelly and some man came by every third day to empty the drum. That was disgusting and it made me sick everytime I went to the toilet. We had indoor toilets in the other place, and not sure why my parents would buy a house in the sticks where you have to venture outside in the dark, wrestle with the spooky spider webs to sit on a smelly drum and hold your breath to avoid vomiting.

Dad was always reminding me that we came to Australia with nothing and had to start all over again. I really did not understand the gravity of that. He would say, "Always be thankful Melody. We came to Australia to give you a better life." I must have heard this so many times that it was etched in my brain. Even in India we had plumbing! However, I had to be reminded of this when we complained, especially about the dirty toilet.

It was 1972, and the house decor was brown and orange, prominent colours of the 1960's mid century era. It was funky and everyone wore multi-coloured clothes that did not match. The carpets were a dirty brown with a dash of green and orange here and there. The walls were a pale purple and it really clashed. What was Mum and Dad thinking? This house was a huge project!

I heard Mum and Dad talking about finding horseshoes outside a few of the windows, and could not understand why. Did the former owners love horses? Mum and Dad were surmising all sorts of things, including some superstition that these horseshoes were used to ward off evil spirits which really did not make sense to me. Why would some evil spirit be afraid of a horseshoe?

The house had three bedrooms and my sister and I had our own room. We didn't have much furniture so Mum and Dad somehow bought some second hand or antique furniture to fill up the house. I had a white bed and brown wardrobe with swirls of some nature that did not match. However, I remembered what Dad said about being thankful. At least I had a comfy bed and somewhere to put my clothes.

My sister Jenny started having nightmares in her room, so she would come and wake me up. This went on for some time, and I felt uneasy in her room. She liked my room better and found it easier to sleep. So often I would awake in the morning, with Jenny in my bed. This happened a few nights of the week, but my parents were hoping that she would settle in time.

Our neighbours across the road were friendly and would often stop and talk to my parents. The Hendersons had two boys Will and Gary and a girl, Dee who was my age. The boys were really into football, and that was the only subject on their agenda. They were always out at football training, football games and Dee played netball. Their father, Mr Henderson was a detective in the police force so Dad said that we were very safe to live across the road.

A few weeks had passed, and Dad was making plans to put the toilet inside finally. I breathed a sigh of relief, not having to smell everyone's poo. Often I found these hairy spiders, just when I sat down and couldn't escape. I did a lot of praying hoping that these spiders would not bite me. I had heard in my new school that some of these spiders were deadly. They called them funnel-webs and I could see lots of webs that looked like funnels. My imagination went wild and it would send me into a panic.

To top it all off, Dad decided to change the colour of the house from white to a teal green! He must have been colour blind or something, because we all protested but Mum said it was okay. I was not sure what she was thinking either. Now our friends would be making fun of us, living in this green eye sore which stood out for miles. Green was a colour of luck and health, so maybe Dad was thinking along those lines.

Now as my sister started to settle in her room, my Dad was waking up with nightmares. He would shout in the middle of the night and scare Jenny and myself. Jenny would then run into my room shivering, and not wanting to go back.

One morning, my Dad told us that he awoke in the middle of the night and saw a little girl with blonde hair in pigtails, and blue-coloured overalls sitting on the end of the bed. For a moment he thought it was me, but rubbed his eyes and realised that she had blondish hair. My Dad said to her, "What are you doing here? Who are you?" He went to wake up my Mum, and she vanished. My Dad was really shaken, and told us that he had seen this little girl two other times.

It was intriguing to hear this story, but Jenny and I just laughed at him sarcastically, "It was just a dream Dad." He used to tell Jenny this about her scary nightmares. So much for the silly horseshoes!

It was July, 1973 and Mum was heavily pregnant and trying to prepare for the new baby. We were always renovating and updating the house, and it was never ending. We often had strangers in the house with building work, extending the living space. Mum would always offer them some food, whatever we had in the fridge from chapatis with meat or chicken curry. It was her way of feeding anyone who visited us, even the workmen! It was a little crazy how an extra baby could make such a big impact on our family.

Jenny and I picked out some girls and boys names, and were excited to have our very own live baby. The baby dolls were getting a little boring, and since I had called each doll Susie, it was getting a little confusing. With a pet called Susie as well, every time I said the word, my dog would appear.

My Mum's brother, Roy, had been staying with us for a little while, so our home was getting a little crowded, hence my Dad constantly renovating and extending the house. During that time, I had to move to my sister's room but that was only for a short time. My Uncle Roy was making plans to rent a house close by as my aunties and grandparents were on their way to Australia.

That was so exciting as I had missed them terribly. When we got together it was a party. Even my Dad's brothers and sisters had come to Australia so we had so many family members. My Dad's family played instruments and sang, so our parties were full of music and singing. It was the disco age, with outlandish shiny outfits, glitter and bling. It was so much fun dressing up and my sister and I loved to dance.

Dad bought a speaker with disco lights and we played our blues, rock and soul music and sang constantly. We learned the dances and the songs, and then became the source of entertainment during the parties.

Our house was too small with both sides of the family visiting, so Dad built an entertainment area at the back of our house. There were three steps going up to a huge concrete area which looked like a stage. We now took our parties outdoors, with coloured lights, music and decorations.

Finally we got a new baby sister, Missy, short for Melissa, during spring. She was a chubby baby with a hairy back, lots of thick hair and big black eyes. She slept a lot and Mum was always changing her nappy.

I went to a local public school a short ten minute walk away, and it was my chance to learn to be independent. However I met up with a friend and we would walk home together. Her name was Leanne and she had the brightest blonde hair ever, with big blue eyes and freckles on her nose. She was very quiet but we found some things in common.

Mum would come to school with my baby sister to buy me some lunch. I was always very embarrassed as Mum still had an Indian accent and would speak extra loud, and wobble her head, "Melody do you want a Pieeeee....?" She would often repeat herself, then shove the pie in my face with the sauce, and it was very embarrassing for me then. My friends would ask me if my Mum was speaking another language, and I would say it was Australian with an Indian accent. They often looked at me puzzled with my answer. I reminded myself that India was still a very foreign and unusual country and many had not heard of Indians. I thought to myself, wait till they start coming to Australia then there would be so much noise, the Australians won't know what hit them.

Mum would often say that I was losing my Indian accent and sounded more Australian each day. Although I did not have a twang, I tried very hard to copy the accent of the English shows I watched from time to time, as they sounded very polished and proper, so I thought!

Jenny and I came home ill with a very bad cold. Mum had us both at home giving us hot lemon drinks and aspirin. The coughing seemed to get worse on day three, and my little sister Missy also picked up the cold. At the end of the week, Mum had taken her to the doctor who sent her straight to hospital far away from our home.

We could not understand what had happened to my sister Missy. She had high temperatures and we were afraid that she would not come home. Jenny and I spent every night praying for her, "Dear Jesus, please make our little baby better so she can come home." It seemed like Missy was away from us for weeks and weeks. The doctors said that she had meningitis, which sounded very serious and life threatening. Mum and Dad were very worried about her, and we did not know if she would live.

Every third day we would all go to visit Missy in hospital at Prince of Wales in Eastern Sydney. I remember it was not far from Bondi, and Ezy Moses' spice shop. We saw a lot of sick babies there, and even remember one baby bleeding everywhere. Jenny and I would just cry and pray for these babies.

It was Friday night, and we decided to take our little dog Susie along with us to the hospital. Dad said we could stop by Brighton Le Sands, have fish and chips and then go see our baby sister. We could leave our dog Susie in the car during the evening for a short time during visiting hours.

There was a circus there on the grounds, with a huge big top tent and lots of animals, even lions and an elephant. How exciting it was to take our dog Susie to introduce him to the animals. Susie could do tricks too. When he was happy to see us he used to smile showing his teeth and then manoeuvre his head from side to side with excitement, whilst wagging his tail. I had not seen any other dog do that.

As we strolled around, Susie got loose from the leash and before long we could not find him. We looked around everywhere from tent to tent but he was nowhere to be found. My mother bumped into a lady who was training animals and asked her about our dog. She shrugged her shoulders and did not seem helpful. She looked at me and something did not seem right to me. I told my Mum that the lady knew something.

It was time to go, and we had to leave Susie. Jenny and I were crying our eyes out as we loved Susie, and could not bear life without him. Mum and Dad assured us that they would come back again in a few days, and ask around. So with that we left, feeling very sad and depleted.

My sister Jenny and I prayed each night, "Jesus please bring our dog back. We really miss our Susie and I know you have more important things to take care of, but please hear our prayers." Mum told me that Jesus loves little children and was so kind and caring. I could not wait to meet Jesus and look into His kind eyes.

It was now five days that Susie was missing and we persevered praying each night and during the day. It was mid-week and we stopped by Brighton Le Sands to find Susie. We searched all the tents, trying to find the suspicious lady, and she was nowhere to be found. I was determined to find her, as I did not want to go home without Susie. I told Dad that the circus could pack up, and leave in the next few days and Susie will be gone.

We waited another half an hour, then finally we saw a man walking out from one of the tents. Dad went over to him and asked him if he knew where the lady was? He was not helpful, pretending he did not understand. Then I spotted the lady, walking near the toilets, and she was totally unaware that we were there. Maybe she thought we had given up and were not going to return. Mum approached her, and she had a guilty look on her face. "Do you have our dog, Susie?" She showed her the photo, and she didn't even look at it.

"Did you take our dog?" I said tearfully. I was choked up because we really missed Susie.

Mum took a step towards her, pointing her comb at her, "If you do not return our dog, I will contact the police and report you." I could hear the anger in her voice.

The lady looked shocked, but she knew that my Mum was serious. The lady motioned to her husband and said something in her language.

The man went into the large tent and brought out Susie. He said, "Sorry, sorry," and I shouted with joy.

"We have found him, yeah!" My sister and I danced around excitedly, thrilled that our prayer was answered. Susie wagged his tail and came running over to us with his sheepish grin.

No-one should mess with my Mum or my God. Mum knew what to say at the time, and the lady looked terrified as I stood close by, proud of her. Now, another miracle to go, my baby sister Missy to be healed. Jenny and I prayed for her each night and also for the other babies in the ward with her. We would be on our knees in prayer, and at times crying, asking God to hear us. He was certainly listening and responding.

Another week went by and my parents told us that my sister Missy was coming home from the hospital. Jenny and I made a welcome home poster with pink balloons, not that she could read. However, when she saw us and the balloons she smiled and smiled. It was so good to see her well again, and we looked up and thanked Jesus for bringing her home to us. I had learned to count on Jesus, which was one of the songs we learned at Sunday school. It was so true!

My extended family came by with food, and lots of noise to welcome Missy back! Mum and Dad were so happy, and appreciated the family support. Whilst the family were noisy and made a big deal about food, they were so kind and caring. I was feeling very thankful. I also told them what had happened with Susie and the circus. Susie probably had a starring role with his sheepish grin.

At school on Monday, I told my classmates about what had happened with Susie, the circus and my baby sister. They were fascinated to hear the story, as nothing so exciting happened to them. They asked me pointedly "Melody, is this story really true? Does your dog really smile?" They had a number of questions, and I invited them to come over to our house to see this for themselves. If only I had a photo to show them?

I also had a best friend at school and her name was Leanne too. She was bright and bubbly and made me laugh with her corny jokes and pranks. Leanne Woodford was the youngest in her family and the only girl amongst boys. She was a little tom boy like me, and she also loved sports and judo, a very handy friend to have in case we got into fights.

There was this one girl, Kerry, that was so annoying. She used to pick on me every morning, outside the school grounds as I walked to school, calling me 'blackie', because I had black hair and was darker than her. She often took out my lunch and threw it over the fence, leaving me with only one piece of fruit for the whole day. She was the bully in our year, and was very tough. No-one wanted to fight her because she was so mean and now she even tried to bash me up on the way home also. I often told her to stop and be quiet, but the more I spoke, the more she would retaliate.

This bullying and taunting went on for at least six months, and even when I defended myself she would become more abusive. Leanne stepped in many times when I was left in tears, and Kerry also went for her. Leanne was punched and her hair pulled. She was such a kind and caring friend who stood by me.

This one day in the playground, I was furious after the taunting and the ridicule. Kerry then proceeded to push me around, trying to punch me. I slammed her in the face, so hard that I hurt my hand, feeling the sharpness of her teeth, and then pulled her hair right to the ground. I found chunks of her hair in my hand. I told her through gritted teeth to leave me alone, or I would give her more of this!!! She had a black eye and bloody nose, and stood crying. The girls around her started yelling "Fight…fight…fight," hoping to see more action. I told them to stop and that I did not want to fight. The next moment a teacher stood beside me and asked me what had happened. Many of the teachers knew what Kerry was like as she had been in trouble many times. They even smiled at me, as I had told them I defended myself and I just could not take this treatment anymore! Leanne backed up my story and thankfully I was not given any detention.

School became more enjoyable now that Kerry left me alone. Days after the fight, I reached out to her and asked her about her family life. Her father had left the family, and she was the only girl. She told me that she did not get on with her mother because she was controlling and strict. I could understand that Kerry was in pain, feeling abandoned by her father and she took out her frustrations on the kids at school, mostly me.

Soon Kerry and I became friends, and I forgave her for the torment she dished out on me. I listened to her talk about her pain, and she cried many times telling me what her life was like at home. I am not sure where this compassion came from, but it was good to be a kind friend. I remember telling her that I would pray for her. She looked at me puzzled, but I just smiled at her.

Chapter 6

Strange Happenings

At the age of ten, I was soon becoming aware of growing up and that soon I would be a teenager. I had heard that teenage life was really tough, with lots of emotions and hormones racing all the time. I decided that I would make the most of my present life and really enjoy childhood.

Jenny kept waking me up during the night with her crazy dreams. She would then jump into bed with me, and I would wake up tired. I was happy to get my room back, but this meant that she annoyed me most nights telling me that she heard someone whispering or a child singing outside her bedroom window. Dad found a horseshoe on her window sill, hanging upwards, so it did not do a thing as Jenny was still being harassed by her dreams. So much for the superstition!

In the early hours of the morning, I saw a white flash hover past my door, down the hallway. Was I dreaming, I thought to myself, but my eyes were wide open? I jumped up and went down the hallway to see this white sheet standing at the front door in the dark. Scared and shaking not knowing what I would see, I pulled the sheet off and there stood Jenny with her eyes open, muttering something I did not comprehend. She was sleep walking and hadn't realised that I was standing beside her. I remember Mum telling me not to wake her as she had slept walked before. She then tried to open the front door. I gently turned her around and directed her back to her room and into bed.

This was tiring and I decided to talk to Mum and Dad about this in the morning. Often I would go into their room but Mum was a heavy sleeper and Dad had to get up at five in the morning for work and I could not help feeling bad about waking them.

Over dinner I discussed this issue with my parents. Jenny said she did not want to sleep in the room anymore and asked if I could sleep on the top bunk. Mum said, "Jenny will probably grow out of this soon, so be patient Melody." So I agreed to sleep on the top bunk, and thought at least I will sleep all night and not go to school so tired with dark circles that seemed to get worse when I did not sleep well.

I asked one of my Chinese friends at school, named Min, about the horseshoe on the window and the front door. She was into her culture and superstitions so I thought she could explain what this meant. She said in a very frank way, "Melody a horseshoe hanging upwards is meant to stop evil spirits from entering your house." I asked her how she knew this and she advised me that her mother did this at their house. She went on to explain that her house had a resident spirit who liked to play tricks by opening the cupboard doors and drawers from time to time. They would get up in the morning and all the doors and drawers were opened. I could not understand how this could happen and was somewhat sceptical. It did not make any sense to me why a ghost would do this. Min said it was in good spirit and did not want to harm anyone, but played tricks. It still did not make any sense to me, even with my imagination.

Then I remembered hearing the stories from my aunties and uncles about spirits taking up residence at our home, the old lady in the cottage, the eerie feeling when I walked by. The stories of practices of 'black magic' which were taboo, all came flooding back to me. I thought to myself, "What if there was a spirit world that we could not see?"

There was some fear there, as I recalled these stories and the fact that there was this awful evil spirit world that was not tangible. That really scared me, but I knew that my Jesus would protect me from this. I told Min about Jesus and she said that He was not real, and she believed in Buddhism, which is part of her culture.

That night I went to sleep on the top bunk after saying my prayers. I slept right through and awoke refreshed and ready for school. I told myself that things would settle down and I was not going to think about the spirit world and the superstitions.

However, it would not leave me alone. The next night, I also had a nightmare which was very unusual for me as I mostly slept through. In the dream I was falling through a big hole, and then seeing fire with people walking through it, burnt bodies that smelt like rotten eggs. The dream was so vivid and it shook me up, and I kept thinking about it all day. I wanted to go back to my room but I decided to persevere.

Two nights later, I had the same dream and this time the people were burning in front of me and calling out my name, "Melody please help me!" They moaned and moaned with terrified expressions on their faces, indicating their torment. I was so frightened that I told my Mum and she tried to console me.

A few nights of the week, I slept in my own room and was fine. There were lots of things happening at school so it took my mind off these nightmares. My friends told me that they had bad dreams too but they went away. Maybe mine would too in time.

My neighbour Dee was playing hopscotch on the road so I went out and joined her. I had not seen her for a week or so, and she had been on a camp with the Girl Guides. She told me about the scary pranks her friends pulled on her. It was very funny. I told her about the scary nightmares and my sister sleep-walking. We laughed and laughed as we hopped. I also asked her about the horseshoes on the front door and my sister's window. She told me about Shelly who was the same age as Dee, and lived in our house before my parents bought it. She sometimes played hopscotch but then she would get very ill and Dee would not see her for months.

The Hendersons were very busy all of the time, with their active boys and sports. One time they were all gardening in the front yard, and the boys were helping too, and Mum with Missy on her hip and Dad went over to give them another shovel to pick up the bark. My parents loved gardening too and we're always ready to give advice. Jenny and I were playing on the grass at the front of the house, and we could see them discussing something that seemed quite serious. We walked over to listen and pretended to help with the bark.

They told my parents that the previous family, the Woodhall's that lived in our house, suddenly lost their daughter Shelly to an illness. They were very private people and didn't socialise with the other neighbours on the street.

The Henderson's liked Shelly and she would come over to their house from time to time. Dee ran inside and brought out a photo of her and Shelly at the front of the white house, a little blonde girl around my age, nine years old with blonde hair tied in pigtails, brownish eyes and loved wearing tunics, overalls and shorts, according to Dee. In the photo she had pink coloured overalls and a cheeky smile. I had told my parents about the little girl that lived in the house previously, but they didn't seem interested in any details.

I looked over to my Dad, who was looking at the photo of Shelly, his face was ashen, expressionless like he was in shock. I was wondering what was going on and my Mum seemed very surprised at his response. Mr Henderson told my parents that the family were Australian that may have had some Aboriginal background. Dad seemed very aloof and asked him about the little girl again as if he had not heard a single thing.

"She was about nine years old, Anthony and died of an illness." Mr Henderson responded, "The parents were very quiet and had told us that Shelly was ill for some time, but no other details. We heard her cry out a few times and she seemed to be in some pain. We reached out to the family to help because they had no visitors, but her parents were not responsive."

Mrs Henderson interjected, "It was all very strange but we decided to mind our own business."

Dad and Mr Henderson had a beer and chatted while we played in the sand. Mum had to go home to prepare dinner. I knew that it would be an interesting discussion over dinner. My sister Missy was getting quite heavy, and she wanted to crawl and play in the sand with us. However, she put everything into her mouth and it sure kept my Mum busy making sure she was not choking on some small toy.

Over dinner, I asked my Dad why he was so surprised about the little girl Shelly. He looked at me and said that she was the girl he saw in his dream. Now he was saying that it was a dream, when he clearly told us that she was sitting on the bed? I think he was trying not to scare us, but I could see that he was hiding what was really going on. Did my parents think I was plain stupid and that I did not pick up on what was going on!? I remember my Dad telling me about the little girl sitting on his bed and calling out to her. She had pink overalls and blonde hair too! I was a little scared thinking that someone had died in the house.

Anyway, she seemed quite friendly and sweet so if her spirit was still around then it was better than some scary evil monster. This is what I had told myself, not understanding what happens when someone dies. Dad was still having these dreams from time to time, and the same girl appeared. It soon became the norm, but the girl did not communicate or say anything.

There were still some eerie things happening at our house from time to time, with a heavy, sturdy ceramic pot suddenly falling down on the tiles, giving me a fright. Also the wooden desk in Jenny's room also rattled as if there was an earthquake, with all her books falling off. Mum and Dad decided to ask our Parish Priest to come over and bless the house. They brought some holy water and walked around dispersing it here and there. It seemed like another superstitious act but I knew that the Bible was really the weapon. We had learned that at the Anglican Sunday School that Jenny and I attended.

It was Wednesday afternoon on 16th August 1977, and my Dad brought the paper home with the front page stating, "Elvis is Dead." I looked at my Dad shocked, and could not believe that this was true. "He died of a heart attack, due to drug addiction," my Dad muttered whilst reading the papers. I stood there trying to contemplate what he was saying. The news on the television was all about Elvis and his last days. There was so much speculation with various stories.

This was so difficult to cope with for a 11 ½ year old as I was a big fan. Mum and Dad grew up with Elvis movies and music and would often play it at home. I cried and cried myself to sleep thinking about a world without Elvis. I didn't really know him, but yet this had such a big impact on me and my whole family. Even my aunts and uncles came over to talk about what had happened.

There was such an outpouring of grief captured on the television and this went on for weeks and weeks. My sister and I made a little memorial for Elvis and put some flowers, pictures and drawings so that we could grieve like the world was.

One of the kids at school brought in a ouija board and decided to have a session in one of the classrooms. I was invited along with my friends. We thought it was harmless and only a game so we went along as spectators. Besides, if we were just watching, we cannot get into trouble. I remember telling myself that, knowing that it was not the right thing to do.

They closed all the blinds to make it dark, hoping that the teachers would not catch them, but left the windows open. There was a slight breeze so the blinds kept knocking against the window. We could hear shuffling and whispering outside the window, thinking it was some kids playing closeby.

Five of my classmates sat around the board with letters, and in the middle there was this glass turned upside down. They began focusing on a dead relative and asking questions out loud like, "What is your favourite colour? What is your name? How old are you? How did you die? Each of them had a finger on the glass. The glass started moving to the letters spelling out answers and my friends and I were commenting on what was happening and discussing who was pushing the glass. We just kept sniggering in the back. There seemed to be two people in particular moving the glass, because the questions were about their dead relative. Leanne and I winked at each other as we figured out this.

The blinds seemed to be moving back and forwards, with the wind, and knocked over some glass bottles sitting on the table, smashing one of the bottles into hundreds of pieces. A couple of the girls screamed at the sudden noise and Jason yelled out, "Tell your grandmother to watch out where she is going?" Everyone laughed and sniggered. This was a perfect set up for a horror movie gone wrong. There was an eerie feeling in the room, and my friend and I were a little anxious, yet trying to make light of this situation.

Then, I suggested they contact Elvis Presley because we could tell if this was fake, so we thought. So the classmates brought out the paper with the heading, "Elvis DEAD at 42" and put the glass on top of it. The two people who had been moving the glass got up to leave, believing that they would soon be found out to be tricking everyone. Jason, one of the boys in the group, started summoning Elvis's spirit, and there was an eerie silence, as the glass slid without a question. Everyone laughed out loud, still believing that this was a harmless game, while Jason asked a question, "Are you Elvis, the King of Rock n Roll?" The glass started moving with the fingers on top, to the letter 'Y-E-S.'

The questions kept coming, mainly yes and no answers, until I suggested a question, "What was Elvis' first movie?" I stated in a matter of fact way. I bet no-one knew this answer and we could see how fake this was. I knew the answer as it was my Mum's favourite movie, but did not say anything to anyone.

All of sudden the glass started moving with the fingers on top to spell the word 'L-O-V-E' then the word 'M-E'... Everyone took their hands off the glass and looked at each other with astonishment. No one knew the answer yet the glass was still moving spelling the word 'T-E-N-D-E-R.' Realising what was happening, all of us in a state of shock jumped up and ran out of the room, frightened. I was really scared and felt myself shaking whilst trying to understand what we witnessed. The other classmates admitted to pushing the glass in the game to start with, but when the Elvis Presley last question came up, they realised that the glass was moving on its own.

My friends talked about this for days, and we all agreed that Elvis visited us that day, and made us all terrified! However, this was still on my mind as

I was trying to find an explanation. Did someone read my mind? Was there a real spirit in the room? I had to find some answers.

My birthday party event was fast approaching and I was so hopeful for the future, and my faith and love for God was really blossoming. I could not imagine what else life had in store for me, and was excited thinking about how big God was and how bold He made me.

There was a girl named Josie who was a redhead, with lots of freckles that I had spent some time with over the years. I felt sorry for her, because people teased her about the freckles and ginger hair, and no one invited her to their party. She was quiet, softly spoken and I enjoyed listening to her about her trips to the country with her family. She was from England and talked about her home life and missing her relatives back home. Her Mum really missed her family in England and wanted to go home for Christmas.

While standing at the quadrangle near my home class room, Josie ran up to me and told me that she could not come to my party as she had a family engagement. She asked if I could meet her Mum and come a week before to thank us for the kind invitation. She had already bought me a birthday present, and wanted to meet my parents also. That was so kind of her.

It was Saturday, and Josie and her mother, Mrs Fletcher came over to wish me for my birthday. Mum had bought a cake and we drank some soft drinks while the two mums had a cup of tea. Mrs Fletcher looked very frail, and even more timid and quiet than Josie. In a soft voice Mrs Fletcher asked, "Melody now tell me what did you get for your birthday?" My birthday was during the week, so I told her that Mum and Dad bought me a real guitar and I was going to learn classical music. I also told her about the softball bat and ball. She was thrilled as she also played guitar, and asked to see it.

I jumped up and made my way to the bedroom to collect the guitar. Mrs Fletcher played a few tunes and some classical pieces. It sounded really good, and Josie and I chatted away. Mum and Mrs Fletcher finished their cup of tea, and went to see Missy in her portable cot. She was telling Mum that she is unable to have any more children but has been trying to get pregnant for a while. She loved children and wanted at least three, as Josie had an older brother.

A couple of hours went so quickly, and I thanked Josie and her Mum for the present and for stopping by. They wished me all the best for the party, and then left. Mum told me to make sure that I kept up my friendship with Josie as she was a genuine and caring friend.

My friends arrived for my party the following Saturday, and I was so nervous but excited all at the same time. I even invited a few boys and they were running around everywhere chasing the girls and acting like crazy animals. We played pass the parcel, pin the tail on the donkey and had a dancing competition and even the boys had to participate.

I wore a red and pink floral pinafore and a blue shirt, a little miss matched but all the rage for the 70's. Pinafores and tunics were very fashionable in those days with a tee shirt or collared shirt underneath. I very rarely wore dresses as I was going through my tomboy stage, and I preferred the drawstring shorts with a shirt instead. Everyone enjoyed themselves and we all ate too much cake, chocolates and fairy bread. Mum put on a good spread of party pies, sausage rolls, cakes, lollies, fairy bread and hot dogs.

It was hard to motivate myself to go to school on Monday after a hectic weekend. When I arrived, I looked around for Josie but could not find her anywhere. The day went by and I thought maybe she was ill or went away with her family to the country.

The next day, a teacher pulled me aside and told me that Josie was not coming back to school for a little while. She had heard that I was asking about her and that Josie did not have any close friends but me. I was very confused but the teacher advised that there was an accident and Josie's Mum had passed away on the weekend. I was shocked because I only saw Mrs Fletcher last week and I told the teacher about Josie coming over to my house with her Mum.

The teacher consoled me and said that Josie will be coming back to school in a couple of weeks when things are more settled. I must have looked really shocked and worried for Josie. It would be so difficult to lose your Mum so suddenly.

At home, I told my Mum what had happened and she bowed her head with sadness. Mum looked up and said, "She was a lovely lady. Do you know what happened?" I shook my head and told Mum that the teacher did not know anything further, but did mention that Josie was coming back to school in a few weeks.

My Grandfather Gerry, Dad's father, was coming over to visit and he was very nice to me, always giving me gifts and praising me for my tea making. He had very dark skin, silver white hair and thick glasses. I did not know much about him, except that he lived alone while his wife lived in India. My Dad drank at least six cups of tea each day over the weekend, so I was constantly making tea, and learned how to perfect it since I had so much practice.

That night, Grandpa Gerry shouted and yelled out in the middle of the night, gasping for air. He slept on the lounge that my parents had made into a bed for the night. I was very frightened and both Jenny and I got up. My Dad joined us to see if Grandpa was okay. He had a lot of whisky to drink that night. It was scary to see him like this, not knowing what could happen next. Sometimes he would be very angry and argue with my Dad. It made my blood boil at times, but he was my Grandpa and we were brought up to respect our elders.

"Something is choking me... this thing is choking me," gasped by Grandpa looking terrified and shocked. Dad kept asking him who was choking him, but he could not speak. He was almost incoherent, and his eyes were rolling back in his head. My Dad thought he was choking so he placed him on his side and started pounding on his back.

Finally he came to and looked around the room mesmerised. Dad explained what had happened and he told him that he saw a man with an elongated but translucent face, very pale who began choking him and smiling. He kept at it until we walked into the room.

My Grandfather was so shaken that he gave up drinking alcohol from that day onwards. It was so surprising because I only saw him with a glass and a bottle of scotch. It made me nervous seeing him like this. It was terrifying for us kids.

Something similiar had happened before at Grandpa's flat and he could not explain it. It was really strange. Now this thing happened in our home, and I was wondering what it all meant.

Still shaking, I went back to bed and prayed. I found it hard to go back to sleep and my emotions took over and I just sobbed and sobbed. I gasped "Please help me Jesus. I am scared ....please help me!" After a little while, I looked up and was shaken to see Jenny standing looking down at me. "Jenny, what are you doing?" I whispered. She told me that she heard me crying and wanted to check on me. I moved over and let her sleep in my bed, knowing that she was also very scared about what we had just seen.

The next morning, I heard my Dad speaking to my grandfather and telling him to cut down on his whisky, as it was not good for his health. Dad was so health conscious. He was very dependent on alcohol. My grandfather had told my Dad that he was so frightened by this visitation of something that was evil, that he was going to repent and not drink anymore. We had heard this before, but I am sure my Dad did not believe him.

Over the next few weeks, Grandpa Gerry followed through and did not touch a drop of alcohol. Whatever happened that night changed him, and he soon became super religious. He was going to church twice a week. He also bought a prayer altar and set this up in this flat, so that he could spend hours in prayer. The family were truly amazed at this transformation. I felt a little better being around him but remained cautious. He still continued to buy me gifts and praise me which was a little embarrassing at times.

We went on a picnic to Warragamba Dam with my cousins and extended family the following weekend. The word had got out and the group grew to almost sixty five people and we took up a large chunk of the grassy area under the trees. It was so much fun, and we loved going on picnics with all the cousins. There was always plenty of food and drink, that anyone would think we were going camping for a week.

My cousin Charlie suggested that we have a rolling down the hill competition, so we found the steepest hill, but it had a gravel part at the bottom. So the ten of us rolled down the hill till we reached the gravel section consisting of small stones. With a few cuts and bruises, we had a wonderful time! Other kids watching on thought they would have a go also, and now we had a queue as if it was some sort of joy ride! With a little imagination, we could make a simple picnic an adventurous and fun-filled time.

It was Monday and the weekend was over, but I was looking forward to seeing my friend Josie again. There were so many questions, but I knew I had to take it slow because her loss was still fresh and it would take some time to adjust to a life without her mother. It made me think of how I would respond if I had lost my mother.

I could see Josie from afar sitting on a seat near the old gum tree on her own, drawing circles in the dirt with her feet. Walking over to Josie, I sat down beside her and said, "How are you going Josie? I really missed you."

She looked up at me and said, "Melody, I still don't understand why she did it." For a moment I did not know what to say, or what she was referring to.

All I could do was sit with her while she spoke as I didn't really understand what it was like to lose someone very close. Josie went on speaking about how her Mum had died and she had found her in the bath. It was a real shock for her, and she talked about the memory of what she saw that afternoon, and described it as a tape player that is on replay constantly.

As a friend I just listened, but wanting to ask questions to understand what she was talking about. The bell rang and we had to go to class, and I said bye to Josie and we could get together at lunchtime.

A boring lesson in Geography, listening to the teacher talk about the weather, rainfall and the process. The teacher would often repeat the same lesson and add on a few extra points, and I was more interested in understanding what had happened to Josie's Mum, and how she was coping with the loss.

At lunch time, Josie asked me to walk with her to the grass area where there were only a few kids getting ready for ball games. I guess Josie wanted to talk, and I chose to listen again, trying so hard not to ask too many questions. Josie explained that she had not been able to discuss her mothers death with anyone, and wanted to tell me what had happened. I blurted out, not knowing what to say, or how to ask the question delicately, "It sounds like your mother drowned in the bath. Did she collapse or faint?"

Josie looked at me with so much sadness, that I felt her pain and as if she was in a very dark hole, with no way out. Josie turned to me and whispered "Mum cut her wrists and there was blood everywhere. I don't know why. Dad said that she was suffering from melancholy."

I looked down at my feet, searching for some words of comfort but there was nothing. Why did I feel so much pain? I didn't even understand what melancholy was. Josie went on to explain that her Mum would sit in the dark for days in silence, and her Dad said she had bouts of sadness. I thought about the day I met Mrs Fletcher and she was bursting with life, and wanted to play my guitar. I could not understand that she had this other side to her. Poor Josie, she found her mother dead in a tub of bloody water, a shocking image that she could not erase. It would take a long time to erase that memory and replace it with a happier one.

At such a young age I did not understand the pangs of death, and how that impacted families. We had watched some sad movies, but this was so different. It was real and it was so messy. Josie explained that she would have to move to the Central Coast to be near her grandparents so that her father could work to support their family. I was going to miss her.

Mum and Dad went shopping that Saturday morning, and I was in charge of looking after my two sisters, and making sure we completed our chores. I had finished most of my chores, but my sister Jenny and Missy decided to make a snack and mess up the tidy kitchen I had just cleaned.

After my first guitar lesson, I had found it tough on my fingers, but the teacher had told me that it would get easier. I decided to practice in the lounge room while my sisters were busy in the kitchen. As I played, I started to feel strange, but could not understand what was happening to me. I was feeling foggy in the head, and cried out to my sisters for help. I couldn't speak and started muttering something to them, but kept crying. I was very scared and could not describe what was happening to me, except feeling that I was going to pass out.

Jenny was shouting, "What is wrong with you? What is wrong? Why can't you speak?" My tongue felt paralysed, and I was trying to say something. Jenny looked very frightened and she started to panic. I motioned to her to get the Bible and she was not understanding. I reached over and she realised what I was looking for and placed the Bible in my hand. Then she and Missy ran out towards the driveway.

At first I did not know what to look for, and there was this fight going on inside of me. I was determined to find something that I could hold on to, and I had learned from Sunday school how powerful scripture was so I went to a scripture about Jesus healing a little girl, setting her free, delivering her from the power of darkness. I asked Jesus to set me free, and cried out to him, making sounds that were incomprehensible. My sisters were still outside on the driveway, terrified at what had happened to me, and were waiting for my parents to come home. I went outside to find them, as I did not want to be alone, and they told me to stay away, as if I had the plague or had become a monster. Maybe I did, because I could feel a struggle within me, and a resistance towards God, but I had a will to overcome this but I needed Jesus' help.

Standing on the driveway, I continued to weep, still praying and holding my Bible. The struggle left me and I was able to speak again. I told them that I had prayed, and that Jesus was with me, and He had made me better. Jenny said that my eyes and expression had changed, and I looked like myself again. I did not know what this meant but I was grateful to be able to speak again.

My sister Jenny and I were discussing what had happened and how we were going to tell our parents. I told Jenny about Mrs Fletcher's death and that Josie had found her. Jenny reminded me about Mrs Fletcher playing my guitar. Filled with superstition and ignorance, I stared at the guitar and thought it may have been the cause. Or was Mrs Fletcher's spirit in our house? My mind went crazy trying to find an explanation for the paralysis of my tongue. I also thought about the ouija board and what went on there, but I was not going to tell my parents about that, nor anyone else. I knew it was wrong to be messing about with stuff like that, and I was ashamed.

Jenny ran out to the car, and blurted out what had happened to me to Mum. I don't think Mum understood and thought she was talking about some movie. I interjected and asked Mum and Dad, if I could talk to them about what had happened. I told them that it was serious and that I was very scared.

Dad could see that I had something serious to talk to them about, and he and Mum went into the lounge room and took a seat. I was nervous to tell them because I was scared of their reaction or whether they would believe me. They sat listening intently and asking me about Mrs Fletcher and the circumstances around her death. I reminded Mum about the week before she died she had come over and played my guitar. Mum looked at me and whispered, "Did she take her own life? Did she leave a note?" I wasn't sure about why she would ask those questions, if it didn't mean anything. Mum was talking to my Dad about what happens to their spirit when someone takes their own life, and they both had different views. Could anyone know what truly happens to someone when they die? Was there such a thing as a wandering spirit belonging to a dead person? Dad brought up the subject of the apparition of the little blonde girl sitting on the corner of their bed. There was so much to understand about this, and the Bible talked a lot about the spirit world, about heaven and hell.

Mum and Dad could not explain what had happened to me, and why I could not talk. I tried to describe the struggle within me, but could not find the right words. After some time, I just gave up. Maybe they did not believe me, but my two sisters had experienced the change in me, and were terrified. Jenny interrupted and told my parents that she was frightened, and that I seemed very different, and not like her sister.

Over the next few weeks I spent some time trying to figure out what had happened to me, and searched the Bible for answers. The event would play out in my head over and over again, as I looked for clues that could give me an explanation. I would often obsess about something until I understood it. Something was certain though, I found it difficult to pick up that guitar again, and it sat there in the corner of the lounge room gathering dust.

This was the beginning of my fascination with spiritual things, magic and the occult, not realising that this was dangerous territory for a novice like me. I would often wonder about what was happening beyond the physical realm, of things that I could not see or understand. I started reading about astrology, numerology and mysticism, looking for answers.

I thought back to the incident at school with the ouija board and contacting Elvis' spirit. I could not tell my parents about this as they were against occultic practices. Mum had told me it was dangerous to get involved referring to black magic practiced in India, but I was bordering on becoming a teenager and they are notorious for pushing boundaries, rebellion and curiosity.

As the weeks rolled by, my parents noticed the fear attached to the guitar and my lack of interest in pursuing the classical guitar lessons. Dad even complained about the guitar becoming a white elephant in the room, and I would burst into tears describing what had happened to me. The guitar was the reminder of the day that something had changed in me. This was no drama, it really happened to me and I was getting more and more frustrated not having an explanation.

One of my friends at school had told me that I had another spirit in me and it took over my body for a while. She saw a movie which explained about possession and how a girl became tormented by this other spirit. It was terrifying me as my imagination went wild thinking how this could impact me. Also the only source for information was the library and it was very limited. I saw one book on possession and how to fight against it. The book mentioned that the spirit is unable to override your will, as long as you have a strong will, you are able to fight against it. Also it mentioned that the spirit can attach to trauma, evil and occultic practices, sexual immorality, jealousy and bitterness.

I also referred to the Bible, and it stated in Ephesian 4:27 not to give place or foothold to the devil and James 4:7 To resist the devil and he will flee from you. I pondered over those verses and what it meant to give place or opportunity to the devil or Satan. The book in the library was written by a christian and it explained what it meant in more detail. I found this difficult to understand, because many sins would give the devil an opportunity. Does it mean that I need to go to confession more often?

I thought to myself that maybe I will stay close to Jesus and He can help me to fight against this evil thing that was taunting me from time to time. At times it was so overwhelming, that I would tremble in fear, feeling very alone in this. I had a friend in Jesus, and I even started journaling and writing letters to Him. The Bible told me that He (Jesus) will never leave me nor forsake me, so I was going to hold Him to it!

During our holidays, Jen and I were so bored that we thought of catching birds to fill up our little metal cage that lay empty as our previous budgies had somehow escaped and flew away. So we found a cardboard box and attached a ruler to hold it up with a long piece of twine. We placed some bread crumbs under the box, and hid in the garage whilst watching for the right moment. Before the end of the day, we had a cage full of birds, from budgies to finches.

Chapter 7

High School Jitters

Going to high school was both exhilarating and terrifying all at the same time. Mum decided to make my uniform quite different to all the other kids, with darker green buttons and a front panel. The girls in my class, especially Colleen, would constantly nit pick how different my uniform was to the others. At times It made me feel even more self-conscious. The original uniform was expensive and we were always on a budget growing up. I also had a briefcase and long socks and looked like a real geek. Who would want to be my friend? Even my best friend, Leanne, went to another school, and I had to make new friends.

There was a girl up the road named Donna, and Mum had arranged for me to walk to the bus stop together. This was all new too, catching a bus and walking to the bus stop, along with our dog Susie who decided to bring along all the other dogs in our area, as an entourage.

I really felt out of place at school at first, especially looking like such a geek. I was so skinny that I looked malnourished and was trying to put on weight. It did not take me long to make some adjustments to the hemline of my tunic, long socks and ditch the briefcase. It took me around three months to settle into the new high school.

Having two groups of friends gave me variety where I had some non-intellectual girls, who were in the lower classes, and then the bright ones who were in my class. They called me 'brainy' and 'Doc' and I was happy with that.

Soon I struck up a friendship with a South African girl, called Lana who had long brown hair, darker skin than I, and big brown eyes. She had some whitish patches on her skin, with two on the side of her face, and she was hoping that they would blend in with her dark skin. She was pretty, and athletic in her appearance. She and I would goof around, playing pranks on the serious girls who thought they were something. Lana was sporty like me, and at lunch time we would play volleyball and basketball with the boys. The boys would whistle at us from time to time, especially when our skirts went up and they could see our tights below. That was so embarrassing! I enjoyed hanging out with Lana at least twice a week, playing sports. It was better than gossiping and talking about fashion.

Jenny and I were sitting watching television in the afternoon, when we heard this loud thump on the window, then calling out in a deep throaty voice, "Where's the boss? Where's the boss?" It was our neighbour old man Grumpy Thumpton or 'Fat man' as we called him. I went out and he asked to speak to Dad. Fat man looked much older than he was, with years drinking and smoking. His face was like a red bulbous melon, and he had put on a lot of weight.

Dad came in with a big bag full of grapefruits and looked at Mum and said, "Fat man said you should eat these and lose weight."

Mum made a funny grunt then said, "Has he looked at himself in the mirror?" Dad had a funny sheepish grin stating that the old man grumpy suggested he gain some muscle, so he could pick up such a weight? It was all very odd.

Then that night after the movie, Dad lifted Missy and carried her to bed, while Jenny and I sat there on the couch, and then realised that Fat man had seen Dad pick up our sister to take her to bed, thinking it was our Mum. He must have been drunk, but could see the silhouette through our back curtains and felt sorry for my Dad, and that is why he suggested she eat the grapefruit. There was no way that my Dad could pick up Mum. We both ran into our parents room to tell them. Then we all laughed out loud, big belly laughs at the expense of our thoughtful neighbour.

We had some strange neighbours with colourful back stories that made our stay in South West Sydney very interesting. It turned out that Mr Thumpton had survived a world war, but came back to Australia severely traumatised at what he had witnessed. Instead he took up drinking to medicate the pain and the reality of war, as he often openly ranted about his terror whilst gustling down beer after beer.

We were friends with his grand-daughter Deb and she often tried to get him to talk about the war and where he served. However, he would lash out at her and tell her that he could not talk about it. It was very disturbing to hear the terror in his voice as he shouted 'stop.' When we looked at some of his old photos of him we were amazed how handsome he was, like a Hollywood movie star, and could not imagine he was the same man. It was difficult to imagine the terror and trauma he endured as a young man that would later transform him into a lonely, old drunkard, waiting to die. He had extensive liver damage from the alcohol, and every year he would say his goodbyes as he headed out in a caravan down the coast to die. He did this for five years, but would come back after three weeks, still alive!

Mr Thumpton liked Dad and would always refer to him as 'the boss' because he had a household of four girls. Dad would sometimes be the one who would rescue him when he came home from the pub drunk and fell under his truck still clutching his bottles of beer, trying to get out. Back in those days, there was no law about drink driving, and Mr Thumpton would often drive home in his truck intoxicated.

One time we were watching television in the family room, when our house shook and we heard a big thud. Mr Thumpton had driven his truck and hit his own house. Thankfully the home was concrete and it split the corner, with only partial damage. He got down from his truck and started swearing at the top of his voice blaming the truck's brakes.

Later that Summer, Lana came over to hang out in the school holidays and we swam, danced and played tennis on the road. She and I were such good friends, with common interests and we just clicked. I really trusted her like a sister. Often Jenny would get quite jealous because we were so close.

After dinner we would share our scary stories and then laugh over it. She also had some frightening experiences in Africa with voodoo, and allowing demonic spirits to take over people's bodies whilst they danced in a circle summoning spirits. It almost sounded like Satanism with blood sacrifices. She saw many of her family members suffer greatly as a result of this, often becoming insane and taking their own lives. It was also something that my extended family had been exposed to in India, with various religious cults, and those practicing black magic.

This gave me a chance to talk about my experience with the guitar, my friend Josie and her mother Mrs Fletcher. Lana was shocked when I told her about not being able to speak, and the internal battle inside me. She believed me, and it was so reassuring to be validated. I could not make up something that was so terrifying, and I did not like the experience one bit.

It was an opportunity to share how Jesus had set me free, by calling on His name and reading His Word. I encouraged her to read the Bible and gave her a small New Testament that I received from Sunday School. We read together the Gospel of John, and discussed it for a good hour. It was great to see Lana so enthusiastic to know Jesus.

It was approximately four weeks later on a Friday night at dancing practice, which was the last time that Lana and I would see each other. That night she was hit by a truck whilst crossing the main road to get her father cigarettes, and killed instantly. It was something we both had done many times before when her Dad dropped me home, but this time I was not with her. My Dad had picked me up that night after they had visited my uncle and aunty.

It was during a school assembly that I had heard the terrible news, and fell to my knees with shock. I was so sad that this beautiful friend was taken from me so suddenly, and I could not understand why. She had just become a Christian, and was discovering how wonderful Jesus is when her life was cut short. Now Lana's parents were afraid that the family was cursed, and their daughter was taken by the voodoo spirits. It scared me how fast life can change, so unexpectedly, without warning.

One night I lay awake for hours thinking and praying that this pain of loss would disappear. I had been reading Ecclesiastes in the Bible at the passage, 'The Mystery of Time' in Chapter 3 where there is a time to weep and a time to laugh, a time to mourn and a time to dance. I contemplated the words, thinking that life is a series of valleys, plains and mountains and there is loss, pain and suffering but there are also mountain top experiences of true joy and peace. The plains are in between times of rest, a time of healing and growth. I surprised myself of the depth of thought not knowing where this came from, but one day would be part of a great book! As I turned over to go to sleep, I was hoping that I would remember this in the morning, as it was too good to let go.

My teenage years were a myriad of emotions, crazy hormone levels, like riding a rollercoaster that could not stop! The heights were fun, and full of fire and excitement as we discussed our interests in boys and who was dating who. The lows were confusing emotions of emptiness, sadness and despair.

There were times at night where I felt very low, broken and scared but did not understand the shame, and the intensity of my feelings. I often told myself that these feelings would go away, but it would linger. I never felt that I was good enough or worthy. It was so difficult to open up and discuss this with anyone. It was like I was in a black hole, and was drifting into oblivion, with nothing to hold onto. Many times I found myself crying uncontrollably but not understanding where this sadness was from. Back in those days you just took an aspirin and got on with things.

I found myself writing letters to Jesus, because I trusted Him and it was my time to pour out all my frustrations, and pain to Him. He promised never to leave me, nor forsake me. I took Him at His Word and it soon became a regular diary entry. I had to make sure that no-one would find this diary, because it was very private. I had to hide it from Jenny, as she was always snooping around, wondering why I was so preoccupied.

I had a picture of Jesus on the wall, across from my bed, and I would look at it from time to time, acknowledging the kind eyes. I often felt the presence of the Lord during my teen years, and I knew that He was with me, particularly during these moments of grief and struggle. Often, I would imagine running into His arms and I would feel the pain dissipate. I would lie in bed and wonder about heaven, and if it was a physical place like Earth, where everyone was kind and caring. These were big things for a girl of my age, thinking about the after-life and knowing that it was not a popular subject to discuss with friends.

Like most teenagers, rebellion set in and I tried to push the boundaries where I could. Dad and I would often clash over things, and I would storm off in a huff. We seldom saw eye to eye, and I was good at baiting him to get a reaction. I also had different views on life, and what I wanted to do with my future. Why was I so different from my parents, so I thought?

I really enjoyed music, and singing became my way of dealing with my pain and sadness. It took me into places that brought healing and calm to my spirit. I particularly enjoyed it when I had the house to myself and I could practice those high notes without annoying everyone. Why was I so good at hiding this pain, that even my parents could not see the turmoil beneath the surface? I was always bubbly and full of life at home.

Gina was in my English class, an Italian girl that was rather eccentric and we became friends very quickly given our common interests in writing and music. She could also sing well, and music brought us together. We even did a duo together, A Donna Summer and Barbara Streisand song, Enough is Enough. From time to time, we spent time together and made an effort to catch up outside of school.

Gina's parents were Opera singers, and performed at the Opera House in Sydney. I found this hard to believe until I went over to home, and met them. She was always making up stories and exaggerating the facts that it was very difficult to separate the truth from her white lies.

One day whilst sitting on her couch practising our song, I could feel something slither at the back of my neck. The next moment, I jumped up and screamed. She did have a python, who her parents used as a prop onstage, something that I did not believe. It was a pet snake, so Gina reassured me that it was not going to squeeze the life out of me!! How could I ever be bored with friends like this, who were colourful and larger than life. Gina just giggled as she watched my reaction.

Getting to know her, I realised that she had a tough life from fleeing Spain after her natural father deserted her, and making their way to Australia not being able to speak English. Gina had abandonment issues, and we talked about her adventure and rough upbringing for hours. She was so trusting of me, and soon we became really good friends.

Gina also introduced me to Mina, who also had that infectious giggle that was both immature and mischievous. I would spend time with both of the girls, carefree laughing at their sledging, then go back to my intellectual nerdy friends, and find myself getting bored. It was a great way to do high school vacillating between groups of girls, avoiding gossip and catty behaviour.

My family really liked Gina and many times she came home with me after school and had a meal with our family. She was so grateful to join in with our family as it felt safe to be part of it. Gina often commented on how close we were, a little envious at times.

One Saturday morning, it was quite early around seven and the doorbell rang. I jumped out of bed, and here was Gina standing on our porch with her suitcase. She had tears in her eyes and stated in a matter fact way, "I have run away from home, Melody. Could I please stay with you?" I was completely shocked, and asked her to come in. Mum was great, and made some pancakes for breakfast and Gina poured out all her frustrations to us.

Mum was so giving and knew how to comfort Gina. I listened and listened, trying to see how we could help her. She talked about going to a shelter or a relative, as she found it impossible to get on with her Mum and Step Dad. We told Gina that she could stay with us for a while until we figured this out.

It did not take long before her Mum was on our doorstep trying to discuss ways of getting Gina to go home peacefully. Mum invited Gloria in and we talked over a cup of tea, and cupcakes that my sister Jenny had made the day before. Gina was a fiery girl with a massive temper, and her Mum was the same. They loved each other but found it difficult to listen to one another without the anger, temper taking flight. My Mum and I were the mediators and we did a fine job to get them to reconcile. Before long, Gina and her Mum left together and returned home to work things out.

Chapter 8

All Grown Up

My years in the workforce started with an office junior role for an oil company at the age of eighteen fresh out of high school, where I learned how to organise board meetings, deliver press releases and networking. It was a platform to land me a job as an Account Executive for a Western Sydney Insurance Broker, after three and half years of experience and extensive training.

I had a lot to learn, but the negotiating, wheeling and dealing side of a broker really appealed to me. I was acting on behalf of clients, and had to negotiate covers and costs with various insurers. Everyday there was something new and exciting, and I was like a sponge soaking in knowledge of the markets, scope of insurance covers, as well as getting my head around technical information and calculations.

It was there that I received the best training from ex CEO's of large Insurers, who took the time to impart their knowledge and experience to me. I had also met some interesting and influential clients from various spheres of society. I had met television personnel, property tycoons, entertainment gurus and small business owners of various industries.

It was just what I needed to catapult me from my mundane, uninteresting world to an exciting unpredictable world of broking. Many times I was invited to client functions where I had to mingle and connect with various people groups. Although I suffered tremendously from social anxiety with a troubling sense of self consciousness, I was challenged to face these fears and work through it. It was the best thing for me, as I learned to courageously fight for myself. Also living in the South West Sydney, I felt underprivileged and judged by these socialites, who were living in affluent areas. Whenever I was asked where I was from, I learned the art of changing the subject.

Sitting amongst these wealthy individuals and hearing their stories of travel, art and money, I thought that these people were seriously content and enjoyed their life. However as I got to know them, I could see the cracks start to appear. They were lonely, confused and discontent with their lives, yet they could buy anything they wanted. Why were they so unhappy? I pondered these questions, and I could see that there was a void in their life, the next big thing, a new relationship or property that would fill this space, something that they desperately needed. Then it dawned on me that one could not buy peace… yes it was peace.

I recall talking to a beautiful middle aged woman who had her name splashed over many magazines over the years, with reporters chasing her to find the big story. Behind closed doors she was hooked on tranquillisers and alcohol, just needed to fall into a deep sleep and find that peace that surpasses all understanding. She opened up to me, and I sat there trying to contemplate the hell she was going through whilst she sat there at the table sipping champagne, dripping in diamonds, expensive clothing and a face one would die for. I tried to wipe the shocked look off my face, and empathise with this beautiful lady.

It became a usual thing for my clients to open up and let me into their life, and I could see that they really trusted me and I had to honour that. Interestingly I found myself sharing some of my own spiritual experiences with them, and talking about Jesus, even to my Jewish clients. They would often snigger at me, but I could be cheeky and tell them to read the 'Dead Sea Scrolls' or the Book of Isaiah. I loved Jesus, called myself a Christian but was not totally committed to Him. He only occupied a compartment of my life, and I was quite besotted with the world, the power and intrigue that came with it.

When I was alone in my thoughts, I was aware of my own void in my life. It was painful to admit that I had made a huge mistake in marriage, and would have to bear the consequences, bound to a life of pain and nothingness. Why did I get married at the age of twenty, still a child in many ways? I had the power to say no but fell for the deception, the bait and switch method. Love does not control or manipulate, yet this is what I had come to know.

Work was a place where I could shine, and build up my confidence as I became more and more competent. It was my escape from the pain. At home, I was ridiculed and abused for having a personality, but at work I was appreciated and encouraged to rise up. I dreaded the weekends, as the heaviness of my failing marriage was beginning to take its toll on me, and I looked forward to going back to work, where I blossomed.

How long was I going to be able to hide the trauma that I was experiencing at home? Soon the seams would come undone, and I would have to fess up to the sham that I was in. I wanted to die everyday, rather than face the pain I was going through. It seemed hopeless, as I did not believe in divorce and the fear of failure was ringing so loudly in my head. I really messed up because deep inside I knew that it was not going to go well. I really did not want this, but I felt trapped by this man who played me like a fiddle, a naive insecure girl that had not grown up. I had to take responsibility for making the choice. I had failed at marriage, and it hurt so bad. It was the truth. I had the choice but I was too afraid to say NO. I had come to believe that I deserved to be treated with dishonour, ridicule and abuse.

It was during this time that the flashbacks of some painful moments in my childhood surfaced, and it hit me like an electric shock. I had buried this so deep within my consciousness yet it showed up in self hatred and shame. This awful onslaught on my innocence had been plaguing me throughout my adolescence and young adulthood. It affected my relationships, my schooling, my choice of life partner and my view of self. It contaminated every part of my being, and made me feel like damaged goods. I was now sabotaging my life on a downward destructive path.

It was amazing that during these dark times, I often felt the gentle calling of the Lord reminding me that he was walking with me through this lonely journey. Then there was Satan and his minions pulling me down with deception and lies. The negative thoughts ran through my head constantly reminding me that I had no value, no reason to live and that I should just die. He was also using various others in my life to do his bidding. I realised that I was in a spiritual battle.

When little Will was born, I was given a chance to regain some hope that things could work out. Will brought so much joy and I was delighted with this precious gift from the Lord. I had prayed for him throughout my pregnancy that He would follow Jesus and be a powerful witness.

After six months it got worse. Yet there was this little whisper, reminding me that God was still on His throne, and He was going to see me through this traumatic time. From one day to the next I did not know if I was going to survive. I was walking on eggshells, afraid that one word would lead to a violent outburst. I was so stressed all the time that my body started to shut down and I got shingles, and a rash showed up on my stomach and upper thighs. I was in so much pain, whilst trying to look after a six month old baby, knowing I had to go back to work full time. I did not want to leave my baby, but financially we could not survive. We could barely pay the bills, or put food on the table. The financial stress was enormous, and money just slipped away.

I was going to have to psyche myself up to return to work so soon in order to keep the house. I knew that this was going to be used against me to contaminate the relationship with my son. However I was reminded by the times I spent at church, that God will put an end to the lies and deception. I held onto this and it gave me hope. Being a mother, I gained courage to fight for my child and myself. I refused to be a victim, but a victor.

Chapter 9

Dealing with Divorce

It was a cloudy day that December morning in 1993 and as I peered out the window of the counsellors office, pouring out my soul. I always felt so emotionally drained after each session, and it felt like lava was flowing out, hot and bubbling molten liquid, then little spouts of fire as the anger surfaced.

The counsellor was a small older man, in his mid sixties at least. He looked pale and gaunt, having lost a lot of weight, as if he was fading away, yet he sat with me so attentive and caring. Besides his physical appearance, he had an angelic presence and I could see the joy emanating inside of him.

Here I was, having been through a damaging marriage, a complete emotional breakdown and I was trying to make sense of the unravelling mess. It was so overwhelming and I was so grateful to have Bill Sykes to help me make sense of this all.

Many times, I wanted to run away from this emotional quagmire, as the further I delved into it, the more stuck I became. I had spent a few years trying to escape from the pain by distracting myself by visiting new places, shopping and taking Will along for a ride. I would return home to the tension and stress which was so difficult to bear. Bill told me that I needed to now walk through it, and that Jesus was beside me all the way. I sensed this supernatural strength and comfort guiding me through the storm.

I recalled the moment that I knew that it was time to pack up and leave. I heard a small voice in my head with firm instructions saying, "Melody, you have to pack your things and it is time to leave NOW!" Somehow I found the courage and strength to listen and obey, not knowing what the outcome was going to be. If I had stayed I probably would not have been around to tell the story.

It was the right thing to do, as I do not think Will and I would have survived. It was time to protect Will and remove ourselves from this abuse, and that was the wake up call. Previously I had planned my exit in my head, but could not follow through, and in fact talked my way out of it. This time it was a clear instruction to obey the call. It was truly a divine intervention.

As I chatted to Bill about my life leading up to the breakup of this toxic relationship, he helped me to see that I had walked into this knowing that it would fail, a form of sabotage of what I truly believed about myself. It was enlightening but I felt this sickly stabbing deep in my stomach of what I had become.

Again, I wanted to cut and run, screaming at the top of my lungs for this all to stop. How could I be so stupid? I had the power to say NO, but was always afraid of letting people down, and I made choices that would affect my life going forward. Bill then told me that pain can be delayed, pushed down but it waits for you, and then you must deal with it. I then realised that the pain went back to my childhood.

As he sat with me while I sobbed and sobbed, letting the pain go, he silently prayed, and I looked up to see the tears in his eyes. I must have cried for thirty minutes, until I was totally exhausted, whilst I listened to his prayer. It made me even more emotional as he showed me the love of Christ. I knew that healing these damaged emotions would take some time and I needed to walk through this, and not avoid or push down the emotions like I had done many times before.

Bill and I met on a weekly basis, as there was a lot to work through, bit by bit. The sessions revealed the effects of a toxic relationship, with years and years of brainwashing and reframing of truth. I felt worthless and unable to even perform basic tasks at home, yet my working life totally contradicted this inadequacy. I channelled my anger and frustrations in my work, where I was proficient and achieving success as an Insurance Broker Divisional Manager. This ambivalence showed me how distorted my thinking was, and uncovered the lies I believed about myself. This realisation was helping me to see reality, of looking through a frosted glass for so long, and then seeing with clarity. This exercise came with a lot of pain and self anger.

I found that the hardest thing to deal with was self condemnation, and forgiving myself for the part I played. I had to take responsibility for my actions, and deal with the consequences the best way I could. I was so fortunate to have my family behind me, as I wrestled with the feelings of disloyalty, self blame and shame.

For weeks and weeks I struggled with the burdens I was carrying, and the hardest part was to forgive. How do you forgive someone who fails to see the truth where there is no admission of guilt or remorse? There was so much guilt that it felt like a solid wall in front of me, clouding my judgments and perception, and the only way was to remove the wall, brick by brick. Bill was so patient with me, and I was to find out later that he had terminal cancer. I only discovered this as I tried to make more appointments with the intake officer and she unintentionally let it slip, as he only had a few months left.

I sat on my bed and cried thinking how this man could spend his last days with me, and I did not deserve such grace. The discussion was never about him, and he didn't even tell me that he had a terminal illness. I was also so entrenched in my issues, that I did not see how much he had deteriorated. Yet he listened intently, his soft eyes beaming up at me, whilst validating my feelings.

The next session, Bill began by telling me that we only had at least eight weeks left, since his illness was terminal, and he was happy to increase the session time to 90 minutes weekly. I looked up at him and sighed stating, "Bill, I do not understand why you would spend your last weeks with me hearing my issues. Could you please help me to understand this, because I do not deserve this."

Bill shook his head and his eyes lit up, as he said, "Melody, I believe that the Lord has put you in my path, and I am supposed to help you to understand that Jesus loves you and He is pouring out His mercy and grace on you." The words penetrated deep into my spirit and heart and I burst into tears. I suddenly realised that I mattered to Jesus.

Bill was an angel sent by God, and I was so greatly appreciative of the value I was given as a child of the King. It was still a rough road to walk down, but I was on my way to healing. Bill handed me a book called Healing Damaged Emotions, and it was a guide through the process. I found it hard to pick it up and allow it to unravel the distorted thinking, and suppressed emotions, but I persevered.

That night I could not stop thinking about the revelation that I was of value to God, and that I was not worthless or hopeless, which I had heard many times over the years. I sat with the thought, mulling it over and over, and it certainly brought a smile to my face. I now sensed the tender heart of God, and it filled me with such warmth and an inner peace.

The following week, I took some bright yellow flowers and a card for Bill and reminded him that he brought sunshine back into my life. God had certainly called him to reveal the Father's heart and what a privilege it was to share the good news of the Gospel message. I told him that I was looking forward to meeting him one day in heaven, and I also intend to take many people with me to eternity. He looked at me with an excited expression and said, "Melody, I believe you will be a soul winner."

Driving back home, I contemplated what it meant to be a soul winner for Christ. I was excited to hear those words, and knew that in some small way, I could share my life with others and tell them how the Lord saved me, and that I could make some difference.

Over the next week, I journaled my thoughts and did the exercises that Bill gave me. It was difficult at times, as I was becoming more aware of the destructive patterns and thoughts. Bill had asked me to highlight the patterns to discuss at my next visit. I remember saying to Bill that I stayed in the marriage because I believed that this was the best I could have, and that this was my lot in life. Once my son was born, I wanted to give him a stable and loving home, but realised it takes two committed people to do that.

I was staying with my parents, having left the family home but this was an adjustment. I tried to have some time out occasionally to gather my thoughts and work on myself, but working full time and trying to help my two-year-old son who was distressed was tough. I tried to overcompensate for the pain and anguish by buying him toys to take his mind off things, whilst providing him a loving and stable environment. I tried the best I could to shield Will from the trauma, but there were cracks from time to time, as I was human.

I wanted my son to believe that I was strong, that a woman should be respected and cared for. I was not a possession or someone that could be dominated and controlled. I wanted to forge a career to make him proud of how hard I worked to provide for our future. There were so many lessons to learn and I had to grow up very quickly in order to manage the coming onslaught that was before me, which was the custody battle.

Through many sessions in court and with my solicitor, I fought hard to maintain custody and minimise the trauma for my son. It really took its toll on me, and many times I felt the enormous strain, that was unbearable. I remember Bill telling me that you fight your greatest battle on your knees in prayer. So I got down on my knees and prayed, calling out to God.

I thought about Bill who was now with the Lord, free from the physical pain of cancer. His administration officer called me and told me that he succumbed to the illness and had passed away earlier than expected. Bill had an assurance of his final destination being Heaven, and he was looking forward to it, as I recalled the excitement in his voice talking about the City of Gold, where the love of God shines upon the whole place leaving no room for darkness. I was so inspired by our discussions which took on a life of itself, exploring the spiritual realm and it was slowly becoming clearer to me. However, he knew it was time, as I was well on my way in becoming a christian, and he did what God called him to do. Still, I was unaware of the battles that were still ahead of me, but I was not alone.

Through many months of being harassed by private investigators, to weaken me and destroy my mental health, I spent some days on the edge of an emotional breakdown skirting around on the cliff face of insanity. There were days when I would sob in the shower, to protect my little boy from the anguish, fear and pain I was feeling. I was fighting the temptation to stay in the pit of despair. I certainly did not want to live as a victim.

Somehow miraculously, I was able to get through it all, with Jesus by my side. I felt His strong hand guiding me daily, and the comfort of many friends and family that held me in their prayers, especially when I was at my lowest. My mother was such a prayer warrior and an encourager. She would uplift me every day, with God's word and remind me that I was a child of God, an heir to His throne. Each day, I fought back the urge to go back to my dark pit, to the chains that once bound me. I remember the soft voice in my head reminding me that I was no longer in chains, yes unchained to sing a new song of praise to my King. So I sang my favourite worship songs all the way to work, in the traffic until I reached my workplace.

Over the next season I battled with the temptation to dabble in worldly pursuits, as I was now free to explore. I missed out on my younger days, being confined to a prison sentence for seven years and now I wanted to party. I loved dancing so off I went to the nightclubs, where I could dance the night away without restraint. Besides it was only dancing, and not drinking so it was not so bad. In those days, the clubs opened earlier, so I could leave around 11.30pm and could get home before midnight.

It was a lot of fun at the time and I took Missy along for the ride. It was a chance to hang out, and feel a little normal, whatever that was. There was a war going on inside me, and the anger that I had suppressed for so long was starting to flow out. While I was dancing I could have some reprieve from the bubbling lava that burned inside me, wanting to erupt.

Bill, my counsellor had made me aware that I was angry with God for the pain I had gone through, and for feeling abandoned at times. I thought he was punishing me for my rebellious ways, of walking into a marriage that He did not approve of. In fact, He let me go and I was on my own for a time, a wilderness experience that took me further from God. He was in the background, and once in awhile He would get my attention.

I was caught in two worlds, going to nightclubs on Friday nights and then church on Sunday. I did not know where I belonged, because even at church I was just not feeling what others were experiencing. I would see these Christians at church get so emotional over praise and worship, while there was a war going on inside of me, my flesh crying out for attention. Even reading my Bible was a chore at times, as I did not always understand what I was reading. There was a blockage of some sort that prevented me from surrendering my will to God, or fully trusting Him. I only prayed when I was in trouble or needed God, but when things were going well, He was in the background.

At church the Pastor spoke about having a personal relationship with Jesus, and having Godly sorrow for my sins. It is by dying to self to be raised up as a new creation. I was sorry that I had to go through such pain, realising that my actions were sinful, yet I had not fully grasped how much pain Jesus endured for me.

The Christians at church seemed to be on some joy kick, yet my joy kick was the dance floor and I could not fully understand this. At that stage, I thought their life was boring, and confined. Were they missing out on going to nightclubs or just having fun? I hung out with a few of them, and was beginning to see that there was something special that they held onto. Deep down I did not belong in the nightclubs either, and would feel lost.

It was Monday that I received a call from one of my school friends, Raina who advised me that Mina was ill in hospital with cancer. I was in shock as I had not heard from Mina for at least twelve months. We had minimal contact due to the issues with her marriage to a controlling, violent and manipulative man, after she left school.

It was an arranged marriage and I did not have a good feeling about this man. He appeared to be arrogant, and self centred, as I asked him about

Mina, and their plans. I also sensed that he didn't like me, because of our close friendship, and the fact that I could see through his facade.

After her divorce, Mina and her son Toby travelled to the Middle East including Israel, and her home Jordan. She was away for at least six months, and sent me a postcard from Jerusalem. She told me about her experience going to the tomb of Jesus, and how meaningful it was for her to see the story of the Bible come to life in such a way.

Mina grew up in a Christian Orthodox family, with lots of religious events and celebrations. There seemed to be a lot of traditions, rules and hoops to jump through to earn your salvation. Even Mina struggled with keeping up with the ceremonies and traditions.

The customs and culture were centred around marriage and family, and it became the focal point for each family. Mina's family were quite wealthy as they owned a number of supermarkets and vegetable shops, so she was always working long hours.

Also Toby had a disability, which was difficult to manage, with Mina being quite young, in her mid-twenties, having married at nineteen, she had a huge responsibility and burden to bear. I remember the discussion during a secret call from her home, as she was not permitted by her husband to contact her friends, telling me that Toby was the result of her husband physically abusing her when she was pregnant. The violence had caused some brain damage and physical disability around Toby's mouth. It made it difficult for Toby to communicate verbally, and the brain damage accentuated this.

It was such a tragic story, and many times it made me angry thinking of how she was coping on her own. Her husband was a typical psychopath, who went out of his way to alienate her from her friends and family, so that he could break her down, as he got off on his increasing power. Mina became his possession, and she was always paranoid that he was watching her. Even when I bumped into at the supermarket, she would look around as if he was spying on her.

Mina was a beautiful person, both externally and internally. She had sparkling brown eyes, that could dance as she playfully looked around the room, and tell her funny stories. She had wavy brown hair with flecks of gold that had a tendency to curl from time to time. Her giggle was infectious and she could make you laugh out loud just watching her. She was mischievous and full of fun, looking for an opportunity to explore places and experiences. Mina was larger than life and she had so much to live for. Then she met this dark, moody man that tried his best to dim the light in her.

As I contemplated the life Mina had, I realised it was similar to my own story. This was a chance for me to get out of the coma I was in and face the reality of my own life. At times I had glimpses of what a healthy relationship looked like, but I felt a form of paralysis when it came to making changes. I guess deep down it was pride rearing its ugly head, of the realisation of failing at my marriage.

On the way home from the city I dropped by the Royal Prince Alfred Hospital (RPA) just on the outskirts of Sydney CBD to see Mina, who is in the hospice area. I was not sure of what to expect, as she hid her diagnosis for some six months. At the back of the main building entrance was a solid historical building, with a sign called The Hospice. As soon as I entered the foyer I could smell the disinfectant mixed with the musty odour of an older style building. It had floorboards that looked over one hundred years old, polished and warm. There was an older nurse at the front desk, who motioned me to the left wing of the building. This was a place where people came to die, a form of palliative care to help patients manage their pain and end of life care. However, it was a sterile environment, and I could not help but think that they could have made this place more homily, creating a warm ambience so patients could feel more like home. As I walked into the room, my eyes moved over to a frail woman sitting up in the bed, her eyes sallow and sunken. I did not recognise Mina, as she had aged more than her twenty nine years. Her body had been so ravaged by this insidious disease, that she was no longer mobile, and had become skeletal.

I moved closer to her bed and called her name to make sure she was actually Mina. She looked up at me with tears in her eyes, looking like a frightened child for a moment. I whispered to her, "I am so glad you reached out to me. How are you today?" I really did not know what to say to her, and it was so difficult to hide the shock, and my facial expression could not hide the pain that I was feeling. Mina told me that the cancer was getting worse and she could not eat very much. She was always feeling nauseous and the pain in her stomach was hard to manage.

I handed her some juice and watched her slowly sip it, as she spoke about how she came to be in the hospital. As it turned out, Mina first became ill in the Middle East and had to return early. She had terrible abdominal pains, and went to see a specialist. Her diagnosis was then confirmed, with the cancer advanced, meaning it was terminal.

Mina looked up at me and said, "I don't want to die Melody. I am very scared. I cannot leave Toby on his own!" I saw the pain and fear in her eyes, and so I just held her hand and we cried together. I did not know what to say to make things better for her, and it was just best to listen and be there for her. After thirty minutes, Mina fell asleep so I left and made my way home.

On my way home in the car, I sobbed and sobbed, feeling the pain of my dear friend. She suffered from the time she got married, with small moments of reprieve sprinklered throughout her life. I prayed that the Lord would strengthen and comfort her, as Mina comes to terms with her illness and the outcome. I also prayed that I could help her with the fear, in some small way.

That night I spoke to my parents about Mina as they knew her too, and were saddened to hear about her tragic past. They suggested that I ask our family friend Rudy to come and pray for her, as he had a pastoral care ministry and spent many times praying for people in hospital. I am not sure if we can pray for healing given she is terminal. Was it better for her to come to terms with her illness, and then prepare for death. Can Jesus heal someone so close to death?

As I went through the Bible looking for the various healings, I read about Lazarus being raised from the dead. Also there was a twelve year old girl who was healed, on the brink of death. I realised that God could do anything, as He willed. Afterall He conquered death Himself. So I thought I will keep visiting Mina and then ask her about it.

Over the next two months I visited Mina three times a week, and she was losing more and more weight, unable to keep anything in her stomach too long. They gave her some chemotherapy but it made her even more ill. I spent time holding a bowl out whilst she vomited, and dry reached from time to time. In between we had conversations and talked about our school days, the music we listened to and our weekly visits to the local cafe to have a cappuccino.

I asked Mina about her visit to the Middle East, Israel and Jordan, and her eyes lit up as she talked about her experiences in Jerusalem. She had a bunch of photos in her drawer that she was looking at from time to time during her bouts of chemotherapy. We went through the photos and she told me about the place where Jesus was buried, and how she lit a candle and prayed. She said she felt a spiritual presence, and wanted to know more about her faith.

I told her about my marriage breakup, and Bill who was my counsellor that helped me find my way back after years of abuse and turmoil. Mina looked at me with tears in her eyes, and she understood exactly what I had been through as she had gone through a similar relationship. She squeezed my hand and told me that things will get better for me. I was able to share with her how my faith in Jesus was helping me walk through this difficult time, and that He even put Bill in my path to guide me for the last eight months of his life. It was this personal relationship with Jesus that showed me that He is real and is active in our lives. I showed her the passage in Isaiah where the Lord says that He will heal the brokenhearted and bind up their wounds Isaiah 61, and Psalm 34,147.

Mina could see that there was hope and as we shared our different stories, we could see the parallels. I showed her photos of our family, little Will with his cheeky face and my sisters. I asked her if she would like to meet my friend Rudy who has a prayer ministry and visits people in hospitals. I was hoping that she was ready, and she looked at me and nodded. Every time I walked into the room, I saw the fear in her eyes and it took some time before she would calm down and savour the moment we spent together.

Later in the week I phoned Rudy and explained the situation to him. He was so enthusiastic and always ready to pray for someone and share the Gospel. I was very inspired by his fervency, and faithfulness. Knowing Rudy from my early childhood, he was a loud party goer, who loved to gamble and drink. Seeing this transformation was a testimony to the power of Christ working in his life. Rudy had done a one eighty turn, was dedicated and on fire for the Lord. God used him in so many people's lives as was not a physically well man himself. In his sixties Rudy spent a fair share of time in hospital himself with various health issues. While he was there he prayed for others and openly shared the good news of Jesus.

The following Saturday, I picked up Rudy in the morning and headed towards the hospital in Camperdown. I warned Rudy that Mina had deteriorated very quickly and could hardly hold herself up. I was hoping that the morphine had not set in and that we could communicate effectively. Rudy and I both spent that week praying for this opportunity.

Mina was sitting up in bed with her head resting back on the pillow. For a moment, I had a pang in my chest as I thought we were too late. She looked lifeless and her eyes were flickering in the light. I walked over to her and kissed her head, and introduced her to Rudy. She put her hand out and shook it. Rudy looked at her and I could see the compassion in his expression as he looked at her frail stature that was quickly fading away.

Rudy asked Mina some questions about her faith, to gauge where she was at with her understanding of grace and Jesus' work on the cross. Rudy was aware of Mina's Orthodox background and the religious traditions which were similar to Catholicism. Rudy shared the story of the cross, our need for a Saviour due to our sin, as we all fall short of the glory of God. He explained that in Ephesians 2 that were dead in our sin, walking according to our own desires, until Jesus took our place on the cross and paid the penalty for our sin, so that we could have a relationship with Him and Father God. He further explained that Jesus was our bridge to the Father, and by His death and Resurrection we can have eternal life. We need to believe in Him and put our trust in Jesus. It is by His grace we are saved, and not by our own works. We cannot earn our salvation, but accept the free gift. Rudy looked into Mina's eyes with a compassionate expression. "Do you believe this Mina?

Rudy was very thorough in his explanation of sin, and gave plenty of examples where we fail. We talked about ignoring God, walking in disobedience and not spending time with the Lord. He further shared his own testimony of his life as a loud smooth talking gambler who drank excessively and had lots of fun. He said he figured that he never murdered anyone, or did any vile acts, and his goodness would outweigh his wrongs. However when he understood the depravity of man, and our tendency to be selfish, and his own sin, he got on his knees and repented. He explained the holiness of God, and that He could not tolerate sin, not even a respectable sin.

Mina broke down and cried as she talked about her own sin, the pain it had brought to her life. It was not tears from feeling sorry for herself because of the pain, but a deep godly sorrow that her sin put Jesus on the cross. It was the realisation that Jesus had to suffer a shockingly gruesome death to save her, an ultimate act of love. I could not help but weep. I could see her heart being transformed before my eyes and I wanted to shout for joy. Yet I was still sitting on the fence afraid to let Jesus have my own heart, completely. I was just not feeling that godly sorrow, and I longed to have the same experience that Mina was having right now. It was just not my time yet.

So Rudy now led Mina through a prayer of repentance and asking Jesus to be Lord of her life. She repeated after him, choking up with emotion. With all her strength Mina lifted herself up, put her hands up to the Lord and cried out for his help, with tears running down her face. Both Rudy and I also had tears streaming down our faces, as we just witnessed something truly miraculous, the greatest miracle; salvation.

Mina now had eternal life and whatever happens from now on, she was safe in the arms of Jesus. I was thankful that the Lord allowed me to be part of this life changing experience for my close friend. I could see the peace in her spirit, and it warmed my heart. I leaned over and whispered to her, "Mina when you see Jesus please put in a good word for me," and we both laughed.

She smiled and for a moment I saw that cheeky expression as she answered back, "I definitely will." Maybe she knew that I was sitting on the fence, going to church and reading my Bible from time to time, but not totally committed. I loved Jesus, but trusting Him completely would take some time.

I held her hand and Rudy put his hand on her shoulder as he finished off another prayer of comfort. He prayed that the Lord would give her strength to face the next step, peace and protection of her spirit. Rudy had explained that the evil one will always bring doubt and confusion to someone who has just been saved and rob the seed of the Gospel message. So it made sense to pray for the protection of the seed that had been sown, and that Mina will continue to pray to Jesus each day.

Mina's family were too terrified to come and visit her in her final days, as they had not come to terms with her illness. They were still in denial, and the pain of the realisation of such a young person deteriorating in such a way was too difficult for them to bear. It was a blessing in disguise, as it allowed Mina some time to spend in prayer without the efforts of making things palatable for her family.

It was Tuesday before I was able to see Mina again, and this time when I entered the room, I saw her beaming smile which lit up the room. For one moment she looked like she was recovering, but I realised that her countenance had changed. She looked hopeful, free as a bird. She had peace. I was ecstatic because of the huge transition from the overwhelming fear and panic that was gut wrenching to witness, to a friend that was content and at peace about her journey to heaven.

Mina kept smiling at me and said in her soft voice.

"Thank you Melody for showing me Jesus. He is truly wonderful and I am not afraid of death anymore. I have an angel that sits on the end of my bed and is waiting for me. This angel will take me home soon, and I am looking forward to seeing Jesus face to face. I don't have any more pain right now, but I know it is time."

For a moment I looked at Mina intently to see if she was under the influence of any pain killers, but quickly dismissed that thought, realising it was my disbelief in what she had told me. She was speaking to me very clearly and had asked the nurse not to administer any morphine. I could not see an angel but I felt the presence of something divine in that room. I told Mina that I was so happy for her, and that I would always cherish this time.

The sterile nature of the room, the smell of disinfectant and the whimpering of the other patients had faded into oblivion for Mina. She was on her way from her temporary dwelling to a permanent one. I could see for a brief moment how temporary this life was, just a vapour and it could be snuffed out so quickly, so unexpectedly. I had seen this a few times in my life so far, but then the god of distraction would set in and take me away on some other whim and I would forget.

It was Thursday afternoon and Raina called me at work to tell me that Mina had passed away. Even though I knew it was coming, it was still a shock to hear those words. I told Raina about my last visit and what Mina had shared about 'going home' and we both cried as we reminisced over the last six months. Raina told me that the funeral was going to be held very soon, and will call me with more details when she hears from the family.

I had to get out of the building and go for a walk as I tried to gather my thoughts. I sat on the park bench with tears streaming down my face, as I recalled our last conversation and Mina's sense of peace. All I could say was Thank you Jesus. Thank you for taking Mina home. I prayed in my head for Mina's family as I could imagine their grief and the pain of coming to terms with what had truly transpired beyond their control. I knew that I would need to go and visit Mina's Mum and Dad and encourage them with her last discussion with me.

That night, my parents were compassionate and encouraging as we discussed how God had worked in her life. It was truly an example of His amazing grace to save Mina from eternal damnation and receive life with the love of God. Mina had only been following religion externally, the traditions of man, but it had not penetrated deep in her heart. She admitted to Rudy and I that she did not have a personal relationship with Jesus. Mum said to me that it was such a wonderful gift to give your good friend, that is eternal life. You know that you will see her some day. However, those words rang in my head as I was not sure where I was going. Was I really saved? I also remember telling Mina to put in a good word for me with Jesus, in such a casual way, and she told me that she will definitely do that. Wow, what a conversation, and what a privilege?

The day of the funeral came, and it was held at an Orthodox church in Sydney. The family arrived with the hearse with Mina's photo on the back, a time when she was healthy and full of life. Those sparkling eyes and cheeky grin were her trademark, and it was always etched in my brain when I think back of her. I thought back to how the cancer had ravaged her body, and features, that she looked like a very old woman who was decomposing before my eyes. For a child it would have been a scary thing to witness. Perhaps that is why her family struggled with visiting her in the last few months.

Mina's Mum could not hold herself up, wracked in grief, she was unsteady on her feet so her husband and brother were trying to help her to get to the front of the church. The service commenced and most of it was in Arabic with a number of hymns sung by a choir. There were moments of wailing and mourning interrupting the Priest at times.

The coffin was a plain and ordinary looking box, sealed up so that no-one could see Mina's body. There were no flowers on top, just the box that was carried in by Mina's brothers. I did not know what was happening, and could not understand the message. I imagined what sort of reception Mina was actually getting in Heaven as she danced before the pearly gates to meet Jesus, with angels showing her the way. There would be singing and praising in Heaven like nothing we have ever experienced here on Earth. I sat clinging to these thoughts and it brought a smile to my face. I looked around and I was the only one smiling, so I put my head down to hide the joy I was feeling at the actual celebration that was going on outside of this funeral procession.

As the hearse with Mina's photo on the back pulled out, heading to the Cemetery, Toby ran after the car, calling out to his mother. I reached out to him and he put his hand up against mine. I felt his pain, and tried to hold back the tears, but I could feel myself sobbing inside. He was only six years old and could not fully understand what had happened.

At the graveside at Rookwood Cemetery in Lidcombe, the family and friends gathered around listening to the Priest who was praying. The Priest had some holy water and was sprinkling it all over the coffin, as it was about to descend into the earth. Mina's brother, Asha threw himself on the coffin to stop it descending and cried out in pain. He had said something in his language and also Mina's name, and I later found out that he was pleading with God to send her back and raise her up. This brought tears to my eyes seeing the solid grief that the family endured with such a vivacious young lady that had been taken from them too early.

Weeks had passed and I was on my way to see Mina's parents. I took a lovely bunch of flowers, yellow roses which was Mina's favourite. Her Mum was decked out in full black and had a lace covering over her head. She looked like she had aged, with the grief and pain etched in her soft features. I gave her a hug and she cried telling me about how quickly this had happened, and she could not understand why God had allowed this.

We chatted over some tea and cakes, and I looked over to her Dad who was sitting with his head in his hands. Mina was his little girl and he had tried to protect her as much as he could. He told me about how he felt about her marriage and the abuse she endured. I listened and listened as they poured out their painful memories, and regrets. It had been at least two months, and there was still this raw emotion, and anger that they were working through.

I reached for Aisha's hand, Mina's Mum and told her that I have something to tell her. I shared with her about Mina's last days and how she received Jesus as her Lord and Saviour. I went on to tell them about the angel that was with her, waiting to take her home. She was not afraid to die. They both looked at me, tears streaming down their faces. There was a language barrier, and they did not speak English fluently so I struggled to communicate this to them. They looked at me as if they understood most things and even asked me about heaven. They wanted to know how certain Mina was about going to heaven. It was my chance to explain what the Bible says about eternal life, and I went on to share this with them, with her parents taking in every word. I was hoping and praying that they were comforted by this exchange, and they themselves could see Mina again.

I wished I had a Bible with me, so I could show them the passage but then I remembered that I had put John 3:16 in the card, with a note of encouragement. I prayed that the Lord would send people to explain all of this in their own language, so that they could be comforted. I left there, with Aisha giving me a long hug as she trembled. She knew that Mina and I were close friends, and I had meant alot to her.

I missed my friend Mina, who died so quickly just before her twenty ninth birthday and yet knowing that she was not here on earth anymore was sad. Death is part of everyone's journey and each one of us must face it. Life was a continuum of peaks and troughs, of pure joy and intense pain.

Even though I had experienced grief along the way, with the loss of some good friends, there were moments of excitement and joy. I knew what it felt like to live in fear, of anticipating the worst outcome and believing that bad things would happen to me, it was going to take time to work through the traumas that were still unfolding in my life.

Deep down, there was the refusal to stay as a victim, but a tenacity that was reeling inside me was to conquer this fear and make good of the lessons that were before me. From time to time the anxiety and fear would unconsciously kick in, and I would have to take my thoughts captive and stop myself from sliding down the slippery dip to the pit below.

I had learned some great lessons from reading some helpful christian books on fear along with scriptures that helped me to speak into the lies that were pulling me down. I found that as I reflected on these scriptures like 2 Timothy 1:7, *"For God has not given me a spirit of fear, but one of power, love and a sound mind."*

1 John 4: 18, *"There is no fear in love; instead perfect love casts out fear."* There was also 2 Corinthians 12: 9-10, *"My grace is sufficient for you, for power is perfected in weakness Therefore I will most gladly boast all the more about my weaknesses so that Christ's power may reside in me. So I take pleasure in weaknesses, insults, catastrophes, persecution and in pressures, because of Christ. For when I am weak, then I am strong."*

Apostle Paul had every reason to feel superior to others due to his stature as a Pharisee and abilities, yet he realised that Jesus was Lord God Almighty, and he needed to surrender to Him. He must have also experienced Jesus' amazing love and grace poured out in his life. This scripture turned me inside out as pride was a true weakness, and not one of power. I learned to submit to Christ, and allow His power to work through me. Every time pride reared its ugly head I spoke these truths into the thought, and it soon helped me conquer the overwhelming desire to puff myself up due to the deep insecurities I felt.

I realised that God had given me the instructions in His word to fight the battle of the mind and the world, but I needed to practice this and build some spiritual muscle. It took some time to reprogramme my thoughts and my secular mindset that was so deeply ingrained. I could feel God working in me, refining me but I had a long way to go yet. I realised that I had been in chains for seven years, in bondage and slowly these chains were being released by the Lord Himself.

The custody battle was intense, with going back and forwards to solicitors trying to find an amicable solution. At the core, my intention was to protect my little boy and that he would grow up feeling loved and secure.

At times, the pain and torment of the constant lies and manipulation caused me to have an emotional breakdown. I was hanging on by a thread, and needed to hand this over to the Lord. The evil attacks were so fierce, and there was no reprieve. I had to stop listening to the lies, and focus on the truth, and the love of God. As I surrendered this battle to the Lord, that is when Jesus stepped in and things began to change very quickly.

Every morning before work, I would spend some time reading my Bible and praying, asking the Lord for strength to face the day. I prayed for an obedient heart. At that time, my mother would be a great encouragement to me, by putting things into perspective, and I knew both my parents had my back. I was so thankful to them for standing beside me.

Some weeks had passed and my solicitor called me to say that I was granted custody, and that the other party withdrew their case. It was over for now... so I thought. I celebrated with my family as they were also committed to protecting my son from the pain and stress of a dysfunctional life.

It was wonderful how the Lord intervened here and took charge as I handed the burden over to Him. My faith was growing, as I learned to trust the Lord, even with the big things in my life. I was so grateful to the Lord, as He was so active in my life. He is close to the brokenhearted and was healing the pain each day.

Over the next few years, the struggle of being a single parent was taking its toll on me, as I juggled a new job, a developmental role in insurance broking. Thankfully the company I worked for was supportive and allowed me to work part-time so that I could be there for my son. In order to work part-time I had a large pay cut, and had to hand over my new car, and was given an older replacement vehicle. I was grateful, and it was worth the sacrifice. I was hoping that one day, my son would understand how much I loved him, and did my very best to protect him the best way I could.

Yet there were still battles going on from time to time, and trying to work out any arrangements were always involved in a power struggle. It became exhausting but I was not going to allow this to bring me down. Listening to christian worship music was always uplifting and I enjoyed praising God. It was my battle cry, and every time there was a hurdle I turned to the Lord for strength and comfort.

Mum and Dad decided to build a new house south of Sydney, and I was so glad to move to have a fresh start. I really wanted to have my own place, but the risk of a violent exchange was too much to bear so I had to settle living with my parents a little longer. Will was also looking forward to having his own room, with all his toys and collectables.

It took some time for the house to be built and finally the day came to move in. It was so exciting moving to this area, which was so leafy, overlooking a small valley with trees and on the other side was the George's river that flowed into the Botany Bay. The place was tucked away from suburbia, with one main road in, down to a peninsula. The homes were built along the ridge, and on hills, cliff faces, and amongst the bush down towards the river. Our home was positioned on the high part of the cul-de-sac on solid rock which was a good foundation.

It was a medium size family home, federation style with decorative stained glass windows in the front porch, along with green and white tiles leading to the front door. The house had three living areas, four bedrooms, and a private yard at the rear. It was comfortable and homely, a sanctuary for our family, including the many visitors that landed on our doorstep, some of which had issues, failed marriages, abandonment and grief. It was an opportunity to open up our home to minister to whoever the Lord brought to us.

It was a time to create some happy memories, a fresh start and a new area to explore. Dad loved fishing and we often went down to the pontoon, and threw our fishing lines out, not sure if we would catch any fish. A few people caught flathead and even mud crabs. One time I even put some fresh meat in a stocking and threw it off the pier. We caught one mudcrab and just as we were lifting it out of the water, it untangled itself and fell into the water. I was so desperate that I was willing to jump in and catch it, then I reminded myself of the big claws and took a step back, remembering the incident of the mud crab chasing me as a child.

Dad looked up with a sheepish grin and said, "Well he got away from the curry pot."

Yes and I could see my Mum standing there in shock with her hands on her head. I am sure she was thinking how many ways she was going to cook this thing. Besides it was only one, and we needed to catch a few more to feed the family.

On the way back home, we went for a drive to the other peninsula, and sat at the river bank for a while, watching Will throw rocks into the water. We both tried skipping rocks like the dam busters book I had read in high school, but it took a few attempts for me to skip the stone across the top of the water. It was so peaceful here, and I closed my eyes for a moment and imagined that all my problems had disappeared. There were no more battles, disagreements and constant bickering and manipulations. How blissful this was, and I needed times of reprieve from time to time to maintain my mental health.

Chapter 10

Free to Sing A New Melody

My job took me to some interesting places along the coastline visiting clients, and I travelled to the Gold Coast and Melbourne a few times for seminars, trade shows and work events. Even though I missed Will, and felt guilty leaving him for a few days, I needed this time to start to refocus and think about the future. I was terrified after such a traumatic period in my life, yet there was hope and it was not too late to reframe a life that had lost its way.

The loneliness was very real, and I ached for a real loving relationship, someone that loved the Lord as much as I did. Yet I was still working out my salvation, and had lots of issues which took time to sort through. I was not good at being patient, and there were still lessons to be learned. I wanted to enjoy life and be carefree, to run away from the stressors and feel a little normal again.

I had always craved affection, even as a young girl but did not know why I wanted it so much. It was a different time, where people were not openly affectionate, and as my parents had also grown up with that 'old-school' mentality, maintaining a tough exterior. It made it difficult for me to show affection, but I was insistent to get out of my comfort zone. I had learned as a child that the world was not a safe place, with people that I trusted. At the age of ten years old, I had experienced an uncomfortable family issue that I could not articulate, and share with others. It was a shameful secret, so I suppressed it deep within my consciousness. Yet it affected my being, my worldview, and caused me to have trust issues. However, as my relationship with Jesus developed, I was beginning to heal the damaged emotions and fractured self, so that my vision and perspective were becoming more clearer.

It was 21st of August 1994 and the big night where I was going to get baptised at church. I was so excited after spending some weeks in preparation with our Pastors. I had written my testimony and invited my family and cousins. For me it was going to be emotional, having spent my time sitting on the fence afraid to make a commitment and now ready to jump in. I recalled that one of the deacons had said that the spiritual battle and onslaught can come before and after you make the commitment to follow Christ. It will be a tough road, and it is vital to have a good support system around you to help you through those obstacles.

The auditorium was full, and I was standing on the platform with a white long garment ready to take a dip in the baptism pool. My Mum, Dad, my sisters, brother-in-law and extended family all came to witness this amazing declaration to follow Jesus. It was all about Jesus rescuing me from the pit that I found myself in. He was the one who opened my eyes to the truth, set me free and forgave my sin.

My testimony declared the struggle I had to commit wholeheartedly. I talked about the pride I had and my unworthiness. It was my family showing me love and compassion that brought me to a place where I wanted more of Jesus. Also seeing the transformation in my Dad, had a profound effect on me, as I knew of his upbringing and the immense struggles he had. I also shared the special time I had with my friend Mina, and witnessing her acceptance of Christ, and the miracle of salvation was truly life changing. I saw the genuine hope in her eyes as she approached her own death.

As I shared my story, trembling with the presence of the Holy Spirit, I felt a warm flame run through my body, lighting up those dark places and lifting my spirit as I soured like on eagle's wings. This was truly divine, and I was grateful that the Lord had shone his face on me. I looked at everyone, and there were lots of tears streaming down their faces. It was truly a special moment in my life.

That night whilst in bed I replayed the experience over and over again, savouring every special moment. I was hoping my testimony touched people's lives that they would seek the Lord and find Him. It was my mountain top experience.

As the months rolled on, I had encountered some turbulent times which drew me back to some dark places. As soon as I felt the bitterness return, I was quick to acknowledge it, and ask for forgiveness. What I was not ready for, was the unexpected relationships that entered my life, packaged in a way that seemed good, but it was misleading me, as I drifted down a distant path. The enemy had a very subtle way of gradually leading me into sin, and I was not strong enough to resist the temptation. Besides I was very lonely, and needed to feel adored and appreciated, after a disastrous experience early in my youth.

Even through these times, the Lord was very patient with me, and many times showed me my sin, as I read my Bible from time to time. I would talk to the Lord about this and pray for his intervention, but on my terms. Again this was a struggle for me. Deep down I knew I belonged to the Lord, and He was going to win in the end. It was going to cause me more pain, but I fought in vain.

It was early in the morning in Hawaii when we landed, having flown over on business class from New Zealand after a stop over. Our flight was delayed a day, so Qantas upgraded us to business class, then flying Air New Zealand to Honolulu, all in Business Class. This was an amazing experience and I think Will enjoyed it the most. He had his own butler who cleaned up after him and even when he dropped all the orange juice on the table and down this shirt. The butler also kept him amused with colouring in, games and lots of activities. It was so good to be served with crockery, fine glasses and tableware. We felt really special, and Dad had his usual grin indicating that he was soaking up this little luxury. The captain of the plane came over and spoke to Will. The next moment both Will and I were ushered into the cockpit to have a go at flying the plane. I looked over to Will, and we could not wipe the huge grin he had on his face, at such an amazing opportunity. I watched as he listened intently to the Captain, manoeuvring the steering column and stick and looking out of the window.

We all were looking forward to spending time with Will, Mum and Dad as we had planned the trip together. Will was at an age to enjoy Disneyland, Universal Studios and Hawaii. Hawaii was a lot of fun, with all the sightseeing, attending concerts and the buffets of endless supply of foods and fruits. Will was fascinated with the tropical birds, and we even posed for photos holding the parrots and Macaws. Dad bought Will a crazy purple puppet that he took along on our sightseeing tours, amusing all the people who joined us with his puppet show. I had so much fun laughing at him, and the joy it brought to the others that watched on. It was so good to get away from the dramas of the custody battles, the constant arguments and bickering. I felt like a child exploring, with a sense of wonder, as I watched my son soak up the experiences around him.

We headed off to Los Angeles six days later, and had the time of our life exploring Disneyland. Who said that Disneyland was for kids? We all become like children as we wander through the world of make believe and magic. Dad enjoyed showing Will the highlights and we even stayed to watch the fireworks. It was truly exhausting but exhilarating all at the same time.

Will really enjoyed the Indiana Jones ride, which was pretty much a four wheel drive on a track going up hills, descending then changing over to a watercraft with giant spiders, large boulders and rubber tarantulas thrown at us along the way. We spent most of the ride screaming and laughing out loud. I looked over to Will and he was so excited and a little scared of what was next.

Will was enthralled with all the Disney characters and Woody, Buzz Lightyear, Mickey Mouse, Donald Duck and the Roadrunner. He actually thought they were real, and we all enjoyed watching on as this make believe world became real in his eyes. We took so many photos and eventually our faces were sore from smiling and laughing so much.

The city of San Francisco was very interesting to see, and it reminded us of our home in Sydney with the picturesque harbour, the restaurants and the friendly people. There were lots of crayfish on the menu and we enjoyed some wonderful seafood meals at the swanky restaurants in San Francisco. This was our last destination with my family before they returned to Sydney along with Will, whilst I flew over to New York, and the East Coast to sightsee, for another two weeks.

Whilst New York was particularly cold and windy, yet an exciting place to experience. The city was so vast with the landscape of the building skyline extending way beyond what I was used to. The company I was working for had an office in the South tower in the financial sector, and I was determined to go up and visit the office. The building was so solid and full of concrete and steel, and the trip to the top of the building took forever. I could not believe the height of the building as I finally reached the top. I also took a helicopter that flew over and through the twin towers, a time when this was allowed and I was able to take numerous photos of the two buildings, using different angles.

After travelling to other areas on the East Coast including Washington, Lousianna, New Orleans I returned home. I really missed Will, and could not wait to show him all the photos and talk about all the memories we made as a family. Will and I made a poster to share with his class showing them some interesting places we visited, and gave him a chance to speak to the class for news with some visual images.

Over the next week I developed a bad cold, and I continued to work through it. Before long, it became worse, developing into bronchitis. Work was so busy, and I was unable to take time out to get well, so I pushed on which was to my detriment. After an X-ray of my lungs, it revealed that I developed double pneumonia and pleurisy which was debilitating and painful at the same time. I was forced to stay home and get well.

Our local doctor lived in our cul-de-sac and visited me at home, because I was too ill to go anywhere. He checked my temperature and it was extremely high, and the only way to get well was to go to the hospital or to receive care each day. So I opted for him to drop by daily with injections of antibiotics, and failing this I would then go to the hospital.

I lay in bed for hours sleeping as I had no strength or energy. I felt too ill to even think, and I was grateful to Mum and Dad that helped me through this. Our doctor told me that the pneumonia was so serious that I was quite close to death. So under his instructions I was to call an ambulance the moment I left I could not breathe well. I recall my constant calling out to the Lord for his strength and healing. My chest was heavy, but it even hurt to breathe. Instead I would take in short shallow breaths as the pain in my chest with my swollen lungs rubbing against my ribcage was excruciating. I prayed and prayed, and spent time in the Word, bargaining with God to let me live. I had to live for Will, to help him through, and give him a chance to forge a life for himself. I held onto this and kept fighting on.

At times, I would gasp for air, feeling my lungs swell up with fluid, and cry out to the Lord for help. I realised then, that I did not have control over my next breath. I was really in the hands of my Lord and Saviour. I battled over calling the ambulance in the middle of the night, and waking everyone up including Will. What was I thinking, my life was hanging on by a thread yet I was thinking about everyone else. What was I to learn from this? What was God teaching me? Deep down I knew it was God's sovereign will for me to come back to Him. I had wandered away from Him, and He was tugging on my heart.

It took at least two weeks before I started to get better, and I was thankful for my family and close friends that prayed for me, sent me encouraging messages and cards to lift up my spirits when I was down. I had lost so much weight that my clothes were hanging off me. I had to give myself some time to recover well, and then slowly get back to my life. Although, something was beginning to change inside me, as I was becoming so much aware of the spiritual pull and the loosening of the temptations that I had been heavily entrenched in. Still I was not strong enough to walk away from this relationship that was clearly opposing God's will for me.

Another six months went by, and I found myself in times of bliss and then remorse. It was a rollercoaster of emotions, yet I persevered. I prayed with a genuine heart, for God to help me to get my life in order and to walk according to His will. I was still very vulnerable having had my heart shattered, and I understood the compassion and mercy of the Lord that I needed time for me to heal, and become a stronger person through it all.

Chapter 11

A Time to Grieve

It was a lovely sunny day, as I strolled to the restaurant to meet up with Peter, a business colleague and his assistant, who I had known for the last eight years. It was Wednesday 5th February 1997, my mothers birthday. I knew I had to get home a little earlier because my relatives were coming over for dinner. It was going to be a day that I will always be etched in my memory.

The food was always delicious in this modern Australian restaurant, and as I scooped up some vegetables, my phone rang. I had missed three calls and it seemed quite urgent. I excused myself then took the urgent call. My assistant was trying to communicate that my Dad had a heart attack and I needed to go to the hospital.

The restaurant was quite noisy, and I thought I heard something about my son. I asked for more details of what had happened and which hospital. I was in complete shock and just looked across the table to my friend, and repeated what I had heard. Peter had a shocked expression on his face, and then told me to leave and offered to get me a taxi to the hospital. I appreciated his thoughtful gesture, but told him that I had my car parked nearby and it was okay to drive there. I left promptly, my head reeling with shock and adrenaline as I tried to focus on where I had parked my car in the parking station. Walking around the car park, I could not locate my car, my thoughts reeling in my head as I did not know what I was going to face. I prayed to the Lord with tears running down my face, please help me find my car and get to the hospital safely.

Finally, I spotted the car and jumped in and broke down in tears. I was hoping that I was not too late. It sounded very serious and my assistant tried to communicate a difficult message the best way he could given that he was young in age and experience. I prayed as I drove towards Kogarah and somehow was able to get there in record time.

My Dad was lying in the hospital bed, on a life support machine and was unable to breath on his own. My Mum was there crying in the corner as the doctors were assessing him. Dad's eyes were rolling back and forwards with the breathing apparatus prompting him to breathe. I walked over to him and asked him to hold on. He had only turned fifty seven, way too young to die. My sisters then walked in and we looked at each other, completely shocked. I saw my Mum's face drawn with the pain etched on her face, as she tried to tell me what had happened.

My Dad was given a clean bill of health only a couple of weeks before. He was slim, healthy and fit as he exercised each day. This was so unexpected, and none of us saw this coming. I was just waiting for the doctors to turn around and tell us that they were able to kickstart his heart again and that he was going to be okay. However, this was not what they were saying. What I was seeing was just the outward shell of his body, and it seemed that his spirit was not present. I tried to put this thought out of my head, and hoped he would pull through.

Mum asked me to call the pastors, her family and ask for prayer. I walked over to the waiting room and called them all. It was a difficult message to give, but somehow I felt the courage and strength to do this. I fumbled the numbers, then took a deep breath before the first call. It was the Lord's presence that was evident in that emergency room, as we quietly prayed.

An hour later, a few of the relatives showed up and one by one walked in to see my Dad. The hospital had given us a room so that we could gather as a family, as the Emergency Ward could only hold a few visitors at a time. They were so flexible and compassionate with us. The smell of disinfectant and cleaning fluids permeated the rooms. The sterile environment with tubes, electronics, and life saving equipment occupied every available space.

I looked around and saw the grief and distress on the faces of those who were waiting to hear how their loved ones were doing. Each one had a story, and it led to this space in time, where we all met and crossed paths for all different reasons, but the reality of our fragility and mortality was staring us in the face. What were we to learn from this? Will we change the way we are living? Will we consider our beliefs and values? Or are we going to soon go back to our normal lives, distracted and controlled by fear, escaping from the reality of our mortality until the next wake up call? These were the thoughts that were mulling around in my head. It felt that my world was ending.

We all felt the heaviness and strain of the shock as reality started to set in that this was a serious heart attack, where my Dad was unable to function without life support intervention. However, It was still not beyond God, as He could raise the dead, heal the sick, and give mobility to the lame. I held on to this hope.

For the next two days, we visited Dad as we could not stay in the hospital Emergency Ward, unless they moved him to another ward. He needed around the clock care and life saving equipment. They were long days, and none of us felt like eating. We could not even think about being hungry or thirsty. Thankfully our relatives took care of us, and made sure that we had food and water. I was so thankful to the Lord for how he moved in people's hearts to provide the care and support we all needed at that time.

When we arrived home in the evening, there were people who lived on the next street who turned up on our doorstep with a cooked meal for dinner. It was so unexpected, particularly as we did not really know them. They had heard about my Dad's heart attack which happened at home, and may have heard the two ambulances that took him and my Mum to hospital. It was so amazing how the Lord ministered to us through caring people, showing His compassion and love for us.

The next day, the neurosurgeon came to visit us whilst in the intensive care unit to assess the extent of brain damage. Dad's heart had stopped for a period of time before the paramedics were able to resuscitate him, and there may be some brain damage due to lack of oxygen. There were a number of electrodes fastened to different spots on his scalp. They were measuring and assessing the brain activity. The cardiologist came in earlier to review the X-rays of Dad's heart, and we were waiting on their final assessments to determine the next step. Thankfully we had a private room so that we could discuss and consider all options.

I listened to my uncles and aunts argue with each other about what was best for Dad. I felt a little annoyed as it was difficult to hear them, and they were talking about our father. I then realised that they also were working through the shock and grief, and this was a lot to bear. They too lost their father, Grandpa Gerry only four months ago unexpectedly so the grief was heightened because of this.

The neurosurgeon came into the room and asked to speak with Mum, and my sister Jenny and I went into the room with her. He looked at us and said in a soft voice, "I have checked Anthony for brain activity and I am sorry to tell you that it appears to have very little function. This means that he will be in a vegetative state, unable to care for himself."

My mother looked at him blankly trying to process the information, yet not surprised. I asked the doctor, "Is it possible for my father to come out of this coma?"

Then the doctor with a compassionate demeanour softly stated, "He is not conscious and with very little brain function, there is limited quality of life. What we can do is remove his life support, one by one and see if he is able to breathe on his own. I can send the cardiologist in and the Head Doctor to discuss the next steps. If you have any other questions, please feel free to page me."

Later that afternoon, the cardiologist then appeared, and advised us that Dad's heart had irreparable damage to it, and showed us the X-rays. He looked at Mum first, then shifted his gaze to us stating, "There is a high chance that your husband and father could have a further heart attack, given the amount of heart damage."

It was very clear on how this was going to work out.

This news felt like a physical blow that left us breathless, and gasping for air. I could feel myself choking back the tears as reality was setting in. My sisters were still in shock, and denial was our friend as we all planned Dad coming home to recover. The specialists were telling us that Dad was not coming home. My Mum already knew that Dad had gone to be with the Lord, but we were not ready to let him go without a fight.

We walked back into the room to my extended family and told them what the neurosurgeon and cardiologist stated. They were firing questions here and there and we just could not answer it. There was a lot of emotion, sadness and anger in the room and all I wanted to do was to run out of there and get some fresh air, so I could process the information.

It was some time later, that the Head Doctor came in to discuss the next steps. He was planning to take Dad off the life support tomorrow starting with the oxygen, little by little to see if his body and brain could function on its own. However, when the doctor discussed withholding fluids and nourishment, my uncles were very annoyed with the thought of this being some form of euthanasia. The plan seemed cruel to me also but we suggested we start with the breathing apparatus first and then re-evaluate. We stayed in the hospital till visiting hours were over, and we kissed my Dad on his forehead and left. The next day, Dad was still in the coma, with very little brain function or response. We were calling out to him, trying to communicate and get some response. I held his hand and asked him to squeeze mine if he could hear me. Still no response or movement. There was such a desperation to get something from him, to know that he was still alive or functioning. Mum kept telling me that God had taken him and there was no point trying to intervene. Yet I could not give up, and Jenny, Missy and I were holding onto a glimmer of hope that he would make it.

The visitors and extended family kept pouring in, taking care of us and offering kind words of comfort. It was such a blur, but we appreciated every gesture of kindness and the outpouring of love we received. That evening the nurses were going to remove the oxygen. The hospital provided some counselling and prepared us for what was next. The counsellor spent some time listening to us as we recounted the events leading up to the heart attack, and the time in the hospital. We discussed the loss and the fact my Dad was so young, yet to retire and take a break from work. His job was very stressful, and he was looking forward to travelling in Australia and overseas. Missy talked about how she was looking forward to Dad giving her away one day when she got married. She was very emotional, and choked up at the thought of losing Dad. Jenny was numb, and trying to hold it together. Her face was sometimes expressionless yet I knew that the tears were welling up from time to time.

With very little sleep over the last two days, we went home later that evening, way after the visiting times were over. The hospital offered Mum a bed for the night but she was exhausted and preferred to go home.

Dad died early that morning. It was such a shock.

The hospital called at three o'clock in the morning, advising that he was breathing on his own, but had another heart attack. He stopped breathing. I took the call, but then handed the phone to my Mum. My Dad has passed away, and it was on repeat in my head. He had only just turned fifty seven, and was still working full time. That heaviness returned to me with waves and waves of sadness, as I tried to take in what the nurse was saying. Mum looked at me and said, "He died on my birthday. He was already gone, Melody." Missy was with me, and she heard the phone too. We both held each other and cried and cried. We sat on the sofa and cried until we fell asleep.

Later that morning, Jenny and I drove to the hospital to be with Dad. I was so sad that Dad died on his own, without us being with him. Although we knew that the Lord had already taken his spirit earlier, and gave us time to deal with the shock. We walked into the room, and he was lying on the bed, with all the machines, and apparatus removed. His eyes were closed and he looked peaceful. I told Jenny he was only asleep and we were going to see him one day in our heavenly home. The tears came again, and I could feel the heaviness of my heart, emotionally drained with exhaustion as we sat in silence. Jenny and I prayed together, that the Lord would give us strength to get through this.

We sat there holding his hand for an hour or so, crying, then talking about some funny memories, then we burst into tears again. This seemed to go on for some time, until we began to feel my Dad turning icy cold as the blood drained from his face and arms. This was another blow to the denial trail, that we wandered down from time to time to suppress the reality of my fathers death. It hit us both that we never got to say goodbye. We wondered whether his spirit was still with us in the room, or was he with Jesus already. I pondered the scriptures -To be absent from the body and to be present with the Lord. (2 Corinthians 5:8).

My Uncle Geoffrey and Aunty Liz walked in and looked at Jenny and I and they gave us a hug. My Uncle was the closest sibling to my Dad and he was so distraught that Jenny and I had to console him. He sobbed and sobbed and held my Dad's hand for a long time, shaking his head with disbelief. "He is too young to die. How can this happen?"

Aunty Liz walked over to my Uncle and put her hand on his shoulder. He was bent over gripped in grief. It was heartbreaking and then Jenny and I started crying again, until we were exhausted. We had not had any water or food but we did not even think about it. Before long the other aunties and uncles arrived, and the tears were flowing, their anguish on their faces. It really felt like our world had ended.

It was now my job to find the burial plot and help organise the funeral. Mum was in a bad way, and was struggling to function and make decisions. She was still in deep shock, as she had experienced my Dad collapsing and then trying desperately to revive him. He lay on the bedroom floor for twenty minutes before the ambulance arrived to try to resuscitate him. They were able to get a pulse and gave him oxygen, then transported him and my mother to the hospital. Our neighbours rushed to help contact us, and locked up the house so that Mum could go to the hospital with Dad. I was so appreciative that our neighbours reached out and supported Mum during this traumatic time.

The funeral was sad but uplifting, knowing that my Dad was a follower of Jesus gave us peace to know that he had eternal life. His life here on earth was very short indeed, but God had plans for him. Our family felt sad with the loss, but not despair as we had the hope of being reunited one day. Although for me, I was not certain of this as I was not living a truly devoted christian life. There was a strong conviction to check my heart, and confess this sin that I had been harbouring.

It was really tough for Will as he was so close to my Dad. He was only five years old, and we would often find him hiding under my parents bed. It was so difficult for him to understand what had happened and I tried to explain this the best I could. He bottled up his emotions and found it difficult to talk about.

I came to understand over the last ten days that Dad had a relationship with the Lord and served Him in quiet ways, never boasting about his deeds, yet he was very generous and compassionate to those in need. He spent time in the Word each morning and was devoted to the Lord. I was so proud in a good way to hear this about my father. He certainly surprised me. So naturally, I got the chance to share this with everyone who came to the funeral.

After the death of my father, I found myself doing some serious soul searching looking for the answers that I needed to have this assurance of my own salvation. I found that the Lord was so patient with me, as I held onto this unconfessed sin of an ungodly relationship which was so difficult to lay down. I was so afraid of being alone, that I tried to fight with God. Everytime I searched the scriptures for answers I was confronted with the truth and this became too difficult to deny any longer.

Having organised the burial plot, the funeral and wake, I had very little time to grieve. There was so much to do and I was grateful for Jenny helping Mum with the finances and the will. Each of us were dealing with the unexpected loss of our father in different ways.

We were so grateful to our church family who called by and checked on us weeks after the funeral. Our Aunt Vee came over to stay with us for a time to help around the house and we were given so much love. I could see God's tender hand throughout this time of sadness and loss as we grappled with a life without my Dad.

My cousins also came over to help finish some of the jobs that my Dad had started and never got to complete. There was such an outpouring of love and compassion that we were all overwhelmed with the kindness we were given. God works through people and it was very evident for the months following my Dad's death.

One night, four weeks after my Dad's death, I found it hard to get to sleep, then just when I started to drift off, I heard a plastic bag rustling in my room, and I opened my eyes and looked up to the ceiling for a brief moment, then closed my eyes hoping that it would stop. The rustling continued. I sat up in my bed and looked around the room. Then I got up and checked on the plastic bag near my wardrobe to see if it was a mouse or rat. Something did not seem right, but feeling tired, I lay back down in bed. I closed my eyes again then distinctly heard my name called, "Melody." I looked up at the ceiling and around my room, as there was a dim light in the corridor but there was no one there. I did not recognise the voice and it was a definite audible whisper. For a brief moment I thought it was my Dad, but remembered that he had died, and his spirit was with the Lord.

As my thoughts wandered, I sensed a dark presence in the room, and immediately my heart started to beat quickly with overwhelming fear, then a cold shiver down my spine. The room became so cold. Moments later there was pressure at the side of my body, as if there was someone in the bed with me. I looked over and I could not see anyone. I was hoping that perhaps Will had slipped in unnoticed. Then this pressure increased and I could feel it move on top of me, putting pressure on my chest like a heavy weight pinning me to the bed, as I lay flat on my back. I had pins and needles in my fingers and toes, and I was terrified, trembling in fear. I was almost suffocating, gasping for breath as I tried to wriggle my body free. It was heavy and all I could do was to cry out to Jesus, "Please, Jesus help me! Please forgive my sin and help me Lord. I need you now. I am not sure what is happening. Can you help me please." I could barely speak, and only managed whispers as the pressure was quite intense. I could not see anything around me, as I looked around afraid of what I would see.

Then miraculously whatever it was left, and I was free. I gasped breathless for a minute while I regathered myself. Then I put my lamp on and got down on my knees and confessed the sin that I had been harbouring, and the relationship that was leading me away from the Lord. I cried and cried to the Lord for a good hour, realising how much I was hurting him. They were tears of Godly sorrow, and a deep desire to repent, and turn away from this sin that was affecting my being in so many ways, while still recognising that I needed the Lord to help me to make the changes.

I fell asleep with my light on, exhausted with fear but so tired that I was not even aware that I had drifted into a deep sleep. The next morning, I recounted what had happened to me and remembered the rustling plastic bag, the whisper of my name and the dark presence in my room that almost suffocated me. I was trying to make sense of why this happened like this, why the dark evil presence, and was God in control of all of this.

I reflected on this event from time to time after talking it over with Mum. She could see how God could use this to wake me up, and lead me to repent of my sin. After all God was sovereign over all, even evil spirits. This was some sort of dark spirit that I had invited in by my continual walking in sin. It was clear to me that the Lord had used this to show me the magnitude of sin, and I could not mess with Him. This terrified me so much and even though I wanted to minimise this, and find a logical explanation, this was so real that there was no way of denying it. I was fully awake at the time, able to move around the room and then this dark presence entered my room. Out of total fear in the Lord, I surrendered myself, knowing that I was completely dependent on Him to transform me.

And He did, Jesus did set me free but it hurt an awful lot. I was again heartbroken and alone but I knew this time I was going to be okay. This gave me a chance to focus on healing my heart, and growing in the knowledge of His will.

In my vulnerable state Will's Dad was pressuring me about joint custody arrangements. I was still grieving the loss of my Dad, a broken heart and the pressure from work. It was a very trying time, and I spent days in tears. Also Will was being manipulated, and was taking out his frustrations on me, also having to process the loss of his grandfather and the instability that brought with it.

To top it all, my Mum's Dad also passed away two months after my father at the age of eighty years old of a respiratory illness. We were going through a very tough time, and didn't need the added stress and pressure that was being thrust upon Will and myself with changes to custody arrangements.

Will continued to act out with tantrums, throwing things with anger. Obviously he felt safe to act out on me, but it was very difficult to manage, seeing him in so much pain. Everytime I tried to intervene with his father, the worse it got and I would be the recipient of revenge attacks via Will. I knew this caused Will pain too, so often I would back down so that he was protected. I was very tired of the lies and deception, wanting it all to go away. I was now grieving my Dad after months and months of tasks to sort through, and it left me so fragile. Sometimes I envied my Dad, going to be with Jesus. I wanted to be there with him, and not experience any more pain and anguish. However I knew that I had to be there for Will and see this through, and there were still some assignments that the Lord had in mind for me.

Chapter 12

A New Vocation

Leaving full time work to take up a Counselling degree was a big faith step, but I knew this was something that I was led to do. I prayed about this for some time now, afraid to make such a change to my life but I had lost the desire to continue with the broking role after fifteen years of service.

Will had moved in with his father and grandmother, after I discovered that the joint custody was actually a change of custody arrangements. Will had been asking to go live with his father for the last three years, and taking out his frustrations on me when I said no. I allowed his father plenty of access but now he wanted more. I was completely blindsided, and felt very annoyed that I was deceived yet again. However, holding onto Will meant more torment for both of us, and I was hoping we could have equal time with Will.

At first, it was amicable but then I soon discovered that it had become a way to punish and control me for speaking up against domestic violence, a subject that was still not openly discussed in the media. There was still a lot of fear and shame attached to it. The insidious nature of evil was trying to crush me, and put out my flame that burned so brightly, but God had other plans for me.

During my time at college, I had met so many interesting people, including fellow students and lecturers. For me this was a time of healing and spiritual growth, discovering the truth of the Word, which challenged my thinking and being in ways that I could not have imagined.

I had started the college degree part time at work and then decided to switch to full time which was a big step away from the corporate world I had become accustomed to. I remember the day that I felt impressed upon by the Lord to take up this calling. I was on the deck of a large yacht at a business function with work colleagues, drinking champagne and discussing some sales opportunities. I wandered over to another part of the boat and looked out to sea, thinking that there was so much more to life than my world, and the thought arrived in my head, "Would you give this up for me?" It was so clear, and I could see that this lifestyle and type of work was losing its lustre. Over the next four months, I had decided to jump in and accept the call, resigning from full time employment to study full time. It was scary and exciting not knowing how my future was going to pan out.

This was a sabbatical period, concentrating on college full time without the distraction of employment. Thankfully I had saved some money during my time of work, even though the divorce settlement and custody battle had eradicated a fair amount, so I was able to buy my car and have no debts. However, sometimes I find myself anxious about the future, and what my life will look like going forward. Everytime I felt discouraged, I would pray for strength. During this time I had learned to depend on the Lord, and the power and promises of His Word. It truly sustained me during this time of uncertainty.

I was really missing Will, and trying to get in contact with him was so difficult and frustrating. I tried to visit him as much as I could, reassuring him that I would be there for him. How could I protect Will from the emotional damage that was inflicted on him by these lies of abandonment. I did not abandon Will, but only wanted him to have a loving and nurturing environment. I wanted to have custody of Will, and for him to maintain a healthy relationship with his Dad, who could put aside any differences for the sake of our son's wellbeing. I realised that this was an impossible task. I was leaning on God to continue to fight this battle for me. Everytime I tried to do something about this in my own strength, it backfired and did not go well. At times I felt powerless, but soon reminded myself that in my weakness, I am strong.

The education of the mind and spirit had a cathartic effect on me, as my self-awareness and perspective became more clearer. I could see the unhealthy patterns of my own life, the choices I made, my own reactions including my character flaws. This was an agonising realisation that my flaws were showing up in times of trouble, but on the positive side my character was developing. I prayed that the Lord would transform and shape me to be all that He called me to be. I was under construction by the Lord, going through the refiners fire, and at times it was extremely painful but necessary. I was learning to die to self, and the old me was being threshed off like chaff, which brought a new found freedom from the bondage of sin.

The course also allowed me to do Units of Theology and Biblical Studies which involved an integrative approach to counselling in accordance with Scripture. That is what I liked about the course, as it incorporated Psychology with a Biblical framework, from a christian worldview.

It was about also relying on the Holy Spirit, to provide Godly counsel to those that were entrusted in your care.

Sitting under an oak tree at the college, I was reading Isaiah and taking in the different lenses and framework, the prophetic and wise Word. In Isaiah 54:17 - "No weapon formed against you shall prosper. And every tongue that rises against you in judgement You shall condemn. This is the heritage of the servants of the Lord. And their righteousness is from Me, says the Lord." This was a scripture that I held onto in times of battle. This was a time of renewal for me, and God was preparing me for an assignment, and it was exciting because every step I was taking I knew I was walking in God's will, and his perfect timing. There was a peace that surpasses all understanding.

The life that I had led up to this time, was part of my journey and experiences to then become my platform for growth and imparting to others wisdom. Life taught me a lot of lessons and I could see the hand of God directing me. I had learned that when you have a mountain top experience, it usually follows with temptation that may lead to sin, resulting in a fall. That certainly happened to me. God allows us freewill, but gently directs us as we follow in obedience, surrendering our will to Him. It really is a daily surrender, as I was quite a strong willed person, and found this to be a struggle. Or I would often jump ahead of God, hoping that He would catch on, and make it alright. However, I was learning that this is not God's way and waiting on the Lord was something that I was going to have to do. Afterall He is God, sovereign, powerful and almighty and I was none of these things. It was pride that reared its ugly head, and I had to keep on top of this but I certainly needed the Lord to help me with that too.

The practical work was part of my course and this involved volunteering through the church or other counselling centres. I decided to work through the church and also a not for profit agency. At church I came across a few christians who were suffering with depression and anxiety, with many of them relying on medication. I was able to offer a holistic approach, showing them the love and compassion of Jesus through His Word. It was the deepest source of comfort.

The voluntary work was so rewarding, and I was learning new skills each day. It was teaching me to be patient, and to listen well. Active listening is not easy. I prayed for discernment and godly wisdom each day and the fruit was becoming evident.

During the next few months, I had listened to parents that had lost children to drug abuse and even a case that had the media attention of a young girl who took a party drug at a concert and died. It was heartbreaking to hear these parents talk about their powerlessness, and the guilt that plagued them following the tragic deaths. Many of these parents looked for ways to deflect their pain by starting up charities or informational companies on behalf of their loved one. I found that people had their own ways of dealing with their loss, and rather than feeling stuck in sorrow, they were able to reach out to help others, and in the process help themselves to walk through the valley. Jesus spoke about the sorrow of death in Psalms 23, and that he would walk through the valley with us, comforting us like no one else could.

The families and individuals that came to me for counselling knew that I had a christian worldview and many of them asked me for my perspective. I was free to answer their questions, and they gave permission to discuss their spiritual beliefs as part of a holistic approach.

The not for profit organisation I volunteered for, was often in the media, with their victims of crime who suffered tragic losses, and I became their counsellor to unpack the events. It opened up my somewhat sheltered world, to a world of horrific crimes and deaths. I had to learn how to process the information with empathy, feel their pain, then disengage from the session when the time was over. That was difficult to do, as often I found myself thinking of the stories as I prayed for these clients. There was a cost to helping these persons, and this was part of being human. Having a deeper spiritual connection with Jesus, meant that I could hand this burden onto Him. I just had to remember to do so.

The media kept putting out stories of how education was going to rid the world of some of the crimes, and the issues of overdoses, attached to substance abuse. Education may help some who blindly walk into this addictive cycle without considering the consequences. However, education that the media strongly suggested did not have the answers for the deep spiritual disconnect, the void and the need for a Saviour. It did not address the human heart that is filled with evil and selfish desires, that is in desperate need of a relationship with Jesus that can transform the heart, and cure the disease of sin. I pondered over the message of the cross, and how powerful it is in giving life to those that are spiritually dead.

Whilst I was involved with a number of volunteering programs and ministry, I decided to go out with a long time colleague I met through the Insurance industry. We had always been friends, but I was now very careful of only dating someone that had the same christian faith. Blake had been involved in a Bible study group through a work friend and he and I would get together from time to time to discuss some of his questions.

He had been a fence sitter for some time, similar to myself and we had some interesting debates. Blake was a strawberry blonde, a ruddy complexion with a cheeky grin. He had the most beautiful icy blue eyes that gave you a chill, but in a good way. It was relaxing being around him, as he was very easy going and not bossy, controlling or intense. I guess it was what I needed. Mum would always tease me and say that this country boy had come a calling, but she did not know that he was really a city guy. The fact that he was so laid back, my mother had confused for a country boy. Anyway I would always say that we were only friends.

Blake would visit from time to time, where we would study various portions of the Bible. We had some interesting debates, particularly on the authenticity of the Word, miracles and the Gospels. It also helped me to explain the things that I had been learning in Theology and Biblical Studies at college, and cemented my beliefs, as I could speak from the heart.

Blake was brought up as a catholic but became an atheist as a teenager, and there were some signs of unbelief and the understanding of a supernatural Almighty God. I had to be gentle and just take it slow. Afterall, I had been praying for Blake for some time. I had invited him to church a few times, and even for a play that I was in at church called Heaven's Gate, Hell's flames, but he was always distracted with other things, and other relationships. For some reason God had put it in my heart to pray for him for the last five years that he would have a revelation and come to know Jesus as Lord. I was not sure why this was the case, but I did it in obedience.

I had known Blake for nine years through the insurance industry, as he visited our brokerage from time to time. He was always approachable and we had good discussions on work topics, as well as spiritual issues. It was encouraging to see him finally take steps to commit his life to the Lord. So I decided to take it slow and work on the friendship and allow the Lord to show me in time.

It was time for the college exams, and over the next two weeks, I spent endless days and nights immersed in my books, and my computer studying the texts and notes. I was determined to do well, having such an interest and passion for what I was learning. The work was truly enjoyable, and during this time I had matured in my faith and understanding of the Word. I was no longer sitting on the fence, but committed to follow Christ and do His will.

Chapter 13

Journey to the East

The opportunity to do a small mission trip and pilgrimage to the Holy Land and Turkey came up, and I could not say no. After hearing Mina's experience, I was so keen to see this for myself. The mission was to travel to Turkey to all the seven churches from the Book of Revelation which was Apostle Paul's journey, witness and pray for the christians who were being persecuted in the various towns. The Book of Revelation was Apostle John's account from a vision given to him at Patmos in Greece for the end times, where Jesus commends and warns the seven churches. It was only a three week trip, but was a way to encourage the Turkish Christians. There was an element of danger, as missionaries were often thrown into prison for preaching the Gospel.

My Aunt Pammy, Mum and I arrived in Istanbul, Turkey at night just after dinner. It was a large airport with lots of people rushing around trying to get connecting flights. The airport was quite modern and very westernised. One could not tell whether this was a US major city, as everyone was well dressed, groomed with designer clothing, except for a few traditional clothed females with their burkas.

On our way to our hotel, the architecture was a mixture of western influence along with the traditional middle eastern flavour, with some period features. It was truly a spectacular city, bustling with people everywhere. It was a city filled with young people, in their twenties and thirties mostly. However, there may be parts of the city where the older folk settled, a little more secluded from this bustling city. Istanbul has more than fourteen million people living in the one city, half of the Australian population, which was difficult to fathom.

The hotel in Istanbul was a quaint boutique one, an older building with Turkish architecture and furnishings. It was quite comfortable with two rooms, a largish one with an ensuite and a smaller one for me, I was hoping. We were exhausted having left home very early in the morning, and I was so excited that I hardly slept the night before. We just hit the pillow after our showers and crashed.

The city was magnificent with the breathtaking harbour, and it reminded me of Sydney, which is really the best I had ever seen. The Bosphorus Straight, a thirty two kilometre sea channel that divides Europe and Asia, from north to south to unite the Marmara Sea to the Black Sea was a must see, with the mansions and buildings lining the waterway. The sea was a gorgeous deep greenish blue, and at places was quite deep, again similar to the Sydney harbour, except for the cityscape consisting of Turkish buildings with large domes, that were unique and typical to this exotic city. Some of these buildings date back to before the Ottoman Empire in 7th Century BC, which was established by the Greeks, then by Rome, so there is a mixture of architecture and designs.

We travelled to all seven churches Ephesus, Smyrna located in Izmir, Pergamum, which is Bergama today, Thyatira in Akhisar, Sardis, Philadelphia and Laodicea. Five of the churches were rebuked by Jesus for various reasons from idolatry, compromising the truth, corruption and lukewarmness. The only ones that were commended were Smyrna, the persecuted church and Philadelphia the faithful church.

The church of Pergamum, which is a modern town of Bergama today, was one that left an imprint etched in my memory. As the bus approached the base of the steep hill leading to the elevated area where the church was located, the blackened landscape caught my attention. This church was burnt, with its ruins strewn all over the hill, with only some large marble columns that survived. It was the compromising church in the book of Revelation, which held 'Satan's throne.' A great altar that survived the Greco-Roman period was confiscated by Hitler, and it is now exhibited in the German museum. I could see that God left His mark on this church, stating that you cannot mess with a Holy God, but fear Him for He is Powerful, Almighty and requires reverence and honour.

Arriving in Tel Aviv I could feel the excitement rising up in me, that finally I was able to see Israel and experience the Bible coming alive, in this Holy land. The city was very westernised with tall buildings and state of the art architecture, the IT capital of the world as Israel was known for its advancement in technology.

As we flew over parts of Israel, I could see the dusty terrain, fields that looked desolate in places and then an oasis of lush green areas scattered here and there. It was so different to other parts of the world that I had visited so far, and even Australia.

We were only spending a short time in Tel Aviv before our trip over to Caesarea where the Gentiles first heard the good news of the gospel. It was situated between Tel Aviv and Haifa on the coastal plain. There were many ruins scattered throughout the city, much of the Roman influence in the architecture.

The next stop was Jezreel Valley, Megiddo where the final battle and Armageddon was to take place, which was a fertile plain that covered quite a large area. We listened to the tourist operator talk about the battle of Saul with Philistines, and the other battles that took place there. Later we drove up to Cana and Nazareth visiting the villages around. Nazareth is now known as the Arab Capital in Israel, with lots of Arabic influences in the culture, food and shopping. Amongst the city, there are some signs of the Jewish old settlements.

The town of Galilee by the sea is known as Lake Tiberias. The waters were so calm and picturesque set amongst the valleys and hills surrounding it. It was difficult to imagine the sea being treacherous during the storm, in which Jesus took control over the elements. We took a boat trip across the lake, and there were small waves but it was a relatively smooth journey. A couple of nuns joined us who were also doing a pilgrimage tour, and they were singing some lovely hymns as we sailed to the other side.

The Dead Sea was what I had imagined, with the amount of salt that prevented any living thing from surviving, we saw many people floating and exfoliating, as the Sea was known for its therapeutic and clinical properties. It was the lowest part of the earth at four hundred and twenty seven metres below sea level, at a depth of 306 metres making the Dead Sea quite deep. The salt in the sea can feel like quick sand and some parts are hard and crusty, crystallised salt that is sharp and can cut your feet. It is best to wear thongs or tight shoes when walking through the water. As we sat along the edge of the Sea, we could smell the salt permeating our senses, and it felt refreshing.

The Jordan River, where Jesus was baptised by John the Baptist, was not far from the Dead Sea. It was a steady river, greenish in colour that flowed from the Sea of Galilee north-south for 125 kilometres. We had a few people in our group that were getting baptised and we went to witness this in the Jordan River. I pulled up my pants above my knee and walked into the water along with the others. I could feel the little fish nibbling at my toes and dead skin. It felt really strange, but I tried to block it out as we sang choruses and praised the Lord. The pastor gave a short introduction and asked the individuals to respond. It was such a special moment, as they made a commitment to follow Christ. I could imagine the angels in heaven singing their Hallelujah chorus.

Bethlehem was a dry and dusty place, and as I looked across at the fields where the shepherds first heard about the Messiah, it was a number of small hills that were quite desolate and not the green fields that I had imagined. Maybe it was a green oasis back in that time.

The hotel we stayed at was very modern and chic, a mixture of Arabic architecture with western culture. I had noticed that the finishing touches of the building were inferior to the type of workmanship I had grown used to in Australia.

We were told not to venture into certain areas, as we explored Bethlehem on our own. We were only to go to the tourist spots, churches and cafes along the stretch. Even whilst in the cafe there was a level of anxiety as it was necessary to be on guard in the event of some unexpected eruption of violence.

The Via Dolorosa was the way Jesus took to go to Golgotha where he was crucified. It was a cobble street, with uneven stones laid with small plaques where he fell from time to time. The religious churches had set up shrines to mark these spots so that the tourists could pray and pay homage. I imagined Jesus walking this path, knowing that He was going to be slain, and endure the most terrible pain, and it made me want to cry out to Him.

Whilst the others walked ahead and visited the burial tomb where the religious declared that Jesus was laid, I sat near the Garden Tomb on a rock and just prayed. I was so thankful for what Jesus had done on the cross, and the reality of my own salvation after the sorrow and pain I endured in my life so far, hit me like a tonne of bricks, and I sobbed quietly, the pain slowly dissipating.

I was praying for the next chapter in my life, of helping those who were struggling with mental illness, addictions, violence and asking the Lord to prepare my heart. There was a struggle within me about my own ability to do what the Lord was calling me to. Yet as I submitted this all to Christ, I knew that He would equip me, as I took a step towards obedience. With my hands covering my face, I bowed my head and felt a soft pressure on my head. I immediately thought that one of the pastors or people in our group were there, but it felt different. I had a warm feeling running through my body, lighting up all the dark places in my heart with a light shining through every crevice. I did not want to move or lift up my head, as I felt this outpouring of love over me. It made me tingle with excitement, yet it was both comforting and peaceful. I could then smell this sweet aroma of a mixture of citrus and blossoms, which I just took in, inhaling and exhaling, letting out every toxic thing in my body. The light touch was still on my head, as I opened my eyes I looked around and there was no one around at all. I was alone. Yet there was this beautiful presence, maybe an angelic being, or Jesus Himself, I was not sure but it was a supernatural experience that I will never forget. I thought about the passage in the Bible in Psalm 37 about trusting in the Lord, to wait up on Him and Isaiah 40 in following Jesus' path.

God was preparing me for a ministry that was going to release people from darkness, yet I was afraid. I had to remember that He was with me, every step of the way and has power over all darkness. This was all ahead of me. I could sense the excitement but also there was a fear in stepping into the enemy's domain. What will I encounter? Was there a risk to this?

The Garden of Gethsemane was a small area, different to what I had imagined, with sparse looking olive trees throughout. There was a gate around the area where Jesus cried out to God sectioned off from the public. Again there were shrines and statues everywhere telling of the struggles that Jesus had as He anguished about His impending suffering and death. The Mount of Olives was just East of the Old city, across from the Kidron Valley. It was named after the olive grove that was there at the time. This was the place where Jesus would return to as King of Kings and Lord of Lords.

There was quite a crowd at all the shrines, and statues which drew in the tourists with historical information. There were candles, ornaments, holy water and other merchandise and people were drawn into, collecting some meaningful souvenirs that they could take back to remember this place. I found it hard to get drawn in, seeing the folly of the tacky items that would only gather dust on a shelf.

As the crowds dispersed, I crawled into the pit in Caiaphas' house, the place where Jesus was held the night before he was crucified. The pit was under the main floor, in a hard rock crevice which was dimly lit. It was cool and smelt very earthy. I sat there on my own and thought about Jesus, the King of Kings sitting here all alone before he died, and I shed a few tears. The reality of it all really hit me, and as I closed my eyes I sensed the peace of God. It was a warm feeling on my skin, and it filled me up with such a warmth, that I could no longer feel the coldness of this dim pit. This must be what it is like to have a closeness with the Lord, to have a humble posture before Him, to worship Him with all your heart. It felt so pure, and so right. I did not want this moment to end. It was so peaceful. I prayed that I would always be in awe of Jesus and could reflect back on this. I prayed that

I would have many moments like this, and that the Lord would continue to humble me.

After twenty five minutes, I heard my mother and aunt call out to me. I did not realise that they had gone ahead. I apologised to the guide for holding up the group, as I had forgotten all track of time. The time spent there had overtaken me, but I was thankful for this special time with the Lord.

That night, we had a lovely dinner in a bedouin tent which were the gypsy people in Israel, situated on the outskirts of Jerusalem. The dinner was in a traditional style reclining on the large cushions on the floor, with a campfire, a low long table where the food was served. The food was a mixture of legumes, chickpeas, lamb, various vegetables, figs and unleavened bread. The wine was served in traditional jugs made by the locals. There was even a rice dish that looked like biriyani, with spices and vegetables. The food was delicious and we had a good taste of the traditional bedouin feast.

Whilst sitting out in the open I thought about the experience in Caiphas' house and the garden tomb. It gave me a shiver as it was so real and special. I was going to have to write this down in my journal so that I could not forget every detail of the moment. I thought about how I could share this with anyone, Would they believe me, or think I was dreaming this up? I guess it was a special time with Jesus that I could delight in privately.

The visit to the Judean desert was even more spectacular than the photos or video footage I had seen. It is funny, how experiencing something with your naked vision is so much better than a screen. The enormity of it, the depth and the linear etchings in the rock were difficult to describe. The rock had different shades of pink, tan and grey and the sun bounced off some parts making it look reddish brown. The desert was very rugged, rocky, with sand dunes. One could see the sand grains being carried by the gentle breeze and settling in patterns that looked like waves on the sea. There were scrubs and scrawny plants here and there. This was the place that Jesus came to pray, and have one on one with God the Father. It was also the place where Satan tempted him. Looking around, the desert appeared to be untouched, and we were taken back in the time when Jesus walked these plains and climbed these rocky crevices.

Over in the distance we could see locals on a donkey and cart carrying piles of wood, and hay. I stopped to take a photo as it appeared that we were right back in time. Before taking the photo I realised that the shirtless boy was talking on his mobile phone which was so funny. I had to take a photo which was hilarious, seeing this primitive looking wooden cart carrying supplies juxtaposed by the modern technology of the time.

We visited a few Messianic churches in Jerusalem, and spent time ministering and praying for the members. It was so encouraging to see that the churches were active in reaching out to the Jews in the local synagogues and had Bible studies in their homes. We also prayed for the peace of Jerusalem and that God would prepare the hearts of those he is calling unto Himself. It was so sad that many of the Jewish people were blinded by the truth that their Messiah is actually Yeshua, a fulfilment of the book of Ezra, where there is a process for restoration, where Jesus is the temple. There is also Isaiah 53, the Suffering Servant and Jeremiah 29: 10-14, with the promise of redemption.

These prophecies were written hundreds and in some cases thousands of years before they were fulfilled, and in Ezekiel 36 was how God scattered His people to exile all over the world, then re-established the nation of Israel in one day in 1948, just as the Bible said. It helped me to trust God, who keeps his promises according to the scriptures. Sadly the Jews had to go through a lot of suffering and this will continue on during the times of Antichrist's reign at the end. God promised that He will save a remnant through this as in Romans 11. It was truly amazing how the Bible clearly shows God's future plan of redemption. As in Revelation 1 we see the glorified Christ who will return to Israel to rule and reign.

The next day we took a tour to sites like the Upper room where Jesus had the last supper with his disciples and the place where He appeared in His resurrected body. It was amazing to experience these places, and it brought back the reality of Jesus walking on this earth, as fully God and man to fulfil his role as Redeemer. I took in every moment of this visit and was so grateful I had this opportunity to be part of this short mission trip.

Chapter 14

Home Sweet Home

Arriving in Sydney Saturday afternoon, we had ample time to make our way home by taxi. It was always good to be home, as I missed Will, and could not wait to see him and give him a big hug. I had so much to tell him. I also looked forward to catching up with Blake to share my experiences and the knowledge I had gained seeing the Bible come alive, and take on a form of its own. I also missed Jerusalem, as there was something there that drew me back, and that it had a special place in my heart.

Blake met me at church Sunday morning, and we went out for lunch afterward. It was good to see him, and he seemed more enthusiastic about catching up than normal. Perhaps he missed me too. I had developed some of the photos in Malaysia and so we could talk about the trip to Turkey and Israel. He was interested in the places, as he was becoming more familiar with the Bible.

I was so encouraged to see that he was enthusiastic in learning more about God, and studying his Word consistently. I often shared my notes and books with him so that he could see that there was actual evidence, authenticity of the Word of God. My prayers over the last five years were becoming fruitful, and I smiled thinking of how faithful our Lord was. Whilst I could not see any results over the years, God had me persevering in prayer for a reason that I still was not sure of.

Will had a beaming smile when I picked him up from his fathers place. He was excited but tried to hold back his feelings so that his father was not offended. I gave him a big hug and told him that I missed him dearly. I was so happy to have him over the weekend, and hear about his stories at school, and the new shows he was watching.

I told Will that we were going fishing with Blake, a friend of mine. I had introduced Will to a few of my circle of friends from college, work and church. It was good for him to see that we had a good support circle of friends, male and female and that it was a healthy social life. Blake had been to our home a few times to study the Bible, and we were simply platonic friends then, but now it had taken a slightly different form. I was afraid to get involved with him in the event it affected this good friendship if things didn't work out. Also I was not going to be involved with someone that was not yet committed to Christ.

It was Saturday morning and after breakfast Blake dropped by to take Will and I fishing. We decided to go to Lilli Pilli as I heard it was a good fishing spot. It was very difficult to keep Will quiet and still while fishing but this was a good test for him. Besides, we wanted to get him outdoors and explore rather than his Mario computer games, which most children were hooked on.

We were there for over an hour, with a few nibbles here and there but no fish. Will was getting impatient, but we just kept talking softly and pretending that the fish were biting. I left Blake and Will to hold the lines while I went to get some drinks and nibbles. While I was sitting there, I prayed, "Lord you know I am afraid of getting involved in a relationship which is outside of your will. I want to be in your will. I would rather be on my own than to be in a relationship that does not honour you. I would like to be equally yoked with a christian who is committed to serving you, as well as someone who will encourage me to be all what you have called me to be. I would like to be that support person who brings the best out of them. Father, please forgive me for this request but like Gideon. I am nervous and afraid, and would like to put out a fleece. You know that I have been spending some time with Blake, and I need to know that You really called him, that as he was baptised, he is truly a follower. I need to be sure, Lord. We have not been catching fish, so if we can catch a few, then I will know that it is okay to get serious with Blake."

I looked over and it seemed they had almost given up. As I was walking over with the drinks and food, Blake got a nibble and pulled in a small fish. It was only 5 inches so I giggled to myself as I watched him take it off the hook and throw it back in. As we munched on the biscuits and dip, Will caught a fish that Blake had to help him with. The fish was even smaller and we had to throw it back in. Almost five minutes later, Blake caught another fish. It was a fighter and I thought maybe this was a keeper. However when he pulled it in, it was no bigger than five inches. I was laughing so loud as I thought Wow The Lord has such a sense of humour! Blake looked at me, puzzled at why I was laughing so much, and I knew I couldn't tell him about my request. One day perhaps I could share this funny story. It was the grace of God, knowing that I needed some reassurance, and I did not want to make the wrong decision.

When we arrived home, Blake and I had a cup of tea, whilst Mum whipped up some dosas. Will loved dosas and samba, and did not mind the spice. I think it was the first time that Blake had tried a dosa, and he enjoyed it. We then played a Monkey in the barrel game with Will, before Blake left to go home.

Missy was getting married to Phillipe after dating for three years or so. My sister Jenny and I were part of the wedding party, along with Cass, Phillipe's sister. We were all very excited, but a little sad that Dad was not there to walk Missy down the aisle. Missy was quite emotional talking about it, but Jenny's husband Mike volunteered.

It was apparent that Jenny was not coping well after Dad's death, and starting spiralling into depression. It all started with post-partum depression and escalated to clinical, for a number of reasons that were too complicated to explain. Jenny's first child, an adorable little girl named Jade, was only two years old when her grandfather passed so she would not remember him, but she did notice that he was missing from our get togethers. Jenny had a little baby boy named Jacob, and he had the biggest dark brown round eyes that looked like marbles. He was so sweet and spent a lot of time with us, while Jenny was in hospital.

It was perplexing for Blake to see, and be part of these trials which had happened in our family, over a short space of time. I was hoping he could see God working in these situations, and that we were still hopeful despite the times of anguish. Afterall, life was a typical roller coaster, of highs and real lows, and it is a time of growth and renewal. There was a cost to christianity, and it was important to weigh up the cost before committing oneself. However, once you die to self, it is liberating. The internal battles of the flesh can go on for a time, and it is a daily struggle as you wrestle against the world, the evil one and yourself. At least we know that it is Christ that wins in the end.

As the days went by, Blake and I were getting closer, and there was a real trust developing beyond the initial friendship. On the weekends we went out for dinner to Brighton Le Sands to a seafood restaurant. Blake always finished his meal in one hundred and twenty seconds, and he sat and watched me enjoy my meal for the next twenty minutes. He was learning to have patience, and I guess we both had to work this out in time. Blake could learn to take his time, and enjoy every mouthful, flavour and texture, while I had to speed up my eating so that the food would not go cold. It was an enjoyable date, and we kept chatting all the way home. He walked me to the door, and we kissed again, a small delicate one. I was going to see him the next morning at church, and it was a forty minute drive home.

It was a warm November morning, and Blake had planned a lunch at the Botanical Gardens restaurant. It was a lovely meal of salmon crusted with almonds and spice, salad and potatoes, coupled with some fine french champagne. Blake chose the duck in a beautiful red wine sauce, along with a terrine of fine vegetables.

After lunch, we went for a walk in the gardens, and enjoyed looking at the beautiful roses, smelling the sweet fragrances as we talked about our families. He proposed to me on one knee and it was official. We were engaged!

Blake and I were attending some marriage preparation classes with a lovely older couple in the church. They were very helpful in navigating around some tricky issues on conflict, resolution, forgiveness, humility and love. It was very important to me that we could grow spiritually together and encourage one another to be obedient to our calling.

It was good to discuss the issues around parenting styles, family background and what a godly relationship looks like. Since we had a different upbringing and parenting style, we had to learn to compromise and listen to one another. There seemed to be so many things to discuss, and although we had known each other on a business level, this was somewhat new. However, we both agreed to work on this together and help one another.

Blake and I were opposites in so many ways. He liked sports on TV, playing golf, hiking and just chilling out. I liked going on walks, meeting up with friends, going out for dinner and having stimulating conversations, and discovering new places and experiences. I also enjoyed reading, writing, singing and listening to music. Our music taste was also different, so again we had to learn to compromise and celebrate the difference.

We both laughed at how different we were, but we had the most important thing in common - that is we both loved the Lord and was committed to following Jesus. Everytime we found a difference, we reflected on our commonality. We also had similar values, and morals which was very important.

What I had admired most about Blake was his love for the Lord, as he faithfully studied the Word, growing in the knowledge of His will. He had such a desire to walk in obedience with Jesus, and by his diligence in searching the scriptures, God was giving him such a boldness. This boldness was outside of his personality trait as he was quiet and reserved, yet God had put a flame in his heart that could not be easily extinguished. I was there to help him fan that flame so that as a team we could expect great things from God, and see his power in our lives and those He put in our path.

I was so excited about our future together, as it was something I had prayed for, that is someone who was equally yoked, passionate about pleasing the Lord, and together we could encourage one another to be all that God has called us to be. I wanted to hear those words from the Lord, "Well done, good and faithful servant," and I often meditated on this to keep me persevering.

The day of the Wedding - 4th March 2000 was a beautiful day. I was nervous about the day, and had so many things on my mind the night before, and struggled to get to sleep. When I finally slept, I could not get up. As I rolled over, I realised that my life was going to change, and I was walking through another door but this time in God's will. What a relief that was to me, to realise that God had given me a life partner to enjoy the beauty and depth of a love relationship, wrapped in the glory of the Lord. It was through our union, that God would manifest His blessing of marriage, and together we could faithfully serve the Lord. I closed my eyes as I thought about the day ahead, and I felt a peace throughout my body.

The sun was shining brightly, so I decided to have my morning coffee on the patio, with my Bible and devotion in hand. I prayed for the day, and all those that were part of the occasion. I prayed for Blake and his family. I also prayed for our worship team who came down with a cold, and needed strength to get through the day. My sister, Jenny had arrived and was talking to Missy in the bedroom about their hair and makeup. Will was still in bed, and I let him sleep in a little as it was a big day for him also.

We had hired some beautiful vintage cars that pulled up at our home to take us to the church. I had my two sisters as bridesmaids. We were all excited about the day, and I had my Mum, Will, Natasha and brother in law Mike in the car with me.

When we arrived at the church, there were a few people who were sneaking in late. I was on time, but we took a few moments to get my dress in shape, with the long train, and a large bouquet of white lilies and greenery. I could see Blake pacing across the front. He looked very nervous, hoping that I was going to turn up, as he kept looking over his shoulder to see if I had arrived.

My beautiful niece, Jade, was my flower girl, so petite and full of mischief was accompanied by Will, who was my page boy with the ring. Will was turning nine years old, and had a cheeky grin. He seemed so excited about the day, and I think he liked having such attention on him also.

As the worship team started to play the 'wedding song' Will and Jade walked down the aisle hand in hand, with a little basket of flowers, both grinning at everyone and chuckling as they realised that they had this attention. It was hilarious as I heard the people chuckle alongside them, sighing with how cute they were.

Then the worship team began the song, "I see the Lord, seated on His throne exalted and the train of his robe filled the temple with His glory" (Isaiah 6 - Isaiah's vision of the Lord). It was just a beautiful song, and as I walked down the aisle I had a glimpse of heaven where I was strolling down a long long aisle going to meet Jesus for the first time, with the angels singing to a full orchestral ensemble. I smiled to myself and then saw Blake at the front, with a smile on his face, a little nervous but excited. I smiled back at him, and all the nervousness went away, as I took in the meaningful union and promise that we were going to make before our Lord and Saviour.

As we both said our vows, our smiles beaming at each other as we made that solid commitment to one another. It was going to be forever, with the blessing from God himself. The ceremony was beautiful and our church family had added a few finishing touches like candelabras, along with the lovely white flowers we ordered, that made the hall look divine.

Everything ran smoothly except for the reception place who were not very helpful with a few issues. I had arranged a string quartet from my college to play as people entered, and served canapes and champagne. However, the night was beautiful and very intimate, and the family and friends celebrated our special day, and the beginning of our life together as a couple.

We decided to have a two week honeymoon, exploring the southern states of Australia on a road trip that took in the Great Ocean Road to parts of South Australia. We both had not done anything like this before, so it was a new experience that we could share together.

While we had pre-arranged some of the accommodation, we decided to find some bed and breakfasts along the way to add a little flavour and spontaneity to our trip. We drove down to Melbourne and stayed in a hotel which had previously been a hospital, then converted over the years to a hotel. It was a lovely room, very clean and bright with the usual amenities, yet it had a strange presence about it. I thought maybe it was because of the history attached to the building, of once being a hospital of those that were ill, those that were dying and the babies that were born.

Chapter 15

Healing Broken Lives

I started work the following week, and it was a slow start with very few appointments. The medical centre was newly established offering a number of services including counselling, sports medicine, physiotherapy and ministry work. It was advertised as a Christian based centre, transparent about our values and worldview. We offered a valuable service to the wide community, accepting people of various cultures and belief systems.

Fulfilling my calling as a counsellor was not only going to help my clients in their brokenness, it was also going to teach me many lessons on human experience, and God's supernatural power. For the reason of confidentiality and anonymity, I will use pseudo names, places or particular details to protect the privacy of those clients. These incidents and events are part of my life's experiences that helped me understand complex humanity and the spirit world. It enabled me to gain some perspective in the happenings of my childhood, which mystified me for years. It helped me to shine a light on the darkness around me, and understand that greater is He that is in you than He that is in the world. 1 John 4:1-4 He is referring to God/Father and the Holy Spirit.

I am going to tell the story of particular clients that presented cases that magnified the power of redemption and also revealed the reality of the unseen spiritual realm. A long period of time has now lapsed between these events, yet they remain etched in my memory. Each of these clients had undergone rigorous diagnostic assessments with our counselling team. Along with our own evaluations, we worked together with psychiatrists, local psychiatric facilities, medical specialists, pastors and ministers of faith to provide a holistic approach. We studied the lives of each of our patients to fully understand their issues. Most importantly we prayed for each of our patients, that the Lord would bring healing and restoration. As a team, we prayed together for Godly wisdom, and that we would be faithful servants dispensing the love of Christ to those He brought to us.

Julie, my first patient, told me she was suffering from anxiety and bouts of depression, and this was her first time in counselling. She seemed much more nervous than I was, so immediately I explained how the session would go, and she was to share what she felt comfortable with. Julie's parents had split when she was fifteen years old and it was traumatising for her. She did not see it coming. Her last three years of school were very difficult as she tried to come to terms with her loss, as well managing the hormonal imbalances and challenges of being a teenager.

She had also recently lost her older brother in a car accident, which left a devastating mark on Julie and her anxiety became worse. She was afraid to go out of her house, and had been housebound for some time now. Julie was still processing the shock of losing someone she loved so unexpectedly. Her world had changed in a short time, and it disrupted her beliefs, her thoughts, and emotions. There was an overwhelming fear that brought on her anxiety and then depression, as she felt that there was no way out of this suffocating grief that drained her to the point of exhaustion. Julie was questioning the meaning of life, and wanted to find a christian counsellor to help her find some answers and purpose.

Five sessions later, Julie was able to manage the anxiety and fear. She advised that her mum and sister had been going to church with her, and she was progressing very well in her faith. In fact Julie, a quiet and shy girl had become bold and on fire for the Lord.

In a space of six months I had seen such a transition from a lost, lonely and depressed young lady to this new creation. What was amazing is that her brother received Christ some months before he passed away, and now the family had the hope that one day they would be reunited. Julie could see how God used her brother to lead the whole family to Him so that they could have eternal life. Julie was so grateful to Jesus for His amazing grace and compassion.

I had three more clients that day, all of them suffering from anxiety and depression. It was becoming more and more common. There was one client who was suffering from burn out, with extreme stress and anxiety, and this was due to ministry work. This was also an epidemic amongst young people and pastors working with youth groups and the demands associated with church life.

It was nine 'o'clock in the morning and I was looking over the calendar for the day. I was prepared for the full day of clients with a small break in between. I made sure I had a good night's sleep so that I would be fresh and able to give my clients my full attention. I realised that listening and being attentive was costly, and it involved concentration, compassion and being emotionally present. Now I understood why Jesus needed some breaks in between to go and pray and have some time alone. I found myself emotionally exhausted, to the point of drifting into a deep sleep early in the evening.

As I was sitting in the room, Diane walked in, along with the receptionist. She had arrived ten minutes early but asked if she could start a little earlier, finding it difficult to make eye contact with me. She had dark curly hair, with the pale sunken green eyes, that showed her tiredness and despair. She appeared to be dishevelled, with her hair not combed properly, her clothes were crumpled and oddly matched. I thought maybe she was not concerned about her appearance, but her face told a different story.

Diane explained that she was suffering from depression and intense anxiety. This strange feeling manifested at times, and it was like a wave of fear that gripped her that she could not breathe, and would often catch her breath. It sounded like a panic attack. I could see her trembling, struggling to make eye contact with me. She went on to explain lots of examples of how this has impacted her life, and all the remedies she has tried to relieve herself of this. It seemed really debilitating as it affected her work, relationships and leisure time. There were no circumstances in her life that she was aware of, that brought on this anxiety and depression.

As I got to know Diane over the next four weeks, her issue of anxiety was somewhat puzzling. She had done a number of medical hormonal tests and everything was normal. However, from the first session, I had made a note while listening to her explain this condition that was starting to make some sense. I had circled her mother and written down - check new age and beliefs. This thought came out of the blue and so I wrote it down. I relied very much on the Lord for guidance, and I soaked myself in prayer about every client I came in contact with, that God would fill me with insight, love and compassion. When I had a thought or a message imprinted, I would wait till there was the right time to ask the question.

I made eye contact with Diane and asked the question, "So can you tell me about your upbringing and beliefs?" I could see her flinch at the question, as if a bullet hit her. The trembling started again, and I could see her trying to compose herself. There was something not right and I was hoping it would become clear as the session went on.

Diane blurted out, "My mother collected crystals and did new age charts so what is wrong with that? Then she asked me to join a small group of young women who practised white witchcraft with spells, prayers, rituals and crap like that, but we had fun."

So the conversation went on by asking another pertinent question, "So tell me what did you enjoy about hanging out with these girls, and what does fun look like to you?"

Diane sniggered, tilted her head and explained the backstory, "I was lonely because my friends were ratbags at school. They bullied me, and made fun of me. I felt very judged and I did not fit in. After all, we had nothing in common because I hated gossip about people I didn't even know. These girls in this group may enjoy some harmless witchcraft tricks, but it was interesting. Life was boring anyway, so playing around with supernatural stuff was exciting and I felt powerful... uh I mean empowered. There was one night where one of the girls, Clare, made fun of me, and this made me so angry, that I could feel myself shaking, so I lunged at her, swearing. My heart was beating so fast, it was ticking like a time bomb. I just wanted to kill her. This scared me because I never felt such rage, that I wanted to crush her..."

Diane went on to explain that she found it hard to sleep after hanging out with her friends, and this continued on.

"There was this... uh dark presence in my room Melody, and I felt so confused and I could not focus on day to day tasks. The fear was paralysing, and I dreaded the night, having to close my eyes... feeling like I was being watched, along with bad thoughts racing around in my head! My mind was troubled, and I was seeing like these images all around the room, spinning continuously. I felt very paranoid and vulnerable, as if I was going insane."

Over the next few sessions, It was apparent that there was a spiritual battle going on. During session four we discussed Diane's beliefs and her upbringing, she was presenting with some facial contortions that were unusual. She kept twitching and closing her eyes, and I could see the resistance building. I had an uneasy feeling about it, as she was another person, a dark presence that filled the room.

In fact Diane made a comment, very softly spoken, "I think there is someone else inside me, and I am scared." It was a scary thought, and something that I was not sure what to do about. She whispered something to me, but I could not quite understand. It sounded like she was asking for help. When I asked her what she had said, she snapped back in a loud raucous tone whilst pushing over the chair, "I don't need your help!" I jumped with disbelief, at what I was hearing. I could feel my anxiety rise, and I tried to calm myself. Diane took a breath, looked down for a split moment and then looked up at me, her eyes blazing. Her demeanour had changed and I could see the intense anger bubbling just below the surface. She began to laugh with a chilling tone, as if trying to intimidate me into retreating with fear. In a deep voice, she snapped back at me, through gritted teeth, "Leave us alone!!! Leave us alone! We don't want your help! She belongs to us!"

It was shocking to come face to face with this evil manifestation. I was trying to process what I was hearing, puzzled by who was the 'us' and 'we.' I did not want to communicate with this thing. It was only going to tell me lies, and manipulate me. I could see the taunting smile on Diane's face, trying hard to lure me into an argument. I reminded myself that behind this 'thing' was a person, made in the image of God. I sat there for at least fifteen minutes, praying in my head, asking Jesus for His help.

Diane sat there staring as if she was miles away. I could see her taking in some big breaths, trying to compose herself. We had another twenty minutes to the end of the session so I asked Diane if she was okay. She wanted to proceed with the discussion, as if nothing unusual happened.

As we were discussing spiritual beliefs, she had told me during an earlier session that her father was a christian. Her mother had walked out on him. Diane had visited his church a few times, and her father gave her a Bible. Was it the right time to talk to her about spiritual beliefs?

With my own fear and uncertainty of what to do next, I asked Diane if she knew Jesus. She looked at me, her eyes opened wide, her jaw dropped as if I had said something so alarming. She began to shiver as I handed her a video on the Life of Jesus. This was a creepy moment and I was trying to talk my way through this, reassuring myself that I was on the right track. I prayed quietly asking Jesus to intervene.

She took the video and put it in her bag, gave me a sarcastic look, then said, "Do you expect me to watch this?"

I looked at her and said, "Diane, Jesus is the only way, the truth and the life, and no one can come to the Father except through Him… He can deliver you from this evil that you have invited into your life… do you believe that?"

Diane looked at me and whispered, "Yes," and I could see the torment and fear in her eyes. That was good enough for me, and she walked out of the room, and immediately the heaviness dissipated.

Inside the cover of the video I inserted a phone number of a local church and pastors' contact details, hoping that she would then contact him. During the session, I asked Diane permission to call him, and to let him know that she may contact him. I was only going to tell him that she needed prayer as she had been involved in the New Age Movement and the Occult. She nodded and gave me her consent. It was a delicate situation of confidentiality but I believed that common sense had prevailed, and Diane was in desperate need of spiritual intervention.

The next day I called the Pastor and gave some brief details of Diane, careful that I was not breaching any confidentiality. I just told him that a young lady may call him and ask for prayer. She has been involved in the New Age Movement and the Occult.

We discussed the rise in the interest in Eastern religions from Hinduism to Buddhism and spiritism all associated with Pantheism, worship of many gods, and all living matter has God in it, including the Universe. It is the worship of creation rather than the creator. This is idolatry, which the Bible talks about as being an abomination, totally despicable to God. As with the children of Israel that fashioned and worshipped the 'golden calf' while Moses was with God receiving the ten commandments. Moses was angered by this, knowing that his Holy God would have to act. During our discussion, It became so clear to me that these statues, idols and ornaments did not have any power, but it allowed Satan access to manifest his power to deceive those that availed themselves of it. None of us really know what sort of power Satan has.

The practice of Yoga was popular even amongst Christians not realising that taking on this form of exercise is not compatible with the Christian faith. I was in agreement about the dangers, that even with Yoga it was a form of worship of the snake god, the Kundalini spirit which is representative of Satan. The Pastor went on to tell me that he was seeing many people who were experiencing severe anxiety and fear, as a result of dabbling in this also.

It was almost two weeks, and I had not had any contact with Diane. I had been praying for her during this time.

I was driving to work and thinking about my day, praying that I would be obedient to the will of God, that He would lead me, as I surrender this day to Him. This was my usual prayer, as I knew that through His power and will, I could do great things for God. I was really beginning to trust and depend on Him.

I had four clients lined up for the day, a full schedule with a small break in between. When I arrived at work, I could see that there had been a change, with Diane inserted as my first client. She must have called late in the afternoon to make an appointment after my first client postponed. This happened from time to time, and I always made a point of arriving early so that I had some time to prepare for any changes.

The aroma of the freshly brewed coffee smelled wonderful, and I sat down on the couch and slowly sipped it, whilst looking over my notes. It had been a number of weeks since I last saw Diane, and did not know what I was going to see. Was she going to be annoyed, curt or passive? I reminded myself that God was in control of this situation and I was just His instrument.

I went out to meet Diane, and she was sitting in the chair looking at a christian magazine that was on the coffee table. Diane looked up at me and smiled, and she seemed very cheerful, unlike how she was last time we met, neatly dressed and presentable. I smiled back at her and asked her how she was as we made our way to the room.

She seemed like she was bursting with news to tell me, and I just listened. She looked at me beaming, "Melody, I am not sure where to start… um… so I will try and tell you all the things that have happened to me since the last session."

I looked at her smiling still, and said, "I am all ears, Diane. Please take your time."

She proceeded to tell me, "Melody, when you handed the Jesus video, I felt this struggle within me, and then this overwhelming terror, which made me shake uncontrollably. I was trying to stop myself from shaking but I could not get a handle of it. Something inside me was terrified of Jesus. I then made myself watch it at home, and I remember screaming at the top of my lungs, saying NO... STOP! My neighbour came by and asked if I was okay, and then saw the Jesus video and laughed as they thought it was some horror or suspense movie. However, the neighbour took one look at me and was a little scared, thinking that I was possessed. In fact I think I was, as this thing was inside me and I could feel myself fighting it, but it kept fighting, giving me negative thoughts of self harm. I even started cutting myself, and I could hear the voice telling me to kill myself. I was scared, but I called out to Jesus." Diane then took a sip of the water I gave her. I asked her if she was okay to go on.

She was getting emotional, her voice a little shaky, "Melody, I was so scared that I would kill myself, so I called the number on the note that you slipped into the video. The Pastor was local and he agreed to see me, along with one of his deacons. I asked him to pray, and told him about my encounter with New Age as you mentioned to me. As he was praying out loud, this thing in me was fighting, stirring and all of a sudden I could hear myself swearing at him. The pastor told me to be quiet and it just stopped. I remember feeling my body writhing and I was hissing, making strange noises and I could not control it. It was like an out of body experience, and I could feel myself in the background, calling out. There was this foul smell in the air, and I don't know where it came from. I was so scared because this has never happened to me before," as her face engulfed in tears as if a tidal wave washed over her.

I went over to Diane and held her hand whilst she sobbed uncontrollably, her pain and torment flowing out of her. I waited till she gathered herself then she continued stating, "The Pastor asked me if I wanted to repent of my sins, and denounce my New Ageism and the Occult. He explained how the occult affects us and how God hates this pagan practices as it undermines Him. Part of me did not want this, and I heard myself yelling out... NO! NO! NO! Melody, there was like this evil spirit in me that did not want this to happen, and tried to resist. Somehow by the grace of God, I was able to overcome this by His will. I felt something inside of me fighting to stay. It was a wicked, foreign entity that was trying to taunt and destroy me. The messages in my head were telling me that there was no hope. It was telling me to run away... from the Pastor. It was making me sick and unable to hear what the Pastor was saying. I remember telling it to leave me alone! It took some time and I felt it depart. I was set free. I asked Jesus into my heart and accepted Him as my Lord and Saviour!"

All I could say was, "Wow! That is incredible... The Power of Jesus! Praise God!" I was still processing this information, realising that yes Jesus had such power over evil spirits, that I recalled in the Bible they shuddered with fear when they were confronted by Him. I shared the story in the Bible about the insane demoniac in the caves at the Gerasenes in Mark 5, of how hopeless his situation was, bound in chains and shackles to try to subdue him, as he was a danger to the public and himself. Yet, Jesus was able to set him free, so that he returned to his right mind. The demons shuddered in fear at the sight of Jesus. Diane had experienced something amazing, indicating God's transforming power over the sin of divination and the occult. It is really an abomination to the Lord! I quoted Deuteronomy 18: 10 -12a *'There shall not be found among you anyone who makes his son or his daughter pass through the fire, or one who practices witchcraft, or a soothsayer, or one who interprets omens, or a sorcerer, or one who conjures spells, or a medium or a spiritist or one who calls up the dead. For all who do these things are an abomination to the Lord.'* Diane understood the seriousness of this sin.

I was truly grateful to hear how the Lord had worked in Diane's life, as I battled my own doubts in the supernatural power. I wanted to pretend that this was not real, as it disrupted my nice, safe christian world, but how can I ignore this? Is ignorance an excuse? Whether I choose to believe that there is a supernatural world with angels and demons or not, the reality is that the Bible is clear about this spiritual warfare which gives purpose to the redemptive power of Jesus' death and resurrection. Jesus conquers sin, death, Satan and his evil angels. How can I stand and watch people suffer from this torment without sharing the Truth? I just wanted to bask in the sun and shut out the unseen but I had a responsibility to get out of the safe world of denial, and find out what God wants me to do with this.

What I had discovered was that the simple gospel message wrapped in Godly love can free someone from demonic possession. The fact is whether we choose to believe it or not, the spirit world exists around us with the principalities of darkness there to kill and destroy us. As I read Ephesians 6 out loud to Diane I explained why Satan is trying to undermine the power of God, by trickery, deception and the things of this world. He uses the occult and witchcraft to entice people to tap into their sinful nature with pride, the need to control others and have power over them. He encourages narcissism and primal carnal behaviours associated with lust. He is set on leading his prey to despair, as there is no love in him, only HATRED! There is so much power in love, a love that flows from God, and dispensed by His fellow servants. Satan wants to be worshipped as God, and if people could see the true reality of his being, they would run from him in terror. So he uses deception, appearing as an angel of light to lure his prey into his web of despair and final damnation!

It was evident that Diane opened the door to allow Satan in by getting involved with New Age and the Occult, which then gave him access to mess with her. She gave him permission to allow his demons to create havoc in her life. I further explained to her that the demons cannot override our will, but because we can be weak through sin, we really need the power of Jesus to set us free.

When a sinner repents or renounces their sin, it weakens the demon's right to oppress or possess the individual. Better still, turning your life over to Jesus as your Lord and Saviour will free you from the clutches of Satan. You are now a child of God.

I looked over to Diane and said, "You need to get rid of every new age item from your home, to cleanse your domain, as you now have the Holy Spirit dwelling in you. It is crucial, Diane… that you do not give place for the evil one to oppress you as he will bring many more minions with him. Please stay close to Jesus, and do not let unconfessed sin reign in your heart. Jesus encouraged believers to remain in His Word, and to stay pure." I could see that Diane was in agreement, taking in every word.

Diane looked up at me, and said that this all made a lot of sense to her. She understood the disgusting nature of evil, and described the internal battle so well, but it showed that with the little will she had, it did not have the power to overtake her completely. Obviously she needed Jesus to deliver her completely, and this meant a daily battle with temptation, especially in times of weakness. God has given her the tools to stand firm, and He will fight this battle for her.

There are cases where God gives the unrepentant person over to the evil one completely and they are doomed. There were also cases in the Bible, where evil spirits are more difficult to expel, and may require fasting and fervent prayer. It was becoming clearer to me, and I was hoping that the intense fear I had for the spirit world would slowly diminish. Secretly I was hoping that I did not have to go through this again, but little did I know that this was not the case.

The session went fifteen minutes over time, and Diane apologised for the delay. My next appointment was in thirty minutes so I had enough time to make my notes. I took the time to give her some direction to continue with her faith through joining a Bible group, a church and a course on christianity. She was very eager to follow through and I finished praying for her. I prayed that the Lord would protect the seed of faith, that He would send people to help her to grow and become fruitful in serving Jesus and sharing the good news of the Gospel. I was so encouraged after this session that I could have physically jumped up and down with joy.

I recall speaking to the Pastor a few weeks after the last session, and Diane had been regularly going to church, and had joined a fellowship Bible group. She was very enthusiastic about her faith and had some great friends discipling her. It was great to hear this, and I thanked the Pastor for the feedback.

I was beginning to see how physical and emotional parts of our humanity interact with our spiritual side. We were all created in God's image, with a deep desire for our Heavenly Father.

I was still trying to understand why some were spiritually dead and just did not understand the things of God. I guess it may be a question that I may never be able to answer this side of eternity.

Chapter 16

Face to Face with Evil

It was a windy stormy day as I pulled into the car park. It was good to have undercover parking to avoid the wind storm. My throat was a little sore, and I thought it was due to the shouting I had done whilst Will was playing baseball on the weekend. I was one of those competitive Mums that could not help but to scream out to their child as they hit the ball. He hit a home run, and it was a big deal, as Will was still learning how to play.

Sitting at the reception desk, I was going through the calendar checking on my clients for the day. I had two cancellations, and I felt the pang of disappointment as they were my clients suffering from addiction. It was so hard to help some of these people because they were enslaved and controlled by their addiction, unable to find the will to get the right help. I was frustrated and annoyed, as they also did not pay their bills. This affected the business and my own budget, and the times I had to repent of my unbelief and remind myself that God was my provider. After earning a regular salary previously, I was going backwards. Blake and I were saving to buy a home and I was not sure how God would provide for us.

At times I had looked at my weekly salary and thought how could I make this work. It was a stretch for us, trying to save for a house when the average home was becoming out of reach for us. Thankfully we had some savings, but we still needed to save enough for a deposit. I found myself frustrated as I wanted to build a safe future for my family, with plans to have children. It was a time of nesting which meant creating a home that was stable and safe. The rental market at the time was unpredictable as many investors were cashing in on the property boom, in which we were uncertain how long we had before we were asked to move. The fact that Blake was happy to rent made me more frustrated as I wanted to settle down.

I found myself at times arguing with God about our future, hoping that He would give me some certainty. I was wrestling with my flesh, wanting this material possession to feel safe. I found myself often repenting of my covetousness and envy of others who were quite settled with their own green patch and picket fence. It had never dawned on me to have this as a priority in the past, but now I was becoming more and more obsessed in striving for my own home.

The Lord was teaching me to trust Him, my provider and it was a difficult lesson. I had given up quite a lot, my son, my previous house, my career, possessions and all that I had worked hard for, and now I had this wonderful vocation, but it cost me alot. I tried very hard to conceal my anguish from Blake, who simply did not worry about anything. He would say that God would provide. This was a painful journey, as I recount the cost to follow Jesus, but I knew in my heart that one day, I would see the value of this journey. I had to keep reminding myself that I was storing treasures in heaven as in the parable that Jesus taught. However, It took quite some time to learn these nuggets of truth from the Bible. I fell often, bruised my knees of unbelief, then repented, got back up again and then doubt would set in. The process would start again, and it made me angry that I succumbed to this struggle. Why could I not just trust the Lord and believe that He was able to provide for us? As I recounted the same argument in my head I put my head into my hands and asked God to forgive me.

Then as I looked up Jessica walked in and I realised she was early for her appointment with Jane, and I was alone with her. I felt so uneasy with her, as she would stare at me as if she was looking into my soul. She always looked like she was miles away. Jane asked me to pray for her at times, as she was involved in some Satanic cult. All our counsellors and intercessors prayed for those that were under spiritual oppression. My spirit clashed with hers, and I sensed the darkness behind those steely eyes.

I was also asked to step in as a counsellor for Jessica when Jane is on leave. That time was coming very soon, and Jessica herself asked to see me. I don't know why, but I was a little nervous about counselling someone with such complex issues. Jessica had a bottle of water with her so I asked her if she wanted tea or coffee, since Jane was fifteen minutes away.

The reception desk was quite high, so I could barely see Jessica as I glanced over a few times. Before long she stood at the desk looking at me, and asked me about my day ahead. She was very talkative and confident, as we discussed her shopping plans, and catching up with an old friend. Jessica seemed to have a personality disorder where she would split off into another person. Jane told me that it helped her deal with the trauma she had growing up with parents that were neglectful and often at times quite abusive.

I found Jessica or Jess as she liked to be called, somewhat unpredictable in nature, and this made it difficult to gauge as a counsellor. Jane filled me in briefly on her traumatic childhood, as the time was approaching for me to step in as her counsellor. I was not surprised that her past had been quite horrific with involvement in cults, given her demeanour. She was very hard to read, and rarely made eye contact.

My clients came in, a couple with some issues with their teenage daughter who had started on prescription drugs. These were always difficult cases and I felt for the parents. The addiction cycle was sometimes a long road with struggles, setbacks and at times victory. I had to keep reminding myself of the victories.

I was looking forward to the weekend, as Blake and I were heading to the mountains for two nights and returning on Sunday afternoon. It was a couple of hours away, and it was nice to get away for part of the weekend. Since my last client cancelled their appointment, I was going to leave work at around three o'clock, and I remembered to stop at Woolworths to get a few things we needed.

The mountains were incredible, and we enjoyed the hiking trails, and stopping off for some hot chocolate on our way back to the cabin. The little home we stayed in had a log fire and it was great to sit back and enjoy the ambience and chat about the day.

After a wonderful time away, It was Sunday morning, and time to head back home to get ready for the working week. We were going to the church for the night service and Blake and I were rostered on to talk to any visitors or new christians.

As we took our seats at church, the praise and worship band were starting up, when I looked behind, and realised that Jessica from counselling was sitting right behind me. She had a male friend with her, and we locked eyes and I smiled. She looked nervous so I was wondering which personality was going to show up today. I had briefly told Blake about her without revealing any names or specific details, but only the fact that she was creepy. It was more than the mental health condition that she was diagnosed with, and I had said this to Jane before. I was able to discern spirits whilst still learning how to exercise it with Godly wisdom. It was something that I had for some time, but I was still growing spiritually and had to learn to trust and obey the Lord.

Jessica looked at me again, and introduced me to her friend Kevin, a good looking man with dark hair, well attired but seemed to be very uncomfortable as he put his hand out to shake mine. I did not feel comfortable shaking his hand so I just waved. I then introduced them to Blake, but did not elaborate on where we knew each other. We turned our heads back to the front and now the band was playing.

While the music was playing I could hear Kevin grunting then murmuring something. I was trying to catch what he was saying, then realised that this was distracting me and I was there to focus on praising God. However, this whispering was going on for some time and I could not keep from being distracted. I turned around and looked at him, and he snarled at me. It was creepy, and I felt a shiver down my spine. There was something sinister about him, and he was not here to hear the gospel message, I was certain.

After the service, Blake and I were welcoming new christians and visitors to the foyer area of the church. I walked over to Kevin and asked him how he found church. He told me that it was not his thing, but was curious to see what happens. He was forthcoming with some feedback telling me that it was like a concert, a show, with people concerned about performance. He said that the message was insipid and syrupy, and at first he was uncomfortable but realised that the leaders were weak.

I must have looked shocked, but he said in a low tone, "Surely you are not surprised by this, I think you know what I mean?" I was probably more surprised about his candid way he came across. I then asked him about his experience of church and that was when I was really shocked at his response. In fact Kevin was a satanist and had been going to black masses for some time. He was very bold and it seemed he was clearly on a mission. I wanted to get away from him, but I thought about the passage, 1 John 4:4, *"You are of God, little children, and have overcome them, because He who is in you is greater than he who is in the world."*

I closed my eyes and reflected on how powerful Jesus was, and then boldly asked Kevin what he was doing with murmuring and whispering in church. He could have told me it was none of my business, as it was an imposing question, but instead he told me that he was performing a ritual, praying against the pastors and worship team that their message would be weak and ineffective. I looked at him, with anger in my eyes, and what I believed was righteous anger, and I could see the mocking wry smile that was forming. He was trying to get under my skin, and was succeeding. As I turned to see where Blake was, he suddenly turned up alongside me, and I was grateful. Blake could see that Kevin was sinister, and he looked at him and told him to leave the church at once.

Kevin laughed mockingly and told us, "This church is weak anyway, and I don't have to do much, in fact the fruits of evil are already at work. Why are you here? You don't belong here!" I was relieved that Blake took such a stance, and as Kevin was leaving I prayed that he would not come back.

I felt disgust as I made eye contact with evil. It made me feel angry, that there are people like that who are deceived by Satan, thinking that they are more powerful than God. How deluded can one get? Blake was also so bold in exercising his authority in Christ when he asked Kevin to leave, as he was trying to make a scene, and draw attention to himself. I had learned that day that Satan sent his minions to church to cause disruption and make the message ineffective.

I was pondering the thought of how a satanist would feel comfortable about entering a church in the first place. It was also unnerving that he stated that the fruits of evil were already at work, and that we did not belong there. These statements were partly true as deep down, both Blake and I were struggling with some of the teaching and practices. How did Kevin know this about us? I remembered reading about some of the satanic powers, where they were able to discern some things, through the demonic power of divination. Demons are intelligent beings, but these powers are limited, and subject to the sovereign God, all powerful, all knowing. God was showing us His will through his Word, preparing us as watchmen, standing up for the Truth. We prayed for discernment and Godly wisdom everyday.

I could see Blake growing in discernment and boldness over the last six months. He loved the Truth and would get all fired up with all the false teaching we had come across through various books and visiting preachers. He would bring up these false doctrines and help me to understand their manipulative ways. We would check the teaching with the Word of God like the Bereans who were commended for their diligence. However, we also found that a lot of the people around us were just accepting everything that was dished out, and we appeared to be divisive in stating our case for sound doctrine. It was strange but we were never encouraged to check the scriptures for the context, but were hearing messages with texts all over the Bible to fit the overall message. Sometimes these texts were saying something else, and this was becoming apparent to us. Thankfully we were also aware that we needed to draw near to Him, rather than focusing on the false teaching, as this was also a method of distraction.

The Lord was really showing us that belonging to His Kingdom would also bring division, and loneliness, as many wanted to hear messages that were motivating and worldly so that they did not have to make any changes to their life. We were learning that the fear of the Lord was the beginning of wisdom. The fear of man was a real issue, and part of our fallen nature. It was more important to please the Lord than to compromise to please others. Thankfully, we found a few like minded Christians that brought encouragement and refreshment to us during this time.

Over a few days, Jane and I had some sessions discussing Jessica's history as I was going to step in for her for the next two months while she was away. I took some notes, as there was a lot to take in. I had not come across such a complex case and was really appreciative of Jane explaining the details of her therapy plan.

We had clients that had been abused in various religious cults including satanism, as small infants until adulthood. The abuse involved putting them through some rituals from a baby, which were sadistic and cruel. The sexual acts became more violent as the children reached school age. These acts were done in a dark cave in various places in New South Wales, whilst they chanted and sang to the angel of darkness.

As Jane gave me a synopsis of the abuse, I could not help but flinch at the torture, and it made my blood boil at how disgusting and cowardly this practice was to inflict such pain on the innocence of a child. Evil was not cool or powerful, as portrayed in movies and television shows. It was disgusting, vile and the lowest form of behaviour.

It appears that Jessica developed a personality disorder to cope with the pain and trauma as a child, being exposed to cultic practices. This coping mechanism allowed her to split off into different personalities to avoid painful memories and flashbacks, which would then bring on traumas.

Jane had been working very hard to understand Jess's coping mechanisms, and help her to work through those memories and flashbacks. Jessica had family but had moved out of home at the age of sixteen. She did not feel safe at home as her mother belonged to a wicca coven, practicing witchcraft, and her father was an alcoholic. She had no siblings that she spoke of. Her only friends were new agers and ex-satanic cult members, some of which were still involved in her life.

This was a difficult and complex case in itself. I had to let Blake know a little as this person was coming to church, and there were some safety issues. I was very careful with what information I shared, although Jessica was open about her involvement in the cult when she spoke to us at church. It was an uncomfortable situation, as she was now my client for a short time. It was comforting to have Blake there to pray through this situation with me.

I had so many questions about Jessica's life and upbringing, but I needed to focus on what she wanted to talk about, develop trust and help her with the day to day management of her life. For now I chose to write these questions down, as they were missing pieces of a big jigsaw puzzle. These questions came to me in my time of prayer and I learned to lean on the Lord for his input.

It was a cool day, the tail end of winter and I was sitting on the couch waiting for my first appointment. Having arrived early, I had some time to get my notes and files in order. The door opened and there was Jessica, always a tad early which was great as she was committed to the counselling process from what Jane had told me, given she had been in therapy for two years.

Thankfully there were other counsellors and people in the centre, as I still did not feel comfortable being alone with Jessica.

She tipped toed into the room like a cat burglar and introduced herself as Cass, one of her personalities. I thought it was best to relax and allow her to feel comfortable about the process. It took some of the pressure off, as I was feeling quite nervous.

This personality was super confident, playful and loved to goof around, easier to talk to than the serious Jess who was anxious and suspicious. She almost looked and acted like another person altogether. I could see her eyes darting around the room, and she got up a few times and stretched, even jumped up and down a few times. Jessica was a lot more intense and would sit hunched up on the lounge.

While I was talking to Jess (Cass) about her day ahead, and how she planned to go for a walk around the National Park with her dog, her demeanour and facial expressions started to change. My heart skipped a beat, as I saw this transformation before me, as Jessica appeared, closing her eyes as she straightened her hair. She looked down then gazed up at me, with a different voice she told me that it was Jessica and that Cassie had to go for that walk as she could not sit still. Even her voice and intonation changed from upbeat and higher pitched to low hesitant tone.

It was difficult not to be consumed or fascinated by these personality changes as they were distinct and it drew you in. I also felt that they were manipulative and playing with my mind, that did not sit right with me. I was asking the Lord for His help with this, that I would lean on His understanding.

As we were talking about Jessica's week, the difficulty, and the fear she was feeling, I asked the question about what the fear looked like for her. She began telling me about how she was watched by the dark one, and how he was speaking to her at night. She could hear him laughing and he was giving instructions to follow. I listened and let her speak. Jessica could not explain what the fear looked like, only the events around it. I thought maybe she was not comfortable with divulging this information.

I thought I would challenge her gently by bringing to her attention that she was not able to describe what this fear was. She then proceeded to tell me that she was not afraid of him speaking to her. They were on good terms. So it meant that she was still in contact with the evil one. Jane had told me that Jessica was a christian, and still working on her commitment. From what she was telling me, It was contrary to christianity. I then challenged her on how christianity fits in with her friendship with the evil one. Immediately her face started to contort, her eyes rolled back and I could see only the whites. I thought she was switching to another personality, and then she made eye contact, her pupils dilated. She sniggered, with hatred in her eyes then laughed at me with a sinister tone. I could sense the anger behind her steely eyes, the fact I had caught her out.

During this time there was a cold presence with the hairs on my arms standing up, and I could feel my body shivering. I recited the passage in John - greater is He that is in me than He that is in the world over and over again so that the fear would not step in. This was super creepy and seeing the display of evil was making me sick inside.

I could not hide the disgust on my face, yet at the same time there was an internal battle in me trying to find love and compassion for this young lost girl. She looked up at me, and started to stand up with her arms on her hip, "You don't like me, do you?" I asked her to sit down and continue with the conversation, not wanting to get into an argument. We sat in silence for at least ten minutes which felt like a really long time, and I asked her if she was okay to continue again. I was feeling like she was manipulating me, and I was trying not to respond in the way she was hoping that I would.

Jess was still in contact with her so-called friends, who were involved in witchcraft and the occult. The witchcraft was about controlling and manipulating people to achieve whatever outcome they were after, the end result was power with evil intent.

There was so much ambivalence to her story, and she sounded that she had not yet left them. I looked at her face, and there was some annoyance as she realised that she could not deceive me. She started to shift again, curling her feet up, then she began to explain how she was often wooed back into the cult, when she felt lonely, as she had many friends. I asked her if she practised any of the rituals and she said that she stayed away from that. However, in my understanding there was no way Satan was going to allow her to leave without a fight. The only way was Jesus rescuing her from the pit she was in.

After Jessica left, I wrote my notes in the file that Jane gave me, with some big questions around her beliefs. I had an uneasy feeling when Jessica was in the room, and there was still a dark spirit present. I could also tell that she was uneasy around me too, so I prayed that the Lord would help me to connect with her. I asked God to break the strongholds that enslaved her.

The next month or so, it was becoming more clear that Jessica had not left the cult. They were still in control of her, and she talked about the 'one' being the dark spirit that was still hovering around her as a friend not a foe. Every time I questioned her about this, she would try to distract me and avoid the question. Then if I probed further, she would become agitated, and her body would quiver, her face contorting as if she was transforming into a beast. It was so scary to watch and at times I had to look away, as my imagination went into overdrive. I had seen parts of the exorcist as a teenager and the reality of it haunted me for decades. I sensed that she was controlled by demonic forces, but I was not sure how Jane would respond to this. I made some personal notes of what I believed that the Lord was showing me, and I continued to pray about it.

Jane finally came back from leave and I was relieved to hand Jessica back. I was not sure if I made any difference, but I gave it a go. Jessica came in and began speaking to me as we were friends, and Jane looked quite surprised. I was also surprised by this behaviour as she was suspicious of me and there was not a lot of trust there. In fact I thought she didn't like me, especially after the scene with Kevin, her cult friend where we asked him to leave our church and to stop with threats and taunting. Here she was again manipulating and controlling the narrative. I was hoping that I could bring this up with Jane, as it was certainly contrary to what she was seeing in Jessica.

Chapter 17

Mental Illness or Evil Possession

Tina, a good friend of mine, dropped by at the counselling centre and we went out to get a coffee. It was a nice stroll through the park and along a side street to the coffee shop. She was such a sweet and caring person, and we could talk for hours. Our discussion was mostly centred on our personal, spiritual growth and our family. I liked the fact that Tina did not like gossiping or talking about anyone at church or people we knew. She had a tough life growing up in South Africa, and yet the Lord was so gracious and merciful to her. Tina had become one of my good friends that was part of my support network. We encouraged each other in the Word and also regularly caught up for prayer. After the coffee and our discussion, we walked back to the centre. Tina had a few errands and left to go to the shopping centre. I had ten minutes until my next new clients, so I spent the time praying and reading a devotional I carried around with me.

Over the next three days, I had two more clients that were presenting with issues around the occult. There were both young guys who through curiosity and peer pressure dipped their toe into the murky waters of deception.

Colin, who saw a tarot reader to find out about his future love life, was accused of sexual assault of a young lady who happened to be the sister of one of his close friends. What is puzzling is that he blacked out and did not remember the event, so he told me. His friends knew him well, and it was totally out of character, as Colin was very shy and awkward around girls. He was a health fanatic, and did not do drugs or excessive drinking, ruling out the effects of substance abuse. His friends had seen a strange transformation of Colin's behaviour to becoming aggressive and violent.

The three friends called me shortly after the session on a group chat to make an appointment. I could hear the hesitation and fear in their voices as they retold the terrifying experience of seeing Colin become another person. "We think Colin was demon possessed. Our parents think he had a psychotic episode but the tests by the neurologist and assessments came back negative. The 'mental illness tag' does not make any sense. We know Colin so well, and it felt like we were looking into the eyes of some…uh evil entity that had taken over Colin's mind. We want to understand how this can happen, so when can we see you?"

What had they seen, I wondered? How was I going to explain this to them? Was there any confidentiality breach in discussing another patient? I would have to get some advice beforehand.

The other new client, Todd, had presented with extreme anxiety brought on by fear. He and his friends formed a Harry Potter book club that progressed to participating in 'Wicker', a form of witchcraft that seeks to control and manipulate to gain power over the individual. They also dabbled into voodoo, making a figure that represented Todd where they practiced rituals of self harm. His friends were playing mind games, causing confusion and paranoia which escalated to violence and stalking. Todd had been the victim with unusual visible physical injuries, as well as psychological trauma.

As it turned out, I had to go to the local court on both occasions to support these two clients. In Colin's case I attended to confirm to the magistrate that he had been receiving counselling, because of the serious allegations. As for Todd, he had brought an assault and stalking charge against the group.

I wondered how can a book club go so wrong? It was rather funny seeing the look on the magistrates face as he peered over at the bunch of guys dressed as warlocks, with a few witches in tow, all with dark heavy makeup. He stated in a tone indicating his disgust, "Is this some freak show or movie? You need to stop with the harassment and go see a psychologist so you can distinguish the difference between fantasy and reality!" I think he was waiting for the director to jump out and say, "cut, next scene" or "you are pranked." Sadly this was reality and I wondered how far can this deception go?

Sitting on the bench at the local park, I pondered over what God was teaching me. It is obvious now that the issues presented to me were not just a coincidence. It was so unbelievable and at times the mental illness tag was a more acceptable option. Yet I knew deep down that there was something more to this, something quite sinister. I thought about my own experiences as a child and it was all becoming clearer. There are consequences for messing with sorcery (magic), the occult and witchcraft, as it invites Satan and his minions to deceive you, leading you on a destructive and oppressive path. It robbed me of my peace, and brought on intense fear, anxiety and confusion. The oppression was so intense and heavy that it sucked the life out of you. Now I can take what I have learned and warn others of this. I wanted to shine the torch on Satan's strategies, exposing his lies and deception.

As a result of this, both Colin and Todd renounced the occult, repented and became followers of Christ, Whatever possessed Colin no longer had the power over him, as the Holy Spirit was now the occupant of his spirit. Even Colin's friends were going to church with him, and on the path to finding Jesus. I was so thankful that the Lord allowed me to help them find answers to the complex questions, and in turn taught me some important lessons too.

Chapter 18

Fear and Protection

I t was a bright sunny morning and I was looking forward to the day. Thankfully there was little traffic on the road and I was there in seven minutes. I had time to make a coffee, and prepare for my new client. I looked at the appointment book and recognised the name from church. It was a single Mum, with a five year old boy, and the father had abandoned her and the child. Her name was Natasha, and she was regularly attending church and Bible study. I had heard one of the counsellors recommend her coming to see me.

I looked up and the receptionist was at the door letting me know that Natasha had arrived. I went out to meet her. She was an attractive brunette, with long hair and big brown eyes. She was around 165 cm tall and seemed to be quite fit, almost athletic in her appearance. She smiled at me, recognising me from church.

We went through the introductions and the diagnostic questions in the intake form, getting a snapshot of her family history and background. Natasha presented with depression, anxiety and fears of abandonment, stemming from childhood. She told me that she was a Christian, and getting baptised in the next few weeks. She gave me permission to explore various aspects of her beliefs and values.

Natasha grew up with one sibling, a younger brother and her mother. Her father left the family home when Natasha was only four years old. As she told me her background and the difficulties they faced with financial struggles, I was puzzled by her facial expressions. She was smiling and rolling her eyes which seemed very disconnected from the emotional turmoil that she was describing.

It was a sad story, and I was empathic of the time she missed out on being a child, feeling safe and trusting that her parents would look after her. I was also wondering what life was like for her in the first five years. The first five years of a child's life were the building blocks for a solid foundation built on trust and safety. She quickly advised that both her parents were quite distanced, and rarely showed her any affection. She felt like she was a big mistake and that her mother becoming pregnant was an inconvenience. Her father had very little love for his wife, and would often go away for months at a time with his mates.

Did Natasha repeat the same lifestyle as her parents, by getting pregnant as a teen, out of wedlock? Her boyfriend abandoned her while she was eight months pregnant, and she had to move back in with her mother. She contemplated having an abortion, but her mother would not allow it. There was so much sadness and pain to walk through.

The smile and cocky expression, would soon turn into grimace, a twitch then back to the smile. As she spoke I could see the light bulb go on as she realised that she had repeated the same cycle as her parents. I knew it would take time and lots of trust for her to open up and freely express herself, and allow the pain to surface.

By the time we reached session four, I had discovered that Natasha was using alcohol as well as her prescription medication to get through the bouts of depression and anxiety. It was a dangerous slippery slope, but she had a few friends from church and her Bible study group that checked in on her from time to time.

We discussed other ways of dealing with the pain, including counselling and prayer. She always seemed so upbeat at first, then slumped into a state of numbness during the session. As I glanced at her from time to time, I could see her fighting back some desire to run away, and feeling her sense of discomfort during the session. This was also quite normal with some, as they faced traumatic parts of their life, or even difficult self examination of their fears and character flaws. There was always going to be this tension with reality and living a deceived life. It was my job to gently show her the true reality, the issues and help her to work through it. It was always going to be her willingness to do the work, and allow the Lord to cleanse and sanctify her.

Jane interrupted my counselling session, and asked me to pray as Jessica was showing signs of violence towards her. I walked in and saw Jessica hunched up in the corner on the floor, her dark black hair over her face, and I could see her bluish grey eyes piercing through her strands of hair. She was panting, and grunting like an animal.

It was heartbreaking seeing Jessica so unstable and unpredictable, considering that Jane had been counselling her for two and half years. It was going to be a long road. I questioned her motive for counselling, and commitment during the time I was seeing her. Jessica was still involved with her cult friends and that was not healthy.

I had another client so then had to leave. After my client settled down, I walked past the room and heard Jessica banging her head on the wall, then she picked up a chair to hit Jane. I walked in immediately and told Jessica to stop, and put the chair down with a firm tone. Jessica glared at me with a blank expression, then put the chair down. Jane looked up and smiled at me, thanking me for intervening, and asked me to keep praying.

We had panic buttons installed in each room, so Jane knew that she could get help if she needed. There were two male practitioners in the centre at the time, who could reach out and assist if required. We all seemed to believe that Jessica was not capable of actually injuring us, but I had great doubts. She was in control of her own actions, and it was becoming more evident as time went on.

We were on our way to church at night, and I remembered there was a guest speaker from the United States. As we arrived I saw a large number of young people walking into the church, and they seemed to be visitors. It was encouraging to see so many young people come and hear the message. I heard that this speaker was an evangelist and spoke in churches on the East Coast of the US.

The message was simple but solid, as he presented the gospel with great stories of conversion. He talked about the problem with gangs in the outskirts of New York, and many of the members repenting and coming to a saving knowledge of Jesus. The churches were working together to reach out to these people with action of love and forgiveness. It is really the Lord that opens blind eyes and draws them to Himself. We are His instruments to help disciple the new believers so that they grow and become fruitful.

The speaker was half way through his sermon, when Ally, a women's pastor came over to me and tapped me on my shoulder. She asked to urgently speak to me in the foyer. I was not sure what she was going to tell me, so I whispered to Blake that I would be back soon and left.

I looked at her expression and she seemed very worried, and had her phone in her hand. She told me that she received a call from Natasha that she was going to end her life, as she was in despair with no way out. She asked Ally to come over and pray with her, and since I was her counsellor she asked me to go with her. I agreed and went to let Blake know, as Ally was going to drive me home afterwards.

I was not sure what to expect as Natasha was difficult to read. As we pulled up at her home, we saw that she had a few lights on upstairs but the light was dim downstairs in her townhouse. Natasha was living there with her son. She was often quite silent about her living arrangements. It seemed that her mother often stepped in and looked after her little boy.

The door was slightly open and we knocked, with Ally calling out to Natasha that it was us. Natasha asked us to come in and her voice sounded a little shaky. She was sitting at her computer screen, with her eyes glazed as she looked over at us. I could see that she had a large knife in her hands, and had cut herself a few times on her arms, close to her wrists. The droplets of blood were trickling down her hand and onto the floor below. Her face was etched with anguish and torment, and she did not look well at all. In fact it was chilling, and Ally and I looked at each other and took a step back. Natasha was uttering something with a deep guttural tone, her eyes piercing with contempt, and on her screens were pictures of Jesus. She was mocking Him, and I could feel a gentle urge to leave. Ally and I could smell something very foul, apart from the alcohol. It was the smell of rotten eggs, sulphur and decomposing matter. It made me gag, and I felt sick. This was another clue of a demonic presence. Ally looked scared and we started to pray, when Natasha screamed at the top of her lungs, "Go away, leave me alone… get out! I want to die… go… leave!" She was swearing at us with lots of vile language. Then she laughed, a mocking tone, as if she was joking.

Natasha had consumed a lot of alcohol and the smell of stale wine permeated the room, with the empty wine cask tossed on the floor. The place was in an absolute mess, with rubbish strewn all over. We called out to her little boy Toby and asked permission to drop him off at her mothers house. It was not safe for him to be there. I had been counselling Natasha for the last four months, and I did not see this side of her. How can a christian be taken over by this demonic spirit? It is not possible.

Ally suggested that we take Toby to his grandmother's house up the road. Natasha's Mum could decide what to do, whether she would call an ambulance or the police, and admit Natasha to the psychiatric hospital. Our main concern was to get Toby to a safe place, and allow the ambulance officers to assist Natasha. She was unstable, and we could not reason with her.

So the ambulance was called to check on Natasha's wellbeing, and perhaps they may admit her into the local psychiatric hospital. Ally and I spoke in the car and we both witnessed something that was gut wrenching, and intense. The chilling guttural tone was not a human voice. What we saw was the insidious nature of evil in its true form, and the hatred it had for us. We had to remind ourselves that behind this 'thing' there was a human being that needed Jesus. Moreover, the Lord was with us, so we were protected by the Holy Spirit. I asked Natasha to stop with the cursing and to put the knife down, while Ally prayed quietly. She held up the knife defiantly, paused then put it down. If we were any closer she could have lunged at us with the knife. I had to remind myself that God was in charge, as the 'what if' alarm bells went off in my head.

It was Tuesday morning, and Natasha's Mum called to speak to me, advising that her daughter was admitted to the psychiatric hospital, and wanted to see me. I was not sure about going to visit, as I had a few patients to see. I decided to pray about it, as it was very confronting being exposed to this type of evil again and again. I was beginning to get a little weary, feeling the heaviness of the oppression. What these clients were experiencing was the torment of feeling trapped in a hell-like state, encapsulating fear, dread and hopelessness, yet eternal damnation is much more intense and endless. It is the opposite of following Jesus where there is freedom, peace and comfort that is everlasting. There was a clear solution. The Lord was teaching me something about His power and authority.

At times I also found myself wanting to run to a place called denial, believing that this was some psychiatric mental health condition that was treatable. Perhaps there was a pill or a ten step program fix. I was searching for some clear answers as I reflected on my own seasons of spiritual battles and confusion. There were so many moments in my childhood that were just not explainable from a secular mindset, but dismissed as 'having a wild imagination'. Clearly I wanted an explanation, given that I was a person of logic and reason.

Whilst I sought counsel on this topic with a number of ministers, pastors and elders, I found only a very few had experienced demonic activity. Perhaps they had not recognised it as such and put it down to mental illness, without investigating the person's life. Is the media responsible for branding evil and insane behaviour as a mental illness? Have we ceased from believing in the supernatural? The Bible is full of the supernatural, and it is clear that if a person is constantly gratifying their fleshly desires, then they open themselves up to demonic spirits. The New Testament Epistles of Timothy and Peter, state that the world will become more evil and deceptive, with Satan intensifying the battle before Christ returns. One would have to look at the explosion of interest in the occult, eastern spirituality and new age in our culture today, and then consider the consequences going forward. The controlling, manipulative nature of this causes confusion by brainwashing the person, so that they are unable to reason or discern. This issue was just not spoken about.

I reflected on the Bible passage in Galatians 5, Ephesians 6 where it talked about Satan being our adversary, hating mankind because we are made in the Image of God. Satan wants to destroy man, and corrupt our identity, but he does this through deception and intrigue, fooling them into thinking that he is the good guy that will provide all the worldly pleasures, then he takes those that are deceived down the slippery slope of destruction. How many of my patients who had opened themselves up to this insidious evil world told me of the constant dark thoughts, despair, and the messaging to self harm, or to take their own lives.

I arrived at the Psychiatric Hospital to see Natasha. There were a number of checks and balances before entering the security zones. I was trying to prepare myself the best I could, being told that there are a number of very unwell people that are mentally unstable and the experience could be disturbing to say the least.

As I approached the main ward, I could see people secured to their beds with types of harnesses, then others in a room with a toilet in the corner, similar to a jail cell where there are minimal walls and no privacy. The nurse assured me that the set up was to protect the patients in care, and also the staff who were regularly assaulted by the very people in their care. I saw a male at one end of the room, his eyes rolling back and he was continually rocking backwards and forwards making unintelligible sounds. It was so sad to see the condition of some of these patients, and I could not imagine how they would function in the world.

The nurse took me along a corridor, then I spotted Natasha seated at the rear of the main room, her feet up to her chin, and she was grinning at me. As I approached her she looked at me and asked me if I was okay, as if nothing had happened. I was bewildered at her nonchalant attitude.

Did she not remember what had happened Sunday night, as Ally and I approached her? I sat down, and looked into her eyes, "Natasha do you know how you came to be admitted into this psychiatric facility?" She seemed puzzled and then said

"No, I don't remember how I ended up here. The only thing I remember is waking up in the ambulance."

I was not sure if she was lying or she genuinely did not remember.

The nurse looked at the records, where it was noted as a probable psychotic episode from substance abuse with violent tendencies, difficult to restrain. Natasha was very slight in stature and these two heavy set male ambulance officers found her difficult to restrain.

Natasha had a smug look on her face, then said, "When can I get out of here? The food is horrible and I want to see Toby." The nurse left and I wanted to check in with Natasha to discuss outpatient care, so I asked the question, "Tell me Natasha, how did this episode happen and what caused this?" There was a long pause, and I could see the hesitation of fessing up.

"I have been binge drinking, and taking my antidepressant medication to help calm my nerves. I feel so anxious and scared that I have been pacing my townhouse, feeling like I am going crazy. The anxiety is so suffocating that I have been scratching my legs, picking the sores that are now infected." Natasha pulled up her track pants to show the sores and pus filled cuts on her legs, which needed urgent medical attention. How could she inflict these injuries on herself?

"Melody, I have these... these dark thoughts in my head all the time, and I feel like someone is watching me. I cannot escape this. Toby is better off with my mother."

I looked at her face, and could see the utter torment as she began to cry, and I was filled with compassion. It was so disturbing to hear her describe that she felt alone, trapped in this terrible nightmare in an utter state of hopelessness.

I tried to compose myself as I wanted to break down and cry with Natasha, "Tell me about these dark thoughts?" I wanted to determine whether these thoughts were suicidal, which would then require round the clock suicide watch.

Natasha looked at me with a shocked expression, trying to hide the fact she told me about the dark thoughts. Why was she trying to hide it now? I persisted, looking into her eyes. Would she follow through in taking her own life? The hospital wanted to release her to outpatient care, but was she stable enough?

"Natasha, please tell me about these dark thoughts, I want to help you." There was a long pause… some fifteen minutes.

She hesitated, putting her head down and then looked up at me, "The thoughts are telling me that I am no good, a failure at everything. I deserve to be abandoned. God has abandoned me too!... No one loves me, and even my mother wanted to abort me! I am worthless and have no purpose to live. God created me with defects but I can kill his work off!" She said in a defiant tone exuding hatred.

The words came forth like explosives, with power and contempt, leaving me speechless. I sat there in silence, asking the Lord for guidance. This was so overwhelming, and this girl was so lost. I knew I had to go and see the nurse again about the results for the mental health assessments, and the care plan but I felt the weight of despair that was pulling me down.

The nurse called out to me and I walked over to the office. I went through the care plan with the nurse and advised that we could modify it once her test results come back. At the back of my mind I was thinking about what Ally and I witnessed that night, and I could not see how further drugs could assist. There was more to this, and I was beginning to see that Natasha required a complete intervention plan, beginning with detox, rehabilitation and spiritual support.

Suddenly, there were screams and I could feel my chest pounding, not knowing what was happening. I looked over and the other nurses on duty were trying to break up a fight between Natasha and another girl called Sienna. Natasha had been cut with a serrated knife across her neck by Sienna, and the girl kept yelling at Natasha with a high shrill voice. It was terrifying watching these two girls, with Sienna in particular yelling abuse and trying to harm Natasha. The nurses were finding it difficult to push them apart.

Sienna was a petite girl, tallish but had incredible strength. Her eyes were rolling back in her head with only the white in her eyes visible. She was shaking all over and swearing using vulgar language and growling like a wild animal. My vision was blurred and hazy and I felt like I was going to faint. The blood splattered like droplets of crimson red paint leaking over the white walls.

The rage in her was off the charts, and she appeared to be having some sort of psychotic episode. The blood was splattered across the floor and the walls of the main area. My eyes were opened to the unpredictable nature of mental illness, and it scared me. It was almost out of control at times, and I wondered how the people here could ever overcome this adversity and have some sort of normal life. All the patients in the area were shouting and calling out for help. It was chaotic and I felt for the nurses that had to deal with this on a daily basis.

The nurse explained that the girls were only given plastic utensils to have meals due to the risk factor of self harming and violent outbursts. She was not sure how they got hold of a serrated knife, but it indicated that there was some premeditated intention to harm someone. The nurse assured me that they collected the plastic utensils after every meal, so one of the girls must have hidden the knife. Thankfully it was plastic and not the real deal, otherwise there would have been a fatal wound.

After leaving the hospital, I was a little hesitant on continuing with Natasha, as she was so unstable and not committed to the process of getting well. She needed to detox first and was not willing to do this. This was something I needed to discuss with my supervising psychologist and the team. We often discuss patients anonymously so that we can bounce off ideas and help each other provide better care.

The week went really fast and I had a meeting with the Supervisor, Andrew. I looked forward to the sessions every month, as it allowed me to debrief, and discuss strategies. I was feeling the pressure and intensity of my caseload, and it pushed me to the edge. My Supervisor had been in mental health for almost twenty years, so lots of experience and knowledge on various disorders. He also had a biblical worldview and he was very understanding of the plight of spiritual issues involving people with addictions. He had encountered demonic activity himself and had some interesting information and advice to give me. He looked up from his notes, and said in a matter of fact tone.

"Melody, demonic activity is part of our world, but we do not always recognise or easily discern it. People with addictions are prone to it, because of the enslaving nature of the addiction. Demons love to enslave people and if they are not a Christian, …uh they can inhabit them from time to time. For an unbeliever, they can possess them, weakening their will, taking over their body and mind. As with Christians they can only harass and oppress them if given the opportunity through enslaving sin, but cannot possess them because the Christian has a permanent occupier - the Holy Spirit."

I had read about this so it only just confirmed that I was on the right track. He also mentioned that some illnesses can be brought on by demonic activity, including physical and mental illness. It was certainly a sticky issue, given that professionals want to diagnose mental health issues as organic, mental health type illnesses, many times ignoring any spiritual implications.

"Andrew, are we so brainwashed by our culture and the secular professional medicos that we take their word as gospel? Or is it because we have been repeatedly told and reported by the media on what they want us to believe… that we are convinced that this is true?

My Supervisor nodded in agreement about the deceiving ways that the enemy works to disguise his work through ignorance, denial and minimising his strategies.

"Has the enemy succeeded in convincing Christians that the spiritual battles are not real, that they are only with flesh and blood, not against spiritual entities (forces)?" I realised that I was speaking with such conviction.

"Yes, he is good at deceiving and distracting Christians into focusing on the physical realm. We always have to try and understand the whole person, before making a diagnosis. Jesus healed people with demonic oppression and possession, some presenting with physical conditions, whilst others with mental illness. These same illnesses exist in our world today.

So Melody, why do you think God is bringing these tormented individuals to you?"

"To make me look like a fruit loop," I sniggered. "I believe God is teaching me about His sovereignty, and given…uh my past in dabbling in the occult, I can warn people not to go there. I believe He is using me to show His love, mercy and grace to these broken souls. God's love is powerful, and He wants me to learn how to love the unlovely. Also Andrew as you know… well… I have an overwhelming fear of evil, and not always understanding how big and powerful God is. I have also seen a lot of bad things happen as a child. My safe world was shaken. I am still learning that Satan's power is limited to what God allows him. Does that make sense?"

"There are a lot of lessons to be learned, Melody. You have made yourself available to God, and by walking in obedience, He is using you to set free those that are enslaved. Yes, as a child we are unable to understand why these bad things happen. An evil monster or an act of evil may appear to be more fierce than God! However, God is much more fierce, and we should fear Him. You know what I mean about fearing God? He is to be respected and honoured... right ...Yeah! He is a Holy God! The wrath of God will be terrifying for those that choose to reject Christ."

I nodded, realising that I was still battling with trusting God to have full control of my life. He is sovereign over the whole spiritual realm. He is Elohim, Almighty God!

Andrew could see that I was thinking through our discussion, and there was more clarity as to where I stood spiritually. He allowed me to challenge myself, and see through my own deficiencies.

"Melody tell me about your methods for working on those presenting with demonic manifestations, given that it can be dangerous."

He could read the fear behind my explanations. "Andrew, there are times when these manifestations are unpredictable, and as you know with the counselling process I am the only counsellor in the room. We now have panic buttons, in case there is any act of violence. At times, if I sense that the person may be demonised, I will refer them to a local church where there is support from the Pastor and Deacons. I did this with one of my patients who was heavily involved in new age and witchcraft. With others that are not so well visible, it may come up at a later session where there is an obvious entry point. I would respectfully ask the person if they wanted to work through this... which means leading them to repentance. As you know this weakens the enemy's hold on them, and they are able to be freed through prayer. Prayer and the Word of God is vital, and Andrew I am constantly praying for my patients. I keep reminding myself that Jesus is the deliverer, and I am His instrument."

"These are valuable lessons Melody, and Satan will try and tempt you with power and pride. Humility is important! If God has called you to this, He will provide the means."

"This unseen world is at war with us every day. I am learning Andrew that the Word of God, our Identity in Christ and love are powerful weapons against Satanic forces. Afterall, Satan does not understand love, and it dismantles his power."

Andrew was so encouraging but always challenging me. It was what I needed to hear, and I left his office affirmed and enlightened. It was like I had left my burdens aside, and was free to continue on the path of gaining a deeper trust in God.

The morning was crisp with a chilly wind that rustled through the trees, creating an ominous feeling as I made my way to work. I arrived twenty minutes early, so I checked the appointment book and saw that Natasha had confirmed, along with some of the other regulars that I was seeing. It was good to work with long term clients, as I could see their development over six to eight months which were encouraging. It balanced out the oppressive, difficult cases that I wrestled with.

The receptionist knocked on the door and entered. She had a distressed look on her face, almost a state of panic, as she mouthed the words that Natasha had a knife in her bag. For some reason the receptionist asked Natasha to see her bag, and when she opened it, the knife was visible. It was a 15cm kitchen knife, small enough to fit in her bag, but sharp enough to cause a fatal wound.

I looked at Wendy shocked at what she was telling me, trying to comprehend why Natasha would do such a thing, and more importantly what was I now going to do about this. A million thoughts were running through my mind. Was she intending to self harm, or was she planning something brutal? Thankfully Wendy had removed the knife from her bag.

I called Natasha into the office along with Wendy as a witness, not feeling safe being alone with her. I asked Natasha why she was carrying a knife, and she sat down on the couch, crossed her legs and looked at me with a menacing expression on her face. She said in a matter of fact way, "You had to be silenced. They were saying that you had to be silenced! I have to get, uh, get rid of you, kill you!" I could not hide the shock on my face, as Wendy responded, mirroring my expression. I felt a pulsating feeling rushing through my veins like an electric current.

"Natasha, who told you this? Who are... they?" The way she answered was so chilling, with no expression as if she was a zombie. Natasha put her head in her hands and started to cry. I wanted to reach out and comfort her, but realised I was being manipulated. Wendy motioned to me to stay where I was, and I nodded and kept the distance. I was thankful that Wendy was with me, as she was a great support, a brave, mature lady with Godly wisdom.

It was so clear to me that this was some sort of spiritual struggle confirming what Ally and I were confronted with. It was a supernatural manifestation in the natural, and the entry point was clear - substance addiction. Natasha had opened up the door to the demonic.

Knowing that Natasha lived so close to me, made me feel very uncomfortable. It was something that I would need to report to the Centre Manager, the Church and maybe the police. Wendy was so great at sorting all this out, and assured me that she would take care of it.

We contacted the police and filed a report, and they were going to send an officer to discuss this with Natasha. Also the Counselling Centre employed a security guard to escort the counsellors to their vehicle at night, as we were receiving threats from the Satanic cults, and also had a number of drug dealers hanging around the centre trying to intimidate me, as I was infiltrating their customers. They would hang out on the stairwell and swear at me as I walked past. It made me a little nervous but I kept praying my way through this time.

At home that night I told Blake about Natasha as he had seen her at church a few times, and he was totally uncomfortable with the situation. The fact that Natasha lived a few blocks from us, did not make it any easier. I kept replaying the incident in my head, and tried so hard not to think of what could have happened if Wendy had not searched her bag. It was clear that the Lord was watching out for me. It was a time we bandied together and prayed through this. I was very grateful to have intercessors praying for me during this difficult time. Although I was afraid at times, I could sense God's peace with me, and He strengthened me.

The police suggested that I not see Natasha as a client for a couple of weeks until they investigate the situation, and may charge her for carrying the weapon with the intention to kill.

I could not help but feel a little paranoid about the situation with Natasha, especially after hearing her say that she was told to silence me, to get rid of me, to kill me! This kept replaying in my head, and I was always looking over my shoulder. I knew that the enemy was invoking fear in me, and it was a real struggle to not allow these thoughts to overtake me. I often came home to an empty house so I would sometimes take my old softball bat and walk around the apartment to ensure no one was there before I could relax.

Four weeks later, I was sitting on the balcony at home reading the local paper, and saw a picture of Natasha on the front page. She had stabbed a local policeman who tried to rescue her from a top floor balcony, as she was contemplating jumping off. The policeman had been stabbed in the arm, and was taken to hospital to recover from the wound. I sat there frozen thinking about the time she came into the counselling centre armed with the knife. She was capable of using it, as she did with the policeman. I was so thankful that it was not a fatal stabbing. I could not help but cry, as I let out the stress and fear that I had been feeling for the last three months.

So Natasha was put in jail as there was an intent to cause harm by injuring the policeman. I was wondering whether I would be called up by the court to give any evidence. I really did not want to be involved at this stage, because I believed Natasha was a threat to society and her own son. So many people from church reached out to her to support her, including the counsellors, yet she rebelled against it. She chose to walk away from God, and was wilful in her decisions. The only way forward for her is to go to jail and be forced to detox, before any rehabilitation can be achieved. It would have to be her will to want to get better, and seek the Lord.

As the months rolled on, we never heard anything further on Natasha. It appeared that her lawyer did not win the case on grounds of mental health, and she was sent to jail. I guess if you attack an enforcement officer, you will need to bear the consequences. I was hoping that Natasha came to her senses and returned to the Lord. I felt very sorry for her little boy, who has to grow up without a mum.

Chapter 19

Deliverance

Blake and I were looking forward to taking a holiday break for some respite. We were approaching twelve months of marriage and it was time to work on our relationship before we had children. We both loved the history of Italy, France and Germany and could not wait to go and discover the ancient ruins, the architecture, art and scenery. Also Switzerland is such a beautiful place, as I remembered that my parents had taken a trip there, before Dad passed away. They talked often about looking outside of their window in the morning at the town of Interlaken and seeing the magnificent snow capped mountain tops like a framed picture, scintillating in the sun. They had taken numerous photos of the beautiful scenic snow capped alps with a lake at the base. In winter the lake would freeze, making it possible to ice skate on it.

While I was thinking about our plans, I remembered that we had a seminar at church that night about deliverance ministry, and Blake and I were attending. I was interested in hearing what the Pastor had to say, given that he was called out of a corporate role to serve in a tough ministry like deliverance.

It was part of my personality that I would immerse myself with something, almost obsessively until I understood it. I needed to find a better way to deal with this, a balance in my life. Blake was good at pointing this out to me, and would often plan little outings to the beach or a drive to the Blue Mountains, to focus on other things. I really adored this about him, as he knew that this was important but rather than cover it up, he helped me find perspective. A truly brilliant man, I thought! I guess he also sensed that God was showing us something, and by bringing these broken people into our life, we were learning about his power and sovereignty. I didn't even realise the fear and anxiety that was simmering below the surface, and at times reared its ugly head, with some sort of panic attack.

It was great having the day off to catch up with Tina, my South African friend, and we planned to have morning tea at the local cafe. She was such a lovely person, who was caring and trustworthy. We shared our lives with each other and she felt like a sister to me, well in actual fact we were related in Christ.

She was sitting in the sun at the cafe as I strolled up, and I could spot her beaming smile from fifty metres away. Tina asked the waitress to come back in a couple of minutes to take our order. She was a full time mum, and was very proud of her role in the home. I liked that about her, as she was unapologetic and saw her role as a privilege. I was hoping that when Blake and I have children that I could be a stay at home mum for a while. I had been working full time for so long, in a corporate role previously thinking that Will would be proud of my accomplishments. It never seemed to matter to him at all. Now I was working part time, and trying to get my counselling business established, yet knowing that in a year or two, I would have to put it on hold, God willing, once I have children. My biological clock was ticking loudly and I could no longer ignore it.

Blake and I walked into the church and were a tad late, with the worship team into the second song. Blake was caught in a traffic incident on his way home. We barely had time to have dinner, before rushing out to the church for the Deliverance Conference. We both could feel the nervous anticipation not knowing what we were going to experience.

The visiting Minister, Don was introduced by the Pastor sharing his background which was quite diverse. He was called out of the corporate career, working for a pharmaceutical company in the United States of America doing extremely well as a Partner, earning a substantial amount of money and benefits, until God called him out. He struggled with letting go, as he was very ambitious, and I could relate to it, having to let go of a career. He then prayed that if it was God's will to resign from his job, then the Lord would show him.

It was eight months in Bangalore, India on a business trip where he began to see his assignment that the Lord had for him. My eyes lit up as he was from the same place that I was born. He saw many people involved in religious cults, spiritism associated with the Hindu culture where they became vessels for evil spirits. Some of these people were tormented continuously, skirting around on the edge of a cliff of lunacy, whereas others were amazingly wealthy and successful, but unknowingly, they too were on the wide road leading to destruction. This ambivalence puzzled him, and he began to investigate it. Afterall, Jesus said, *"I am the way, the truth, and the life. No one comes to the Father except through Me"*. (John 14:6) Was he a liar, a lunatic or telling the truth?

So here he was after the rather long introduction of his calling into ministry which was very insightful and encouraging to hear, he was invited to visit various churches all over the United States, Australia and Europe. God was using him to free people from enslavement to these demonic spirits.

He explained how wandering spirits can only enter or oppress you when you give them permission through habitual and unconfessed sin. God had created man to have free will so this means that we can ask these unclean spirits to leave. This can only happen through true repentance by turning away from that sin, and clinging close to Christ. These demonic spirits can oppress and torment the true believer if they give the enemy a foothold. They will use any area of vulnerability, trauma, unconfessed sin and deception to attack a Christian. They cannot possess a Christian because they are not empty (Matthew 12:43-45) but are occupied by the Holy Spirit.

As he dispelled all the myths of possession and oppression, where preachers had mystified the subject, and corrupted the teaching by introducing heresies that promoted the abuse of power, paranoia, control and superstitious legalism. He made it sound really simple in accordance with the teachings of Jesus. He suggested that we read CS Lewis ' The Screwtape Letters', where one will discover that there is a real devil, and demons which interact with our natural world.

Don also explained the deception of necromancy (that is communicating with a dead relative or person to gain future knowledge). That is another form of magic and witchcraft. He confirmed that the dead relative cannot come back to our natural world. This is explained in the Bible in the story of a rich man and the poor man and believer, Lazarus, having died, and gone to Hades. (Luke 16:19-31) There is a deep chasm between two regions of Hades. One region was Abraham's bosom (a heavenly state), where Lazarus went and also the Old Testament saints dwelled after they died, and the other a place of torment for unbelievers.

The rich man found himself in Hades (a form of hell but not the final intense state) where there is torment, learning that the worldly possessions and comfort meant nothing in the afterlife. He did not show any mercy to Lazarus during his earthly life, the poor man who begged for food and shelter, yet Lazarus was comforted when he died. The rich man, not given a name in this story, desperately begged Lazarus to dip his finger in water and wet his scorching lips. The rich man could see Father Abraham in the distance and begged him to warn his living family of the place called Hades. Yet he could not reach them because of the great chasm between them. There is no way out, only endless despair. At that time, the rich man could communicate with those of the two regions, but not those still living. He also had a heightened awareness of his own sin and judgement. In Hades he had become an evangelist wanting his loved ones to accept the truth, and not the fate that he was facing.

At the cross, Jesus paid the penalty for all those that died believing in God. The resurrected Jesus went down to Hades and released all the old testament believers and took them to Paradise with Him, separating the chasm of Hades (hell-like state) so that there is a complete division. Now those that die as unbelievers go to Hades awaiting judgement, and the believers go to be with the Lord. There is no intermediate state.

Don confirmed that the enemy uses this situation to deceive the vulnerable who are grieving the loss of a loved one, where a familiar spirit can take the form of a deceased person. It helped me understand the deception of playing around with the ouija board as a child with my school friends, as we tried to communicate with dead relatives. Instead we may have attracted other evil entities.

It was all making so much sense to me, as the missing pieces of the jigsaw puzzle were coming together. Don walked down the steps of the platform as he was giving a command or nugget of truth, "Do not give Satan any power, as He is no match for the Sovereign God! He is a created being, and not the Creator! He is trying to destroy and corrupt God's creation including You. However, (*pause*) he is to be respected, as he is capable of causing you much pain! We need to understand his strategies so that we can stand firm. The Word of God is our weapon! As you feed upon the Word of God, you will overcome the sins of the flesh. Do not be afraid brothers and sisters in Christ, God has marked you as His own, and He will be with you till the end." The crowd clapped and roared. I really felt that he was speaking to me. The intensity was building and I could sense a resistance simmering, ready to explode.

Then Don continued to walk along the first row explaining that a close relationship with Jesus was the key.

"It was about knowing your identity in Christ, so that Jesus goes before you, so that you are always attached to Him, through a personal relationship… a complete surrender to Christ."

As Don put his hands up describing the complete surrender to Jesus, people in the church started manifesting. There was chatter, disorder and people shaking uncontrollably. Then Don motioned a command of silence, as he prayed for the presence of Jesus to be exalted and lifted up. There was silence for another fifteen minutes as he called on people to repent. There was such peace as the believers cried out for the presence of the Lord. Then the chaos started again.

Blake and I looked at each other, and we saw so many things happening. It was scary, unpredictable and intense. Don asked people to come up for prayer and there were pastors at the front to deliver them from their infliction. We were one of the leaders called up to pray for people at the front. I could see some of the pastors shouting at these people as they were shrieking and writhing like snakes. This was beginning to get out of control. There were people vomiting and hallucinating, eyes rolling back in their heads, as if they were under some spell or drugs. Thirty minutes ago, there were regular people taking part in a church service, and now there was chaos. It was like the veil had been lifted, and we were seeing into the unseen realm.

I was afraid, but I remembered that demons were terrified of Jesus, and those that belong to him. I also recalled the story of the sons of Sceva in the Bible Acts 19:15 who were trying to copy Paul and cast out demons, yet they did not know God, and tried to do it in their own strength. The evil spirit beat them up and they were badly injured.

While I was standing at the front, I prayed that God would tear down the strongholds of falsehood and lies that wage war against the truth of the Bible, then one of the leaders pushed a girl over to me and asked me to pray for her. She was Sienna, a girl that was a regular at church and Bible study, who was completely insane and out of control. She was disruptive and caused a lot of division and harm to her Bible study friends. Sienna was a regular at the local psychiatric hospital, and had stabbed my client Natasha with a serrated knife the day I visited.

Sienna also attempted suicide on a number of occasions, and the counselling staff were often asked to step in. She would call the counselling office each time she attempted suicide, and we would have to keep her on the phone, trying to talk her around. We each took turns but it felt like we were being manipulated. Yet she only got worse and worse. One time she overdosed on sleeping pills in the counselling centre, and we had to call the ambulance.

Her parents were highly regarded in the legal world, wealthy and accomplished in their careers. After sending Sienna to so many rehabilitation clinics with no positive results, they built a granny flat on their property and locked her away every night. She was free during the day, and continued to play havoc at the church and the friends that had shown her mercy.

I felt inadequate in handling Sienna in this condition, and she could easily assault me. Her whole body was trembling uncontrollably, shaking and unsteady on her feet, yet she had this sarcastic smile on her face, trying to ridicule me, like she did to many others. I made eye contact with her and held onto the scriptures of my identity in Christ. I asked her to stop with the taunting, and she did. I was respectful, yet kept addressing her by her name. I prayed that the Lord would fill me with compassion, and love for Sienna.

I asked Sienna if she knew Jesus and how He was able to set her free. I shared with her the gospel message of John 3:16, and explained sin, and why we need a Saviour. She may have heard this before, but I had her full attention. Sienna looked at me, making eye contact and she was still and quiet. "How long can you go on like this, Sienna?" My voice broke with the emotion and sadness that I was feeling. "There is a better way!" I could see the tears start to form, and I was finally getting through to Sienna herself, and we prayed asking Jesus to forgive her of her sins, and she boldly named them, then she asked Jesus to cleanse her. Sienna surrendered her heart to Jesus that night. I hugged her and went to get a Bible from the back of the church. I gave her the Bible and asked her to read one of the gospels - John, then all the others. She repeated John 3:16 and put her name in.

She took the Bible, gave me a smile and said thank you. Sienna then left the building, quietly and she seemed like a different person. There was no dramatic response, just a simple understanding of the message of the cross. I was not sure if what I did was enough because I had not seen anyone so out of control, and completely insane in which that part of me thought it was not possible.

On the way home, I told Blake what had happened with Sienna, "I am not sure if I did enough." Blake pulled me up.

"Melody, the good news of the Gospel is more than enough. Jesus is the deliverer."

" Yes you are right. The simple message of the gospel is powerful. I asked the Lord to help me with compassion and love for Sienna, and I sensed the outpouring of His love. Sienna broke down in tears, and I had never seen her react like that before."

"We easily forget that there is no greater love than Jesus laying down his life for sinners."

That night we had seen so much theatrics, shouting at the demons with abuse of power, disrespect and disorder that I soon realised that the demons were not deaf, or dumb. Jesus' presence, through the Holy Spirit, was enough to set them free.

It took me some time to process what I had seen. I saw people that I knew in ministry go crazy as if under some sort of spell, behaving out of control which was unlike their character. Was this real? Were they hypnotised, magic or mind control - witchcraft? These were the questions I was asking as they seemed to be followers of Christ. Then I remembered that not all that call on the name of the Lord are actually saved, and maybe these so-called Christians were not true believers. It left me feeling a little disillusioned how people could talk the talk, but not live what they preach.

Blake and I were always praying for discernment and Godly wisdom as we navigated some crazy things that were happening in churches. We saw totally insane things like being drunk in the spirit, with Christians laughing uncontrollably, falling over chairs and being disorderly. Is this behaviour unbiblical as it does not glorify the Lord, nor produce fruits of praise and obedience? The Bible talks about a God that likes order and respect.

Although we were seeing some extraordinary things happen, I was still questioning the source. I regarded myself as a believing sceptic. The enemy comes as an angel of light and can easily deceive people into thinking this was God's work, when it was actually the work of Satan. The proof of the pudding would be the person becoming a Christian and producing good fruit. There were a few people that I knew from church who went up for prayer, so time will tell. I could also see the trap for the ministry team in believing that they had the power to deliver, or there was a special technique or formula that allowed the person to be delivered from their strongholds. I know that this was evident as I almost fell for this myself. After exercising the gift, you could easily take pride in your performance, and this was not of God. Jesus was the deliverer and He used earthen vessels like myself to help people. I had to remind myself of this from time to time, so that I would not get puffed up or feel some sort of superiority.

Over the next few weeks I had watched my friends who were delivered from their afflictions, start to produce good fruit by getting involved in ministry, becoming more generous and showing acts of kindness. It was encouraging and reassuring to see this. I also saw some of these colleagues become more volatile, with ungodly behaviour, leaving the church in a worse state. I realised that God had His way of sorting out the wheat and tares, and this may continue to happen for some time until He Returns to take His bride.

Summer had arrived and it was getting humid earlier than usual. I had arrived at work and was driving into the car park when I heard my name called. I stopped and saw a young lady approaching my car as I parked. She was dressed in a lovely linen light blue dress with a tie at the waist, and flesh coloured sandals. I didn't recognise her at first, but then realised it was Sienna. She looked so feminine and beautiful, with her long blonde wavy hair glistening in the sun. Her demeanour was so calm and poised, that I had to blink to make sure I was seeing right. She seemed very excited to tell me her news, and I looked at her with such a surprise, anticipating what she was going to say. She told me that her life was on track, and that she had a new job in an office doing some administrative work.

It was truly remarkable to see this beautiful young lady in her right mind. She thanked me for praying for her that night at the Deliverance Conference and reassured me that she had found a great church not far from her home, and was excited about her relationship with the Lord. She was very grateful that Jesus set her free from the years of torment. She made my day, and my heart soared to hear what the Lord had done with this girl that most people wrote off as a lunatic, a child of the Devil.

I could not wait to tell the other counsellors, who had been praying for her since the day she was delivered. Even they thought she was a hopeless case, but the Lord showed us that He has the power to deliver those He chooses, and only in His time.

The next day, the church pastors advised us that they had received a phone call and card from Sienna's parents. They were amazed with Sienna's transformation and asked what had happened. The Pastors had told them that Sienna came up for prayer and was delivered from her affliction by Jesus, through prayer by one of our counsellors.

Later we received a huge bunch of flowers and a card thanking us for praying and supporting their daughter over the years. We continued to pray for Sienna's parents who had suffered many years watching their daughter's torment, not knowing how to help her and or what to do. They were given so many diagnoses by experts in the field of mental health, even sent their daughter to expensive rehabilitation clinics, and retreats, but to no avail. This was a way that we were a witness in the community that dispensed God's grace, mercy, love and power. Even the local hospitals and psychiatric services sent their outpatients to us, knowing that we would take good care of these clients, and the help was beyond the physical realm. We were developing a great reputation in the community for providing relief for the outpatients.

We had not seen Jessica for some time. She had cancelled the last two appointments and Jane was getting a little concerned whether she had gone back to the cult. I had seen some unsavoury looking persons outside our building and when I asked them if they were looking for anyone, they sniggered and swore under their breath. Some of the members from the cult lived in the vicinity and would make it their mission to pray against the work we were doing in the counselling centre. They prayed to their satanic god that the centre would be destroyed, implode and disappear. It was really annoying to have these people outside of our centre, chanting some meaningless prayer, but I reminded myself that Greater is He who is in me than he who is in the world.

Chapter 20

European Vacation

I was so excited about our trip to Europe which was finally happening, as we were scheduled to leave Sydney by the end of the week. That morning, I was getting ready for work and thought I would do a quick load of washing. As I put my hand into the basket, I felt a sharp pain in my right hand, but thought it was a safety pin or a broken clasp. I looked at my hand and it was getting itchy and red. It looked like some sort of bite, so I thought maybe a mosquito, but it was starting to throb. I could feel a strange sensation up and down my arm, like I had been given a tetanus shot. I took a drink of water and left for work thinking that I would return early and put the washing out.

Once I got to work I was feeling faint and almost passed out, so my colleague drove me to the clinic to check on what the intense burning pain was about. It turned out to be a spider bite, the culprit being a red back, which is quite painful. I stayed at the clinic under observation, until the pain subsided.

This was the beginning of the shenanigans for the week prior to our departure.

The next day the fridge thermostat went, so now all the frozen goods were thawing out. We had to get a technician out as soon as possible, to minimise further food spoilage. Whilst Blake went to get the ice to salvage the food, he lost the house keys with the unit number on the tag, meaning we had to replace the lock for the door. Thankfully we were able to get a locksmith out that day.

Then that night, Blake was cleaning his backpack for the overseas trip and snapped the cords so that they could not be fastened properly. That was it! I lost my temper and almost screamed. I had to go for a walk around the block to cool off, rather than yell at Blake which was such a temptation, as he remained so calm, and shrugged off the misadventures saying, "That's life." This riled me up even more and I wanted to pick up the esky of ice and throw it over his head to knock some sense into him.

Whilst I was walking I wondered whether God was telling us something. We had prayed about this trip for some time, requesting that if it was His will and timing that He would make a way, and everything had fallen into place, except for these mishaps. I was thinking whether we should have invested our savings into buying a house. Yet Blake did not seem to be too concerned about buying a property at this stage. For me, I was thinking about starting a family soon, and having a secure and safe place for our children, rather than moving from house to house in rentals.

Finally, after the dramas of the week we were seated in the plane, flying Qantas to Rome, when the notice came on the loudspeaker that the departure was going to be delayed by one and half hours due to air traffic issues. I thought to myself, "What else?", better this than an air crash, but

I did not want to overthink this. Then Blake and I both bent down to get a book from our bags, and bashed our heads together! We both started laughing out loud and everyone on the plane were wondering how possibly we could be laughing about being delayed so long! After the week of mayhem, this was the final straw that broke the camel's back, but we both saw the humour in it and let out our frustration in laughter!! I looked over to the couple staring at us with a quizzical look, so I told them that we had a crazy week, and to top it off we just accidentally banged our heads together. They took awhile to respond but then smiled back, maybe thinking we had lost our minds and they had to spend the next twenty something hours with some looneys sitting alongside them.

My eyes were stinging, as I did not get a lot of sleep last night thinking about all the things I needed to do to prepare for this trip. Then it suddenly occurred to me that all these mishaps may have been an attack, to rob us of our peace, and time of rest. Some weeks prior to this we also had the car broken into twice, and an attempt to steal it also. Blake's golf clubs were stolen by the car thieves. We both had such an eventful crazy year at work and in ministry. We were in the enemy's territory, doing God's will, hence the constant darts aimed at wearing us down. The holiday was an opportunity to create new memories and to have a time of reprieve, before the next chapter of family planning. So after fifteen minutes of trying to read, I was seeing blurry print so I decided to close my eyes and listen to music instead.

We reached the city of Rome, and it was quite early in the morning, and we were able to get a shuttle bus to the hotel. The Hotel was an older style building with a solid stone entrance, decorated with chandeliers and period furniture. The sides of the building were brick of various sizes and textures, that looked hand made rather than mass produced. It truly felt that I had stepped back in time, with this quaint style with a touch of glamour. We left our bags with the concierge and they assured us that it would be locked away. They gave us quick safety tips and told us to return after lunch, as our room would be ready. I was looking forward to having a shower and taking a quick nap, although I was told that it was better to go to bed early and have a good night's sleep.

Rome was an amazing place, with ruins splashed here and there. We walked the cobblestone streets close to the hotel, and there was so much history everywhere we turned. All we could hear was the traffic, horns and sirens of the police and ambulance. I could not believe that every five minutes you could hear these sirens. These Italians must be crazy drivers!

It was a beautiful city with lots of historical buildings that stood the test of time, and the architecture was breathtaking. Rome was known as the 'eternal city' as the Ancient Romans believed that no matter what happens in other cities, Rome will remain standing. However, this was certainly not the case, as mankind no matter how brilliant and gifted is finite, and we have an infinite God. The builders and architects at the time, used the best quality products, and built things to last. There was also so much intricate detail on the buildings, with the etched columns, lintels and arches.

The Colosseum was such an imposing structure, known as the Flavian Amphitheatre where the great battles of the gladiators took place. It was also the place where the Christians were fed to the lions or used as human candles to light up the structure. It was a place of sport, entertainment, persecution and painful deaths for the Christian believers. If only the walls could speak, what would they say? It was a place of death and barbaric acts of murder indicating the evil hearts of mankind.

The guide went on to say how the Romans at the time went to lengths to eliminate the stench of burning flesh with perfumes and lavender, yet the smell was so vile that they installed vomit troughs for people to throw up. I could almost feel the heaviness of death and pain, that it brought tears to my eyes thinking about the early Christians. It was hard to see the beauty and grandeur of this place when it represented such a heartbreaking history.

The smell of the stone, earth and dust permeated the air, and I touched the walls to see how strong and solid the structure was. The wall had a thin film of sandy dust that rubbed off on my hand and it was difficult to comprehend that this structure was more than 2,000 years old.

The Sistine Chapel was also extraordinary, and both of us loved the work of Michelangelo, having read his biography. He was asked by Pope Clement VII until his death, then Paul III, to paint a number of frescoes of the various Biblical events like the crossing of the Red Sea, Jesus' ascension, and the Last Judgement. Michelangelo had a good way of depicting the good and evil angels and the torment on the faces of those that were snatched by the evil angels.

We stood at the Last Judgement painting and took in all the detail, the facial expressions, the joy of believers who were welcomed to Heaven by the disciples contrasting with the evil angels and demons that tortured the unbelievers. Seeing the tragedy of those that were being snatched away by the evil angels with anguish in their faces, brought home the reality and finality of judgement. We were both looking at this through spiritual eyes, understanding the message that the painter was trying to convey.

I could relate to seeing many of my clients who were controlled by demonic forces, displaying similar expressions of utter torment, and insanity. They had terror in their eyes, chained to their addictions of various kinds, controlled and manipulated by these entities. Some were given over by God, and their final judgement awaits them. Some were able to find mercy and set free to follow Christ.

The colours and texture was amazing, as the images looked life like, with the body shapes, and facial features. There was also one odd looking man, his face distraught and languishing which I believe is meant to be the humble, miserable Michelangelo, himself. According to his biography, Michelangelo detested the idolatry of the church, and even his artwork which he believed took people away from the true Saviour, Jesus. The focus was on the art form rather than the person of Jesus. It was only due to the Pope insisting on him finishing the work, that he persisted, while losing interest in the very talent, and gift that was given to him.

The other paintings of the conversion of Paul, Moses receiving the ten commandments all had similar colours and textures. Michelangelo captures the expressions of the faces of the disciples so well, telling the story of the odd bunch of men, who did extraordinary things by faith with Jesus' teaching and instruction.

We could have spent the whole day looking at the art, experiencing the finer details but we had a tight schedule, and hoped that one day we could come back here and experience it all over again. We really appreciated the way the historians and artists restored the paintings, preserving them and keeping with the vibrant colours typical of Michelangelo's style.

We finished up at the Vatican later in the afternoon and headed over to the Trevi Fountain for a quick lunch and coffee. The Trevi fountain was beautiful with the marble backdrop of statues and baroque architecture along with the Ancient Roman ornate style. The fountain contained many coins, as there was a belief that if you throw one coin over your right shoulder you will return to Rome, If you throw two you will fall in love and three you will marry. Since Blake and I were already married we just threw in one for good measure, and chuckled at the myth told by the tour guides. In summer we believed that many children played in the water and collected the coins.

It was difficult to get accommodation in Venice as there was a Carnivale which was a celebration of culture and traditions, and thankfully we pre-booked as it was overcrowded with tourists and visitors from other parts of Italy.

It was a spectacular city, set amongst the canals and waterways, with no roads or traffic. It was so unique that I had never experienced anything like it. There were water taxis if you were in a rush, and the gondolas that were much more economical. The canals were a dark green in colour, indicating the depth maximum of five metres, and you could not really see the bottom with the murky water. They also had a pungent smell of the pollutants. I tried not to think of that, instead deciding to take in the vibrant atmosphere. Amongst the canals there were small arched bridges connecting the buildings and shops from one side to the other.

The Architecture in Venice was a mixture of Venetian Gothic, Renaissance, Byzantine and Islamic. The churches and cathedrals were gothic, with gargoyles on the outside of the buildings, to guard against evil spirits and protect those inside of the buildings. It was ironic as these gargoyles actually look like demonic beings. They were grotesque and not welcoming to say the least.

Blake and I went into The Basilica of St Mark which was situated in the famous St Mark's Square, often appearing in many of the Hollywood films. It was very similar to the Cathedrals in Turkey, that had the Islamic domes and ornate etchings on the exterior. The interior of the building was cold and damp, typical of a full stone building thousands of years old. It had been restored well, and there had been several changes over the years, but you could smell the age, and history of this grandiose structure.

There were so many young people here exploring, walking through the streets and the crowds were overwhelming in some areas. Also I could not get over how many pigeons were there, and when they decided to fly, the feathers and noise was astounding. If you had a fear of birds, Venice was not a place for you. Blake was so excited about this place, the culture and his enthusiasm was infectious. The place was certainly tantalising all of our senses, from the beautiful colours, architecture, smells of food, the water in the canals, the sounds of the music and chatter everywhere you turned. The people were dressed in various costumes which were part of the Carnivale, with colours and designs, theatrical masks and traditional decorations. Blake and I were wondering whether we should buy some costumes so that we could take part in the parades. We watched the performances of the street theatre, dancing and singing, which were very entertaining.

We sampled some typical Venetian dishes with pastas, marinated sardines with a twist of lemon, cuttlefish and mussels with loads of garlic, olives and small cherry tomatoes. The flavours were strong, yet they worked well with the pasta and breads, washed down with an Italian Moscato. We enjoyed the variety of ways to make pasta, and the combination of breads drizzled with olive oil, and grilled vegetables. Blake was still dreaming about his huge steak, but I caught him a few times, really enjoying the cuisine in Italy minus the meat dishes.

Florence or Firenz was a much smaller city than Rome, and it was breathtakingly beautiful in every way. The historical buildings with Renaissance architecture, were intricate yet solid structures. The Duomo was an amazing Cathedral and you can climb to the top and see the city from different angles. The top of the cathedral was this reddish dome, with cappings made of stone and the base of the dome decorated with etchings. The Cathedral had the paintings on the ceiling from Michelangelo, preserved and restored to perfection. It was common in Florence to have decorated ceilings and cornices. Even the pensione where we stayed, which was a type of bed and breakfast accommodation in Italy, had these decorated ceilings. We could lay in bed and be inspired by the beautiful artwork above.

Exploring Florence was truly magical and this was certainly one of my favourite cities in the world, and I had only spent one day there. It had a homely atmosphere about it that felt warm and embracing. The people were lovely and friendly, not hurried like other cities. They enjoyed their lives, making time for social interaction in the evening after work at the Piazza's, where they enjoyed wholesome Italian food, pizzas with only three toppings and red wine. I thought it was certainly something that I could take back to Australia, creating a social haven amongst my Christian friends so that we do not lose touch with the important things in life.

At night Blake and I were craving some meat, and really missed the juicy steaks in Australia. The Italians did not seem to have much meat in their diets, and very little on the menus, so we found this restaurant just a short stroll from the Ponte de Vecchio, an old bridge across the river to connect the towns. We enjoyed some succulent beef slowly cooked in butter and red wine, with some potato mash.

After dinner, feeling content, we continued to explore this interesting structure. On top of the bridge was a selection of shops and businesses that had been there from the 13th and 16th centuries. It was such a unique structure that has stood through World Wars and battles over the years.

We strolled across the bridge venturing into the shops, and there were numerous types of food stores and clothing. I found a lovely cashmere scarf in a warm yellow which was soft and of high quality, so I bought it and wrapped it around my shoulders. It would remind me of Florence, this remarkable city of art, culture and love.

I could smell the sweet fragrance of boiled lollies and chocolates as we walked past the candy store. In the window were handmade chocolates, delicate pieces of soft fudge with nuts and other decorative toppings. They also looked like a work of art.

The bridge looked amazing at night as the lights shone, reflecting off the water below which would be a marvellous painting or drawing. Blake and I took many photos of the bridge from different points of the canal so that we could hang it in our apartment when we got back to Australia. It was such a unique piece of architecture, nothing like anything I had ever seen before. Looking at the digital photo through the lens, there was an olive glow in the photo, where the reflection from the green water canal below to the yellowish and cream coloured buildings on top of the bridge spanning the entire width. Only a fine detail photo or painting could capture the unusual structure that was too difficult to describe.

Later we returned to the Duomo Square, and were amazed how accurate the copy of the King David Sculpture was. We sat down in the Square and had some afternoon tea, chocolate cake and took in the atmosphere. There were so many tourists amongst the locals, and it was easy to pick out the locals. They were loud and vibrant, talking with their hands, and shouting at times. Blake fitted in so well, as he was quite expressive too! I often had to keep an eye on him otherwise he was bound to hit someone one day by throwing his arms around and pointing out various sites. I had a bit of fun teasing him about his spatial awareness, while he reminded me about knocking people over with my handbag. It was great that we could laugh at each other's idiosyncrasies.

San Gimignano was a beautiful and picturesque town in Tuscany, set amongst the hills in Northern Italy. The town was historical with lots of older buildings, along with farms and family run wineries. There were lots of stone roads, walkways and steps throughout the little town, with some families having roof terraces that looked out over the luscious hills of the Tuscan villages,

The town was situated between Siena and Florence and when we arrived Blake looked at me with a huge grin. The town was exactly what we imagined a Tuscan village to look like, with the character filled stone homes, tiny rooms, roof terraces for entertaining and kicking back. The Italians really knew how to have a good life, enjoy the company of family and friends, whilst savouring the lovely home cooked cuisine from the freshly picked vegetables from the garden.

We walked up to a family run winery where there was a little restaurant overlooking the valley. We enjoyed tasting the delicacies of the land consisting of marinated eggplant, artichokes, salami preserved in fennel seed, with sun-dried tomatoes, pecorino cheese, olives with fresh homemade bread. The family served us a tasting platter along with the red wine made and fermented on the farm. It was so tasty, and the wine accompanied the dishes so well. In the corner of the room was an old wooden piano, and an older man was playing a melodious Italian folk song. The owner's son was serving other visitors, singing in a rich baritone, an opera ensemble that echoed throughout the small room, and down the valley for everyone to hear. The sound bounced off the walls, a perfect vibration of passion of a God-given voice, in perfect pitch and tone. I paused to take in the sounds and smell of this place, tantalising all of the senses in so many ways.

The bus trip back was bumpy, along the narrow roads winding through the hills. It was such a lovely drive seeing the countryside and small villages scattered here and there. The homes were working farms with lots of vegetation, olive plants and even grape vines. Some of the properties were a little run down, quite rustic I would say, and it would have been very difficult to do any major renovations in these remote places. Yet these people were content and were not concerned about building 'bigger barns' so to speak.

Back home, it was all about the great Australian dream to own your home with a plot of land, a white picket fence and that was all in the name of success. For us we were renting an apartment, and not knowing if we could ever afford a home in Sydney. I was trying to establish a part-time business as a counsellor, as I believed it was the ministry that I was called to, while Blake had only just started in Insurance Broking. I was feeling a little deflated about the possibility of settling in an area, and having more children, when the house prices were going skywards. I had to keep reminding myself that doing God's will was super important and that He was going to provide what we needed. This was a daily thing for me, to remind myself how big God was and that even the impossible was possible with the Lord.

I would often glance at Blake over dinner, and would be truly thankful that the Lord had put him into my life as my husband. We were such a fierce team, both passionate about serving the Lord and doing His will. His blue eyes were mesmerising, as they revealed his gentle loving soul, which always created a spark in me. I enjoyed listening to music together, while we chatted about our family planning, our vision that was solely dependent on our Lord and Saviour. We both knew that being in God's will would truly bring us peace and an everlasting joy, a different type of success than the world would employ. At times when we were tempted to do things our way, we could gently remind each other of this.

Afterall, we were surrounded at times with successful worldly people with great wealth, power and status, yet their lives seemed so empty as they were chasing the next big thing. As in the book of Ecclesiasties, it was like chasing the wind under the sun which amounts to nothing in the end, and is meaningless according to God. Our vision was around creating eternal wealth that could not burn up and would be pleasing to our Lord.

However, knowing all of this we really had to fill our minds with the Word of God to resist the pull and influences of the world, our own fleshly desires and the enemy who was trying very hard to destroy us, cause fear and make us ineffective Christians. That is why it was important to be aware of Satan's strategies, so that we are not caught off guard. The Bible talks about being prepared as a soldier, an athlete and farmer who all had to be disciplined, trained and intentional in their actions. Yet, at times we forget, and leave ourselves exposed, hence suffer the consequences of being lazy or foolish. Thanks be to God, who often protects us by His grace. I often thought back to the times, where my life was protected, and even recently through counselling some disturbing demonically controlled clients.

I thought about my recurring dream as a young child of people on fire, calling out to me to help them, their flesh burning in what seemed like hell. Their torment was so evident on their faces, as I stood there wondering what I could do to help them. It was sharing the good news of Jesus who does not want anyone to perish but come to a saving faith. It dawned on me how precious the gift of salvation was, and I had the life raft to help as many people that God put in my path.

Blake and I were thankful that we could have this time to travel to these beautiful places in Europe and create our own memories for our life together as a couple. It was clear to us that our old life before becoming committed followers of Christ, was part of the growing process, but it was nothing compared to the new life we have been given through our Saviour. As per Apostle Paul, an elite Pharisee stated that his life was rubbish before he came to know Jesus.

The streets in Nice were lit up at night, and the glow of the yellow painted stone buildings provided a warm ambience that was embracing. There were people everywhere having dinner together, laughing and enjoying the company of one another. The older part of Nice had the narrow cobblestone roads similar to Rome, which were tough on your feet. It was also very clean as people made an effort to upkeep their apartments and villas.

The next morning we were on our way to Paris, having bought two rail tickets, with no sleepers available. Blake suggested that we could find an empty sleeper or enough seating for us to sleep through the night. Unfortunately the train was overcrowded and we could only find one seat which meant we had to take turns sitting over the seven hour journey. That was so tough, especially at night. Thankfully we were both still young and could manage standing for a period of time. However it was really tough in the early hours of the morning when we wanted to sleep, and could barely open our eyes. I wanted to get off the train and find some accommodation in one of the towns along the way, but Blake had booked a hotel in Paris, and we had to get there by tomorrow so we decided to persevere the best we could.

It was a long journey, even longer than we thought with nothing to do. I tried to make a game of it, by creating a life story out of each person seated opposite us, hoping that they could not understand English and get offended with what I was saying to Blake. It kept our minds off the journey. I also decided on having a long sleep when we reached Paris. Blake reassured me that usually there were plenty of seats on the Eurail, but something must have gone wrong and the seating was limited.

There were a few people snoring and talking in their sleep, and I tried very hard not to laugh. Blake would drift off to sleep a half an hour or so then give me a seat. I tried to sit on the handles but I would only fall into his lap as I felt my body give way to sleep. I was finding it more and more difficult to keep awake, and at times I felt like I was going to faint. I imagined a nice cosy bed and it only made me more frustrated.

At last we arrived in Paris and we both staggered out of the train like drunkards after a heavy night of booze, yet it was only the lack of sleep that caused us to be unsteady on our feet. I was sure that the cab driver thought we both were either drug induced or intoxicated, as he hesitated in picking us up. Blake's eyes were red and bloodshot and I had dark circles along with smudged mascara, mimicking a panda bear with my dark grey fluffy jumper. We told the driver that we stood most of the night and hardly slept, and he looked at us with compassion.

Once we arrived at the hotel, we were told that our rooms were not prepared and to come back in an hour. Blake and I were so exhausted and we did not know what to do, as all we wanted was to sleep for a few hours. We went to a cafe and had hot chocolate with a croissant. We sat in a booth at the rear, hidden from others and had a quick nap leaning on each other. It was enough to give us a little energy to get back to our hotel, collect our luggage and find our room.

It was lunch time before we awoke, so we had a much needed shower, put on fresh clothes and took a walk. The streets were narrow, with some type of pavers similar to Rome. It was a beautiful city with lots of hidden nooks, amazing buildings of French architecture. We must have walked for two hours before we decided to sit along a fountain to watch the locals gather for lunch and afternoon drinks. There were lots of people everywhere, talking, laughing and riding scooters without helmets.

We found a lovely French bakery where we indulged on savoury croissants, cheese bread and coffee. It was quite cold and it had snowed the night before. We were hoping to see it snow here as it would be a great memory of Paris to take back with us. As we headed along the narrow street, we saw some children playing hopscotch on the pavement, counting in French and it reminded me of my childhood, the innocence and total trust in the world that things would be safe and well. I had a little flashback of my ten year old self, and it made me smile.

We returned to our room, which was cosy, with black and white decor. It was very art deco in style, with a balcony with wrought iron balustrade with enough room to sit and watch the activity below. There was also a lovely hanging basket of flowers that were slowly showing signs of its final bloom before the cold winter. Anyway it was enough colour to enjoy. The television was quite small, and everywhere we went Blake had to turn it on to see what was playing. He was so much like his Mum, who would have the television blaring all day, and I guess she liked the constant noise and distraction. Most of the shows were in French, with not much in English.

That night we ventured out for dinner, and it was freezing. As we were walking along the street, there were fine flakes of snow falling. It was beautiful and we enjoyed the stroll to the restaurant which was fifteen minutes away. The little restaurant had a fireplace, and was very cosy. We enjoyed some lovely french cuisine, of a buttery sauce over the duck, potatoes and long green beans. It was homestyle cooking with the delicate french sauce that we enjoyed after our long long train ride.

The Eiffel Tower was closed that night, so we had to postpone our visit to the following night. After dinner, we strolled along the Seine River, looking at the beautiful gold around the street lamps, the ornate corbels and French architecture. It was a truly beautiful city, and I could now understand why this was such a romantic getaway.

The next night we lined up for the Eiffel Tower, and had to wait forty minutes, then due to a proposed terror attack, we were asked to leave and return the next day. I was so disappointed as we had planned to experience this together. However, a terror attack was serious so we could certainly wait another day.

Before we knew it we were back again at the Tower, praying that it was all clear. Finally after waiting another twenty minutes we were given the green light. We both were so excited, and I could see that Blake was so thrilled to be sharing this time with me. His eyes were glistening in the moonlight, the blue tone, turning a deep green with the reflections of the light. We hugged each other tight and looked up at the Tower, as they motioned us to pass. Blake and I took some great photos of the two of us at the top of the tower, before we were summoned to leave with the group. It was such a cold night, with a chill wind, and a few snowflakes that glistened in the moonlight as they tumbled down from heaven.

The Champs Elysees was iconic to Paris and we strolled along the street at night, as it was even more spectacular when lit up. At the end of the main street, was a huge ferris wheel that allowed you to see the city up high, with all its splendour, lights bouncing off buildings and street lights. Blake and I, our teeth chattering in the cold, still managed to take in this magic night on the ferris wheel. Our carriage stopped at the top, pausing for five minutes rocking to and fro, and we were able to pause and take in this experience that will always be with us. I could not feel my cheeks, as they were frozen in time. Blake's eyelashes were filled with snowflakes as they glistened in the lights. I was so grateful that I had a warm hat that kept my head warm as I could not feel my toes.

We were exhausted from all the walking we did in the cold, and could not wait to have a warm bath in our tub when we got back to the hotel. It was still only the end of autumn moving into winter, so the city was usually blanketed by snow by the middle of the month. It was a good time to experience Paris, as the summer months were even more crowded and it was very hot.

The Louvre was an unusual building in the heart of the traditional, period French buildings, where you have this modern piece of architecture that simply does not fit. The artwork was amazing, and I could have spent two days there as there was so much to see. The Mona Lisa is the most famous of the paintings and I was surprised how small it was. It was protected by thick glass encasing it, and we took some photos without a flash. There were quite a number of biblical paintings including the Last Supper which is often copied. Blake and I both enjoyed exploring the artwork, dating back to the different eras in France, and then comparing it to the modern pieces.

The city of Paris was such a huge city, and having a panoramic view from a tall building one could appreciate the vastness, structure and order of the place. The streets were planned and layed out, along with various precincts, sections and open spaces. It looked like an ordered city that had been carefully thought out, with heaps of character and spectacular architecture. I loved the gold touches on the statues with lampstands along the bridge over the Seine River. It looked even more amazing at night.

Blake and I travelled up to Switzerland, Germany and Austria via the Eurail system. Switzerland was amazing with the huge snow capped mountains, the deep blue lakes, the pine needle trees and landscape. We would look outside our window in the morning and it took our breath away to see the picture framed landscape that even a photo could not replicate its beauty and form.

The Dachau Concentration Camp in Germany was the place where the Jews were imprisoned and tortured for some time during the war. In the entrance, there was a huge black and white picture that extended across the wall of the building of the faces of the prisoners before they were sent to their death in the gas chambers. Their faces told the story of fear, torment and pain as the Germans stripped them of their identity as human beings. They were treated worse than any animal, more like vermin that needed to be exterminated. I stood there and felt the tears roll down my face, stinging with the cold air as I imagined what it would have been like for them. I also thought about how it would have grieved the Lord to see this atrocity. I could not believe that six million of them perished. How could the Germans commit such crimes and be totally brainwashed by Hitler? It was truly appalling to see the ovens where the Jews were burnt alive. The guide told us that the stench that came from the ovens caused the guards to vomit.

We moved along to see the mass graves of some tens of thousands of Jews, of children, women and men who had perished. Along the perimeter there were trenches where soldiers were free to shoot victims as they tried to escape. I felt the heaviness and sadness of the place, where the blood of the victims were spilled all over this land, and the souls of many cried out for justice. There will be justice one day, when the Lord returns to the earth to judge the world, those that have died and the ones left that remain at His coming.

Blake and I walked across to the gas chambers and listened to a guide explaining the events surrounding those that perished, believing that they were showering. So many children and young people perished this way. It was so deceiving and heartbreaking to know that many had lost their lives.

I could not wait to get out of this place, as it was hard to see the depravity of man, slaughtering other human beings like they did not have any value. The snow started to fall and we headed back to the bus to wait for the others.

We were looking forward to getting home, and getting back to our life, after a wonderful holiday and experience. Blake and I learned so much about the countries we visited, and the people we met along the way. I had also learned that I was a chameleon that in most places I visited, people thought I was a local, except in Germany and Switzerland of course. In France and Italy in particular, people would often approach me and speak in their native language, believing I was a local. I also experienced this in Israel and Turkey.

It was such a buzz to see the Harbour Bridge, Opera House and Centrepoint building as the plane flew into Mascot. It is always so good to return home, and we were looking forward to seeing our family and Will, who we missed so much. Looking over this peaceful harbour and contemplating the safety of home, I had no idea of what was ahead of us, the next chapter in our life. The world was about to change, and yet this moment in time was both captivating and pure. I took a deep breath and savoured the moment.

Chapter 21

Shock and Awe

It was September 11, 2001 and we had awoken to the attack on the World Trade Centre. I was in shock, having been there myself not that long ago. I went in the lift to the top viewing floor in the South Tower, and it was such a solid structure, especially the foyer area with the huge columns of concrete and metal. I remember standing on the top floor near one of the office windows and taking a photo looking down with my feet on the edge. I could see small people like ants scurrying around frantically. It seemed impossible for this building to crumble like a stack of cards. It appeared that the US was under attack, and the world had changed.

Blake was on his way to work, and I called him with the news. We had received a call in the middle of the night from his brother who had seen the first plane fly into the north tower, but we thought it was a prank call and did not answer. He left a message telling us what he had seen in real time. There was rolling coverage on each of the television channels, with images of the planes flying into the buildings. Now both towers had collapsed or imploded in a cloud of dust and debris.

When Blake got home, I walked over to him and asked him, "How are we to bring up a baby in this world of such evil acts?" He smiled realising that I had my pregnancy confirmed and then gave me a big hug and turned me around. I could not wipe the grin off his face, and he then took in what I had said, and reassured me that the Lord holds us in the palm of His hand, and we are safe. I was six weeks pregnant and the baby was due at the end of May 2002. In my moments of such happy news, I felt the pang of grief for the people that were enduring such atrocities in the United States.

The next day, I drove over to see my Mum and told her the news about the pregnancy. She was delighted and gave me a big hug, excited about gaining another grandchild. We talked about the terrorist attack again, and I shared with her about my concerns about bringing up children in this world, where terror and evil acts were increasing in intensity and frequency. Yet she also reminded me again that the Lord is still on His throne and controls all things. We are all safe in His hands. Whenever doubt came knocking on my door, I was reminded of this.

Our whole world changed that day, with these attacks that were televised around the world. The fear of man had penetrated through so many spheres that now security and safety were high on the agenda. People were terrified to travel, and it brought the economy and our way of life to a standstill.

When I arrived at work each of the counsellors had been inundated by phone calls, with people wanting to see us. The next few weeks we had a huge intake of clients.

It was difficult to know how to best help people when we were still processing these attacks ourselves. I then realised that they just needed someone to help them discuss the events, and help them to grapple with their own beliefs and worldview.

Over the next few weeks, the clients continued to come through our centre, with issues of fear and anxiety. I thought to myself that this was something that the church was capable of handling, yet many were not comfortable about turning to the church for help. There may be exceptions as the media were reporting that the attendance level for mainline churches had increased in the last month or so. Again, the doomsdayers were promoting 'the end of the world', and even the media jumped on the bandwagon with the end of days, apocalypse type movies. This obviously fuelled the fear, as the world had become unsafe, unpredictable and scary for so many, particularly those that did not have the hope and comfort of eternal life as in the Christian worldview.

Some months later, Jane went on leave again and I filled in for her in looking after Jessica, her client with the dissociative identity disorder. My workload was easing off now, since life started to get back to some sort of normal. I thought that the disruption and intensity of the last six months would eventually settle, at least it was what I was hoping for now that I was pregnant.

Jessica came in early one Tuesday morning, and sat in the reception waiting for me. I was running a little late, hoping I would be there earlier in time to review my notes, and answer my messages. I was not feeling the best with morning sickness but there were only two counsellors on the roster this morning, so I tried to make myself well and get to the centre as soon as possible.

She came in and sat on the couch. Jane had prepared some notes and I was to follow on from there. I had looked at her file last week, so I was familiar with the tasks that were set. Jane had uncovered an order to her transitions now, whereby some years ago Jessica was all over the place.

She looked over to me, while I made some notes and told me that my baby was moving. I could feel the flutter on and off as I was around eighteen weeks, but it was very faint and I had not shown any expression or signs of any surprise of the movement. I asked her how she knew, and she gave me an impish smile, and shrugged. She then said, "I just know." The thought of her knowing brought a shiver down my spine. It also made me annoyed, because I knew that she was operating with an evil power of divination.

I quickly moved on, not wanting to give into this power, and checked in with her on the exercise that Jane gave her to do. She took a piece of paper with some drawings. Jessica began to explain in the drawings how the different identities and alters back each other up. In times of crisis or stress, the different identities step in to protect the vulnerable one. In the drawing there was this black cloud with lightning reigning down. It looked dark and angry, and Jessica made a point of explaining that this was the dark spirit that controlled some of the alters. It had power to control and even cause harm. I noticed that there were exclamations of messages from each of the alters, such as, "Help! Don't harm me! Stop you are hurting me. Stop, stop!" Jessica went on to explain how the dark spirits would inflict harm and pain on her, and that is when she would split off into one of the alters. It became her coping mechanism. However, I was a little concerned about the ability to cause harm and injure others.

I listened intently to Jessica explaining in detail how the alters operated, with each of them having special abilities and levels of control. Something was just not right, and the question was how could one be a Christian and operate or function in this way? Jessica was insistent that she was a Christian, whilst attending church and even joining a Bible study group. She was not a stable person, and these alters had power over her from time to time. I put big question marks on my notes, highlighting specific details of the discussion. I was also asking the Lord for wisdom in how to deal with this, as it messed with my mind and spirit. I could feel the effects of this controlling and manipulative force, so I prayed against it. I had come to believe that once the person became a believer through genuine repentance, and trust in the Lord Jesus, the Holy Spirit took up residence in the person's life so that any other spirit that does not bow down to Jesus will leave immediately.

I put this in my notes, as it seemed to me that Jessica was under the control of something else, and she in turn operated to control and manipulate people in her life. She was also capable of bringing harm to an individual, as she had explained moments of rage and violence. She had tried to hurt Jane on multiple occasions with various objects in the room.

It was apparent to me that Jessica was uncomfortable with our sessions, and then often the older mature alter would take over and become very defensive. The queasy feeling started to come back again, and I tried to breathe to avoid the reflux and urge to vomit. We sat there for ten or fifteen minutes as Jessica refused to speak. Jane advised me to expect moments of silence as Jessica would be overwhelmed and tired. The time was eventually over, and I admittedly felt relief, as it was very difficult to be in this presence.

With a series of spiritual encounters I was learning to understand the strategies of Satan and his minions. Most cases were not like the exorcist movies with spinning heads, levitation and material manifestations, even though these things can happen. Afterall, Satan was not purposely trying to scare us, but in fact was trying very hard to disguise himself as an angel of light, as he is a deceiver. In fact, after researching the cases, one could see the entry point, sometimes it was trauma that occurred in a person's life, unforgiveness, addictions, idolatry, violence, pornography. It was like allowing mice or rats into your house to take up residence, and before long they would multiply and affect the order in your home. The person would then become demonised which would infiltrate into their thinking, and translating into their actions. The only way is to repent of the sin, which means to do a 180 turn, close the door of entry, call on the name of Jesus as your Saviour and Lord, and the demons will flee.

In addition, it is important to maintain a Godly life, or they will return. If the Holy Spirit does not take up residence in the person, then they are exposed to unclean spirits. After several encounters with the demonic I soon recognised the signs: enlarged dark pupils, facial contortions, refusal of eye contact, guttural tone of voice, a sudden change in personality, and trembling. I could feel the hatred emanating from the individual towards me, and it was chilling to say the least. I imagined that it would be like looking into the eyes of a serial killer.

I had also learned that Christians can be oppressed by these demons, if they continually walk in sin, gratifying the flesh. Sometimes it is their carnal nature with no demon activity, but sometimes it is demonic activity. As I studied King David and Saul in the Bible, I could see that both had sins, even murder yet King David had a repentant heart and turned back to God in humility. Saul did not do this, even when God sent an evil spirit to harass him and steal his peace, he continued in his sin.

Jesus also indicated in his gospels where the spirit of infirmity was cast out of the woman in Luke 13:11, where she was bent over for eighteen years. It was a physical condition, indicating that these spirits can affect humans physically as well as mentally.

Blake also made me aware that my concentration with all things evil was a trick used by Satan to distract me, giving him more power than required. I did not like being told this, and it was my carnal nature to defend myself, yet I took this to the Lord in prayer and repented. Satan and his minions were seducing many of our counsellors into believing that they had the power in knowledge to deliver people, when in actual fact we were the earthen vessels used by Jesus to do His work by grace.

Whilst I was trying so hard to figure all this out, I was also being deceived. It really hurt coming to terms with how cunning the enemy was, using pride in my heart to deceive myself. Blake and I would argue about this, and I could see that he also was so used to the Hollywood version of evil, when in actual fact it was often disguised and repackaged in everyday life, albeit through the media, entertainment industry, social media and addictions of various types and regular people.

It was crucial to be discerning and have a balanced view of the spirit world. The enemy used various ways to do his bidding, and each one of us can be deceived. We had to have a holistic understanding of humanity, and explore each before making any diagnosis. Also it was extremely important to have a close relationship with Jesus, as He was the source of strength and sovereignty. It was only by His authority and His alone that we can help people that are demonised.

I reflected on the scripture in 1 John 4:4 Greater is He that is in you that he that is in the world. I knew that no one could touch me unless Jesus allowed it. Jesus had me in the palm of His hand and whether I lived or died, I belonged to Him. I did not enjoy this confrontation and looking into the eyes of evil, but I found it a great joy to see people set free, unchained from the bondage of sin.

It was evident that we were in a spiritual battle, and the enemy was putting up a fight to change our culture, breakdown the family unit, contaminate the purity of children, murder, violence and lawlessness, just to name a few strategies. As Christians we were here to restrain evil, through the indwelling of the Holy Spirit, and to fight for our families. Paul encourages christians to protect their families from Satan's attacks and stand firm for the truth of the Gospel (2 Thess 3:1-5 and Ephesians 6).

That night, I cooked a chicken stir fry for dinner, when Blake arrived home. He had a good day, and told me all about his encounter with some new prospective clients. He was building a book of business, and it seemed to be rolling in, which was such a blessing. He was the breadwinner and in a short time, I was going to stop work to look after our baby.

A few months on, I was getting more movement with the baby, a flicker now becoming little jabs here and there. It was exciting feeling this little life slowly blooming inside of me. I would try and get Blake to place his hands on my tummy, and he felt the little jab. He was so tickled by it, and we would laugh thinking about this small person forming a combination of both our genes. "Maybe this little one may be a footballer, or at least like football," he stated with such confidence. We were both so excited and looking forward to meeting our little baby that was forming, a life that God had created.

The week went so fast and it was already Sunday. After breakfast Blake and I headed off to church, and we were on the roster to meet visitors and or new believers. It was always exciting meeting new people and hearing their story. As we were chatting to the new couples, Jessica grabbed my hand. I turned around to see her with a reddish stain on her shirt, which she was trying to cover up. It looked odd, and it felt a little strange. Blake also saw her, and pulled me over to the side, away from her.

She had cast a spell on a lot of people at church, those that could be easily manipulated and fascinated by her transformations. I believed that Jessica, knew that I could discern what was happening by her divination ability, and was trying very hard to control me also.

On the way home, my mind was wandering thinking about Jessica and the mark on her shirt that she was trying to cover up. It looked like dried blood, or maybe it was coffee or chocolate but something did not feel right to me. I did not want to talk to Blake about it, because he may try to convince me that It was something explainable.

We were sitting on the couch watching the end of Sixty Minutes, when Blake turned to me and said, "Did you get a strange feeling about Jessica, that she was trying to hide something?" I blurted out, "Yes I was thinking about it on the way home, and something does not seem right. I had an uneasy feeling about her tonight." I was amazed how intuitive Blake was, and he trusted my judgement. It was so good to be able to talk to him about it, without him dismissing the notion.

The next morning I was sitting on the balcony having a cup of tea and raisin toast, when breaking news came on. There was a missing girl around fourteen years of age that disappeared from a train station at Waterfall. Her parents reported her missing on Saturday night when she failed to return home from shopping. They thought that she had gone to a friend's place, and were frantically searching for her, because it was out of character for her to go missing without advising her parents. I thought she may have run away, as fourteen is a difficult age.

It was hard to motivate myself to get ready, especially when I knew I was seeing Jessica. I had to be alert and vigilant because she was a difficult client, and I was feeling a little vulnerable not feeling like myself.

Thankfully there were a few people in the medical centre when I arrived. I did not want to be on my own with Jessica. This was the last session with her before Jane returned from holidays, and I was grateful to be handing her back. She arrived and took a seat on the couch. Jessica was pulling at her sleeves and adjusting her shirt, looking somewhat uncomfortable.

She came into the counselling room with her water bottle and handbag. I was wondering whether anyone had searched her bag, so I asked her to open it. Since our encounter with Natasha carrying a knife, we were vigilant on checking particular clients for weapons. Jessica had her phone, wallet and some tissues. I asked her about her weekend and she told me that she went to Bundeena on a bushwalk, after meeting up with some friends at the station.

As I looked down at her feet, I saw some red stains on her shoes. It looked like blood stains, so I tried not to be alarmed, and asked her whether she had fallen and cut herself. She looked at me a little shocked and tried to tuck her feet under the chair. She seemed guilty of something and was trying to hide, and I could see she was feeling uneasy about the line of questioning.

As I desperately tried to disguise my thoughts, Jessica switched, telling me that she fell when she went bushwalking resulting in cuts and bruises on her body. Jessica did have some bruises on her arm, so the story seemed legitimate, but there was something more to this.

It was difficult to remember all the identities, and Jane had dutifully written them in the file for me. I think this was Martha who showed up and was a motherly type, although somewhat bossy. She bossed all the other alters around and was certainly the caretaker. When things got tough for the younger alters, Martha stepped in and took over. I was certainly seeing that now. Martha would speak so fast, and was very eloquent in her language, her choice of expressions, which showed her worldly experience.

Martha often talked about the places she travelled to, from Europe to the Middle East. She even went to India and was very interested in the mystical and spiritual worship over there. She often talked about her collection of incense and fragrances that meant different things. There was also an array of wooden artefacts and ornaments that represented the natural and supernatural worlds. She even carried these ornamental gods around with her in the backpack that became her signature look and her source of comfort.

As Martha kept talking about the bushwalking, the trails were filled with lots of shrubs with spiny leaves that were sharp. It would explain the scratches on her legs and the bloody spots on her shoes. I found that my mind was wandering thinking about the idol she pulled out. I tried to focus on what she was saying, and I could feel the presence of something sinister that was messing with my mind. I stopped, took a breath and prayed, as I could see a wry smile on Martha (Jessica's) face. She was manipulating me, trying very hard to distract me.

There was a heaviness in the air and I could feel this cold draft, making my hairs on my arms stand up. Martha (Jessica) began to show signs of switching, with her face contorting and her eyes rolling back in her head. I could see the whites of her eyes looking at me, her mouth twitching as she panted. It was terrifying watching her transform, but sensing that she was being overtaken by some other spirit.

Whilst many mental health professionals saw this splitting as a psychological illness and sometimes it can be, I was seeing something quite different with Jessica, a spiritual battle manifesting before my eyes. I asked her if she was okay, but her eyes were rolling backwards, and then she stared at me, a cold heartless stare, and I could see pure hatred in her eyes. It was chilling, and my heart skipped a beat. Was I looking into the eyes of an evil entity? The blood had drained from her face, and she looked like a corpse yet I could hear her heavy breathing and panting. She kept inhaling loudly and blowing out, as if she was fighting for every breath. What was happening?

I held my breath as I prayed softly to Jesus, asking Him to help me. Jessica closed her eyes again, and I was hoping that she would keep them closed. I did not want to look into the eyes of the evil spirit that had manifested before me. I reached for the panic button, then paused when she started to say something in a low guttural voice, a tone that I had not heard.

It was so scary, and I did not know what I was hearing. It did not sound human, but a base tone, whispering some words that I was trying to catch without flinching. It was trying to tell me something, and it repeated the phrase, "I took her... life... I... snapped... her throat...I drew her blood... she is gone... (*a long pause*) Leave me alone! I hate you! I hate you!" She shouted back at me. I did not want to communicate with this thing, and I told it to stop and be quiet. I sensed the presence and comfort from the Holy Spirit, and I didn't even realise that I had called the name of Jesus out loud. Jessica started to tremble, then shaking uncontrollably, and she abruptly got up and left the room, slamming the door.

I remained on the couch, my body trembling, as I was feeling vulnerable being pregnant and unable to properly defend myself if she became violent. I knew Jesus would protect me, so the fear was slowly dissipating. I sat there thinking through what she was saying, making sure I wrote this down for Jane to follow up. I did not know whether this was something to report, as Jessica talked about taking someone's life. Was it a dream or just a threat of some sort? I was not sure if she was talking about some sort of satanic ritual. I decided to discuss this with my supervisor, hoping that he was available to see whether this was something that the police needed to investigate.

I was so nervous but had to make the call, despite not being able to advise Jane of this. After speaking with the senior counsellor and Supervisor we made the decision to contact the police. The policewoman took down the details, and told me that she would follow up the lead.

For weeks I did not hear from anyone on this. Jane returned from her break and we told her about the decision to report to the police. I could tell that she was not very happy with the news, and Jessica had not returned to the centre for some weeks now. I could certainly understand her disappointment as she had spent years counselling her. I could see that Jessica was often falling back into her cult. It was best to hand this over to the police to investigate, and see if there are any links.

I was getting ready for work and I overheard the news stating that they had found the body of a young girl in the mangroves at the back of Kurnell. I waddled to the television and turned up the volume. The body was badly decomposed so they were trying to identify her. I was wondering whether it was the girl that went missing a few weeks ago.

When I arrived at work, I discussed this with my colleagues. The girl was in a shallow grave, and they showed the site on the news. There were some markings on the trees and a chain between one tree and the other, and a fire pit of some sort. It looked quite strange. The police were trying to identify what had happened at the site.

A few days later, I called the local police station to follow up, but hung up, realising that they could not provide me with an update until they completed their investigation. The news report mentioned that the body had some unusual markings on it. I remembered years ago before Will was born finding a goat's head with a green pentagram on its forehead on my front lawn, and later realised that it symbolised some satanic ritual.

I froze at the thought that this murder may have been satanically inspired. Was the satanic cult behind this? It all made sense, that Jessica seemed very suspicious, trying to hide the blood stains on her clothing and shoes. I had a strange feeling when speaking to her, and I wondered whether the police interviewed her. Was it just circumstantial evidence or did Jessica witness murder? Was she involved? My mind was racing with hundreds of thoughts thinking back to the words she said during the session. She had suddenly disappeared, and had not kept her last two appointments which was unusual for her. She was always on time, and did not miss appointments unless she was unwell.

A week later, the police confirmed that the body they found in the mangroves was that of the missing fourteen year old girl. I felt so sorry for the family that were so grief stricken, and heartbroken to hear that their beautiful daughter had been taken from them in such a brutal act.

I only had two more weeks before going on maternity leave, and I wanted justice for this fourteen year old girl. I knew that I needed to hand this over to the Lord, praying for His power and justice over this horrendous crime.

The next day, two policemen showed up at the counselling centre and asked to speak to me. I took them into one of the rooms, and was feeling a little nervous. They advised that they have some leads on the case of the murder, and were still investigating. I was also asked not to see Jessica until they made an arrest. I mentioned that Jessica had not turned up anyway for her last two appointments. Unfortunately Jane was not in so I would have to convey this message to her. Hearing this warning from the policemen, was a little scary as it indicated that there may have been some possible link with the Satanic Cult and the murder.

I had no actual contact with the other cult members, except a few that cussed me when I walked down the stairs of the centre. I wondered how many people went missing that were not investigated, in which these satanic cults had some links with. Were they still practicing human sacrifices and torture as part of their worship? There was human trafficking going on involving children and young girls in various parts of the world. I had heard this from an international mission group who reported that these children were subject to satanic ritual abuse. This ritual abuse involved heinous sexual acts. I felt sick in the stomach and angry that this was going on. I prayed that the Lord would rescue these children through these mission groups, and that the government would put an end to this. God's wrath was going to be poured out on these perpetrators that corrupt the innocence of children.

After the policemen left, I called the prayer team and asked them to pray for our safety at the centre, not knowing whether this was going to escalate. Then I called Jane and explained what the policeman had told me and asked her to contact them for any further clarification. Our church leaders were initially unaware of how infiltrating and intentional these new age and satanic cults were, in bringing us all down. Thankfully they installed panic buttons in the rooms and hired a security guard for the after hours appointments.

As I conversed with christians from various churches and ministries, they were unaware of the dangers of new age and witchcraft infiltrating their churches. They had fallen prey to the Hollywood spin doctors who deceivingly glamourised it, disguising it as entertainment. It was quite subtle at first, but it became more dark and evil, corrupting the minds of little children. Why wasn't anyone warning people about this? Were the church leaders afraid to offend people? Jesus warned so many times to watch and pray and let no one deceive you.

Parents were buying fantasy, sorcery and occult books, delighted that their children were encouraged to read, as the magic was good for their imagination. How deceiving was this, because it was a gateway to the world of the occult? I experienced this myself and fell for the lie.

Teenagers have a heightened spiritual awareness, and may have the desire to explore the enticing and sexy world of the occult. It gave them power over others, but the cost of dabbling into this was dire as it encouraged an escape mentality, repackaged as entertainment. It appeals to the creative part of the brain, tantalising the natural sinful desires. I saw the web of lies, layers upon layers of deception taking people further down the road of fantasy to the edge of insanity where one could not discern the difference between true reality and a self created world.

This was the slippery slope into lawlessness because of idolatry (creating your own god including the god of 'self') where people did what was right in their own eyes. It creates a culture where there is no respect or care for the governing laws or authority, or the value of a fellow human being. It creates a world that is cold, heartless and selfish rather than others centred. We were hearing about mass shootings where young people were acting out their fantasy of taking out targets, ignoring the reality and consequences of taking the life of a human being. It is not a game!

I watched those that were caught in this trap of deception live in a constant state of anxiety and fear. They described the fear as if their body was under a constant assault with no reprieve, no peace and no love. They once felt the excitement of power, but it quickly entangled them in a web of lies, a prison where there was no escape. They were under surveillance and felt the prying eyes of a demonic being watching them. Satan had seduced them, with the bait and switch trick, and now they were enslaved. Satan does not understand love, only hate fills his being. He wants to enslave and take people to hell.

This is the old strategy that the enemy uses to lure people to become a god of their life, to have control over other people, creation and mess with God's order.

The boundary that God set was for our own good and to protect us in Genesis 1-3. Once we delve outside of this boundary, we invite Satan and his minions in to terrorise us and rob us of our peace and well being.

As I was becoming more aware of the cunning deception, I reached out to warn fellow christians of this, but sadly their response was defensive. Were they threatened by something that was disruptive to their neatly packaged safe Christian world? They did not want to rock the boat, but clearly addictions, idolatry and sorcery brought confusion, extreme anxiety and disharmony. God is not a God of confusion but order, reason and truth. It was clear, as in Galations 5: 16-22. Why would they not listen? I was so thankful that Blake was so discerning and backed me up one hundred per cent on this. Together we were a strong force, but we had to remain vigilant, watch and pray.

Chapter 22

Blessed by Two Princesses

Little Sarina was a beautiful baby, and the doctor gave her a clean bill of health. She brought a lot of joy watching her observing us, watching our expressions and facial movements. She seemed quite fascinated with everything that moved, like a little sponge. Blake would play his guitar and she was beaming up at him with her gums showing, indicating the delight in music. Maybe she was going to be a musician, as she loved hearing him strum his guitar.

I was going to protect this little baby, and show how wonderful life can be with parents that loved the Lord. It was going to be different this time, and I was certainly a person who had grown spiritually and emotionally. It was such a privilege to know that I was going to be a stay at home mum for a while and enjoy motherhood. I realised that I could not hand this baby over to the care of others, even family members as she needed the assurance and trust that I was going to be there for her. The first five years of a child's life were the building blocks in creating trust and safety, so I was determined to make whatever financial sacrifices we needed to make in order to be obedient to the Lord. I also understood that in our world, a mortgage was such a huge expense and sometimes it required both parents to maintain employment to make it work. This time, I really felt the Lord impress on me that this was the way to go, and that He would provide our needs.

I was able to finish up with my counselling for the time being, but it did not preclude me from assisting with pastoral care work through the home groups and other mums that needed care. However I kept in touch with my colleagues at the counselling centre from time to time. It seemed that there were some financial constraints, along with spiritual opposition from a number of sources that would eventually make the business unviable.

It was such a disappointment to see the centre going through this difficult cycle, as it serviced a large community of people that needed support. I could not understand what God was doing here, and the scars of disappointment and disillusionment kept festering internally, and I knew I would have to work through it, and allow forgiveness to reign in my heart.

I bumped into Jessica at church and she boldly approached me at the base of the stairs of the church. I was not sure what had happened with her and why she had disappeared for the last few weeks. I decided not to enter into any discussion, but she asked me about my baby, and whether she could hold Sarina. I turned to her and said No!, and I continued to walk up the stairs. It really gave me the creeps, as I did not trust her one bit, and I was not going to be pressured into handing over my precious daughter to her. She gave me a wry smile, so cold and calculating and I just ignored her.

That was the last time I saw Jessica, and my colleagues advised me that she had moved away towards the Central Coast. The murder case for the fourteen year old girl was still unsolved, and the police had no witnesses or proof to arrest anyone, although they had a number of suspects, but because the body was badly decomposed, there was not enough evidence or DNA of the murderer or weapon to make an arrest.

I was praying that they would find the persons responsible as it was so suspicious. This whole situation with the cult seemed suspicious but there was not enough evidence. I knew one day, justice will prevail. God knows the truth and He will bring whoever is responsible to account. Even though these terrible things had happened, the Lord still sits on His throne and is sovereign. I had to remind myself of this from time to time, as the fear set in.

We finally bought a house in the south west of Sydney and it was a modest three bedroom home that needed updating. It was close to all the amenities but some distance away from our family. It was a little daunting at first, being so far away from our friends and family, knowing that we would need to make new friends and find a church close by. I convinced myself that it was all going to work out, having prayed about this for a number of years. The housing market was at a peak, and with one salary our choices were limited. The market was crazy, and good properties got snapped up quickly, so we had to act very fast.

It was a cozy home, with a spacious lounge and main bedroom. The other areas in the home were quite small. The kitchen cabinets were atrocious with wood grain finishes on the cabinet, but we would have to make do with it until we could renovate. Whoever built this house did not have good taste with the decor, and even the bathrooms were an electric blue colour. However the house was clean and in good condition considering it was built in the 1980's and was now around eighteen years old. The carpets were brand new and were beige, so it was easy to adapt a neutral colour scheme.

It felt really great to be able to decorate our home without having to consult the landlord for their approval. We also needed to renovate and add some value to the home. The backyard was spacious and relatively flat so it was safe for our young toddler. Will was now eleven years old and would come to visit from time to time. It was tough not having him around regularly, while trying to negotiate more time with him without Will being affected. I felt for Will, having to be in this situation with a split family, but I was always reminded to keep away from any power struggle and to put his well being before mine. At times it made me very sad, as I could only do my part to bring some normalcy to the situation.

I was more determined to make my marriage and family work, so that we could thrive as individuals and a team under the authority of our Lord and Saviour. It was this commitment that gave me the grace I needed to work through times of pain and difficulty. I knew that any relationship was a myriad of ups and downs, and that whatever happened, if the husband and wife are submitted to God and one another, we could work through any issue together.

I saw myself as the gatekeeper of my home, and in that I would do everything I can to maintain our christian worldview, morals and our Christlike identity. I did not know what was next in God's calendar, but I was learning to trust Him, knowing that He was holding me and my family in the palm of His hands.

As a stay at home mum, life was so different but I was up for the challenge. At times it was lonely not having another adult to talk to, but I was so busy teaching Sarina new skills, and experiences that the day went quickly. We also ventured out for walks and made friends with the locals.

I missed my previous home, where there were local parks, and community within walking distance, including friends from church. I also missed my friend Tina who was a great support to me during my times as a counsellor. She was such a good listener, and allowed me to open up without interjecting and turning the subject back to her. I had come across so many narcissistic conversationalists that found ways to circumvent the discussion back to themselves. They would ask you a question, but not wait for the answer, before interrupting and relating the answer back to them. Maybe they enjoyed hearing the sound of their voice, and were not aware of their need to monopolise the discussion. I found myself shying away from people like that because they did not seem genuine enough to care about what was going on in my world. Trust was still an issue in my life. I needed to grow in grace, and bear with others better, not write them off.

They say that each person would only have two or three close people as friends that genuinely cared about them, and as the years passed by I found myself shrinking back from only acquaintances to working on deeper friendships. This took effort and time, but it was valuable in the long run.

Sarina was two years old and she was full of life, a little climber and I had to watch her continually. She was full of mischief, and wonder as she explored everything around her. It was such a blessing to see the intrigue through the eyes of a child, as we tend to lose this sense of wonder as we get older and routine sets in. I could see how children were such a blessing, as it reminds us of our own innocence and wonder. I did not want to lose that sense of wonder or inquisitiveness as it keeps you youthful.

After the miscarriage three months ago, I was still dealing with the loss. I had seen and heard the baby's heartbeat through the ultrasound, and the excitement of conceiving so soon after Sarina was approaching fourteen months, it meant that the next baby would be close in age.

At times I would cry in the shower, as I let the grief spill out freely. I did not want Sarina or Blake to see me breakdown like this. I guess there was a lot of pent up grief that I had held onto since my Dad passed away, then letting Will go to live with his father. It was all just spilling out of me in waves. I did not know that one can hold onto such pain for so long, and then it is triggered with the loss of a child. Even though the baby was still an embryo, it was still a soul, a child with a spirit. It was our little baby, that we would not know until the day we stepped into Heaven, and hoped that we would be greeted by this sweet human that was our child. It was something I kept reminding myself of and it brought me some comfort.

Eight months later, I was pregnant again and I was so excited. It happened a lot sooner than I thought, but I was looking forward to the new baby. I kept this pregnancy quiet for a little while until it was twelve weeks. Sarina was so excited to hear that she was getting a new sister or brother, someone she could boss around.

Thankfully I did not get morning sickness too bad, but instead it was reflux at night that made it difficult to eat. I had to eat small meals all day, and very little at night. I had to sleep upwards so that the reflux would not burn my oesophagus with the acid rising up from my stomach. My mother and sisters were very excited to hear the news of the pregnancy.

As I arrived in the hospital on the Friday afternoon after the doctor triggered my labour that morning during my antenatal visit. Having decided to take an epidural due to the position of the baby, things went a little wrong. The anaesthetist had given me the injection incorrectly, paralysing my lower part of my body, my legs and now it was working up towards my lungs. Before long, the hospital emergency button was triggered and a bunch of doctors barged in, with Blake looking astonished and helpless not knowing what was going on. However, I did not panic as I usually do but felt a sense of peace, and I asked him to pray, whispering and gasping at the same time, as I felt my whole body becoming numb. Was this how it ended for me? My breathing became harder and I could feel myself slowly drifting asleep. Something had gone horribly wrong and the doctors were panicking, trying to neutralise the effect of the epidural. I prayed for the little baby inside the birth canal, trying to find its way out.

I slowly began to feel my upper body and could breathe, but only shallow breaths. I kept fighting it and I could feel the tears streaming down my face as I looked over to Blake who was talking to the doctors and asking a bunch of questions.

Noelle was born, and looked identical to Sarina. She was a little princess, beautiful rosy cheeks and red lips, with a perfect little nose. How sweet it was now that little Sarina had a baby sister. After the scare, I tried to push it back for a bit and enjoy the beautiful little girl that God had given me, my little precious Noelle. I prayed that she did not have any adverse effects, or abnormalities due to this medical procedure. She was in the Lord's hands and I thanked him for this lovely gift. How could I have enough love that I experienced for Sarina for little Noelle as well? Somehow, I knew that there was a capacity deep within me like a well of spring fresh water that bubbles up to the surface and dissipates in a circular motion. I hung onto this picture and it brought a smile to my lips.

Some weeks had passed and I was enjoying motherhood, with two small infants that filled my world up with so much wonder, excitement and delight. I was so thankful for this experience, and wondered how I even deserve this. My heart was so full, that I felt it could burst!

Noelle was six months old now, and we decided to take a road trip up to the Sunshine Coast. It was a brave thing to do, given the fact I was still breastfeeding and we had quite a drive, so we decided to break the journey up and stay at Coffs Harbour and The Gold Coast.

Along the way Sarina sang her little lungs out, just as Dr Child prophesied when she was born : she was going to be a singer! We were amazed to hear her sing, 'The Prayer' in her own Italian language! Noelle blew raspberries to accompany Sarina throughout the song. Blake and I laughed and laughed with joy.

We had exposed our girls to opera, musicals and tenors so that they would have an appreciation for various types of music. The pop music of the day was becoming increasingly toxic, and a bad influence on the younger generation. At times it really concerned me about the unwanted influences that were polluting our children. It was becoming more and more difficult for Christian parents to police, and we had to learn to live in the world and not of the world.

Noosa was such a beautiful place, and little Noelle cooed her way in the car, smiling at us singing, and hearing her sister giggle from time to time. This was such a lovely time that I will always cherish. I looked at Blake who was smiling at me, also thinking the same things. My heart leapt for joy, and I was very grateful for this time with my beautiful family. I missed Will, and wanted to take him with us, but his father would not allow it. Also he was in school, and now living with his grandmother so I knew that he would be taken care of. It was heartbreaking at times, as I wished he was regularly part of our life.

Chapter 23

The Visit

I was getting ready for work, and needed to drop off Sarina and Noelle to school first. It was great working part time for a broker, a work that was familiar to me. I could not find a flexible part time job as a counsellor, so this part time role was certainly helping to pay the bills. Better still the job was only twenty minutes away, so I was not too far from my girls.

Sarina was excited about school, as she had a friend next door starting at the same time. She was shy, but liked to make friends and was full of life and mischief. I knew that she would eventually fit in and enjoy her time at school. I was a little hesitant about sending her early but she did not like pre-school and wanted to join her friend next door.

Noelle was more of an introvert and was happy to play on her own. I wanted her to join with the other kids at pre-school, but she loved to hide in her little corner. Her teacher told me how she enjoyed getting the naughty boys in trouble by encouraging them to do mischief. Noelle would laugh at their antics, particularly during afternoon rest times and the teachers would catch them out not realising that Noelle was part of the group. She would close her eyes and pretend to be asleep. There was a lot to Noelle, and she only just showed small snippets of her personality at a time.

It was hard leaving the girls, even though it was a part time job. I was attached to them, and I wanted them to feel safe and assured. I understood that separation anxiety for a little one is a real thing, and I waited till they were ready for school before deciding to go back to work. Afterall the pre-school fees were quite high and the extra income helped.

The day was going really slow, and there were not many phone calls. The office manager was out trying to drum up new business, and I was manning the phone. I tried to offer some help, given my experience in new business, meeting budgets and deadlines but he was adamant on doing it all himself. At times I made some calls myself and instigated the sale. It was small business packages, so clearly within my parameters. I had to do a refresher course to update my qualifications and credentials before I was able to provide advice.

The girls were happy to see me, although I was five minutes late to pick up Sarina. She was with her friend, crying looking for me. I told her to wait near her classroom, and I would be there to get her. The traffic was crazy that afternoon and even though I left early, I got stuck with the traffic. I reassured Sarina that it was all okay, and that she did not have to go to after school care yet.

When I arrived to get Noelle, I found her playing with puppets in the corner, and she ran over to give me a hug. She was excited and a little nervous. It was great to be able to take them home, and have the time to play with them. Sarina had a little kitchen and we often used her china set for tea. Even Noelle would sit with us in the small chairs and try to sip on the warm tea and scones. It was so much fun, and I would watch them giggle as we talked about their day.

There was a knock on the door, then the doorbell rang out. It sounded like the person was impatient. I quickly got up, told the girls to stay seated and went to open the door. They continued tapping, so I peered out to see a female standing there, but could not see her face. I thought it may be one of my neighbours. I opened the door, and little Sarina was standing near me. I looked at the lady standing before me, her chilling blue eyes like an icy lake staring at me as if she was looking into my soul. She looked down at Sarina and smiled, then looked back at me. I immediately recognised this woman, and my heart sank.

I felt the anxiety race through my body, and the dread of seeing this person again, now grown up. The flashbacks came back to me, and that feeling of pure evil that resonated from her being. I was hoping to never see her again, and that she had been locked up in jail for assault and murder. I had tried so hard to block her out of my mind, yet it was so hard to forget the physical and emotional damage she caused my colleagues. Why was she here.? Was she intending to cause me harm? I was going to fight back to protect my family. The questions kept rolling around in my head. Then I remembered the scriptures 2 Tim 1 :7 For God has not given me a spirit of fear, but of power, love and a sound mind.

I could feel my cheeks become hot, and the anger was rising up in me. I was alone with my young girls, and I did not want Jessica to come anywhere near them. She had aged over the last seven years, looking a little drawn with that deadpan face, where there was no emotion.

She was void of any empathy, a narcissist who had controlled those around her, a form of survival and coping mechanism she had learned from childhood. Having been surrounded by monsters all her life, she had also become one. I looked past her to see if there were any others, and realised that she had driven to my house, and there was a male in the passenger seat. I wondered if it was Kevin. I could not see the number plate. I closed the door on her, locked it and then called the police. I sat on the couch with the girls and prayed, asking the Lord to protect us.

References

The Holy Bible, English Standard Version ESV Copyright 2001 by Crossway Bibles, Copyright 2002, By Crossway Bibles, a division of Good News Publishers All rights reserved.

The Holy Bible, New International Version NIV Copyright 1973, 1978, 1984, 2011 by Biblica Inc used by permissions, All rights reserved worldwide.

Amplified Bible Copyright 2015 by the Lockman Foundation
All rights reserved
La Habra CA 90631
Zondervan

Author's Bio

Jacqueline Clark is married and has three grown children. She and her husband are followers of Christ, and share the vision to proclaim and live out the Gospel message. Jacqueline has held positions in the corporate sector in management and has undertaken various tertiary qualifications in Business, Insurance, and Counselling. Jacqueline has also studied Theology and Biblical Studies at Wesley Institute For Ministry & The Arts, Sydney, Australia, with a postgraduate degree in Counselling. She has been actively involved in pastoral counselling and ministry work over the years. Her hobbies include reading, writing, singing, serving and mentoring others.